Other Books by Jan Yager (a.k.a. J. L./JANET BARKAS)

Nonfiction
Friendshifts®: The Power of Friendship and How It Shapes Our Lives
Friendship: A Selected, Annotated Bibliography
Single in America
Victims
Creative Time Management
Creative Time Management for the New Millennium
Business Protocol: How to Survive & Succeed in Business
Effective Business & Nonfiction Writing
Making Your Office Work for You
The Vegetable Passion: A History of the Vegetarian State of Mind
The Help Book

Fiction
Untimely Death (with Fred Yager)
Just Your Everyday People (with Fred Yager)
The Cantaloupe Cat (illustrated by Mitzi Lyman)

When

Friendship

Hurts

How to Deal with Friends Who Betray, Abandon, or Wound You

Jan Yager, Ph.D.

A FIRESIDE BOOK
PUBLISHED BY SIMON & SCHUSTER
NEW YORK LONDON TORONTO SYDNEY SINGAPORE

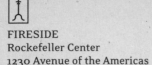

FIRESIDE
Rockefeller Center
1230 Avenue of the Americas
New York, NY 10020

Copyright © 2002 by Jan Yager, Ph.D.
All rights reserved,
including the right of reproduction
in whole or in part in any form.

FIRESIDE and colophon are registered trademarks
of Simon & Schuster, Inc.

For information about special discounts for bulk purchases,
please contact Simon & Schuster Special Sales:
1-800-456-6798 or business@simonandschuster.com

Designed by Diane Hobbing

Manufactured in the United States of America

10   9   8   7   6   5   4   3   2   1

Library of Congress Cataloging-in-Publication Data
Yager, Jan, 1948–
   When friendship hurts : how to deal with friends who betray, abandon, or
wound you / Jan Yager.
      p. cm.
   Includes bibliographical references (p.) and index.
      1. Friendship. 2. Interpersonal conflict.   I. Title.

BF575.F66 Y345 2002
158.2'5–dc21   2002021212

ISBN 0-7432-1145-6

Author's Note

Researching and writing *When Friendship Hurts* provided me with a unique and valuable opportunity: to return to one of my areas of expertise, friendship, but to look at a very specific aspect of it—namely, betrayal in friendship and how to deal with and overcome destructive or negative friendships. My first written treatise on friendship was my sociology dissertation, "Friendship Patterns Among Young Urban Single Women" (City University of New York, 1983). I followed that with a scholarly, selectively annotated book on friendship and related references, *Friendship* (Garland, 1985). I continued my friendship research of more than 1,000 people by conducting original surveys and interviews, including a study of 257 randomly selected human resource professionals who were members of an international association. I relied upon all the research I had amassed on friendship to write *Friendshifts®: The Power of Friendship and How It Shapes Our Lives* (Hannacroix Creek Books, 1997; 2nd edition, 1999). That book covered everything from defining a friend to perspectives on friendship in history and in the social sciences; how friendships are formed, maintained, and end; friendship through life's stages, including childhood, single years, marriage, and the older years, and an application of the friendship principles I had learned to improving marital, sibling, and parent-child relationships. I was interviewed on *The Oprah Winfrey Show, The View, The Today Show, The O'Reilly Factor,* on programs on National Public Radio and BBC Radio, and on dozens of other network and cable television and radio shows, as well as by web site, newspaper, and magazine journalists for articles in *The Wall Street Journal, Time, Glamour, USA Today, Newsday, Redbook, Reader's Digest, Seventeen,* and numerous other publications.

Yes, there was lots of interest in friendship, and in my research and my book *Friendshifts.*

It was exciting to help increase the awareness not only that friendship was an important social relationship, but that researchers had found having even one close friend could extend someone's life, as well as increase the likelihood that someone would recover from breast cancer or a heart attack.

But I noticed that some topics were "hush-hush," even though the letters I was receiving from readers of *Friendshifts,* as well as the e-mail inquiries following a network morning talk show appearance, often posed questions like "When is a friendship no longer worth saving?" or "Would competition be damaging to a relationship of friends?" or "Why would someone betray her friend?" People were asking how to recognize and get out of harmful friendships.

I was also being told about men and women, and boys and girls, who were afraid of friendship and did not have even one friend. Could facing their worst fear, coping with the end of a friendship, help them to get the confidence to initiate one?

When Friendship Hurts benefits from all the friendship research I have been conducting since 1980, but it expands on the prior research with a new study I have conducted over the past five years. That study is based on responses to more than 180 friendship surveys, including responses to a questionnaire posted on my web site (www.janyager.com) and selected follow-up in the form of extensive telephone and in-person interviews.

The 180 questionnaires were completed by 41 males and 139 females ranging in age from 13 to 72 (with an average age of 34). In addition to getting responses from practically every state in the United States, I received questionnaires from more than a dozen countries around the world. The respondents were men and women who work for medium-sized to large corporations, as well as entrepreneurs, small business owners, homemakers, publicists, writers, artists, consultants, executives, human resource managers, social scientists, speakers, computer programmers, teachers, secretaries, and military people. Most questionnaires were from individuals who had no connection to anyone else in the sample, although six women who have been part of the same close friendship network that began when they all worked at the same company 20 years ago and six men and women who work for the same consulting firm, with more than 10,000 employees, also completed the survey. Included in the total are 34 male and female adult survivors of childhood sexual abuse from throughout the United States and Canada; of that group of survivors, 28 completed an expanded 104-question survey related to their abuse as well as to their friendship patterns.

These written questionnaires about friendship, betrayal in friendship, and related issues were distributed not with the intention of compiling quantitative data, but as a preliminary method for gathering qualitative data.

Quotes in this book not attributed to a secondary source are from original research I conducted, in the form of in-person or telephone interviews, completed questionnaires, or other written communications; whenever possible, they are reprinted verbatim but, if necessary, they are excerpted. Editing may have been required for either sense or clarification. If words are missing or terms need to be explained, that is indicated by brackets within the quote. If anonymity was requested or required, a fictitious first name has been provided; other identifying details, such as occupation or hometown, may also have been altered to maintain anonymity. However, care has been taken to preserve the integrity of each example.

Secondary sources cited within a chapter also have complete bibliographic entries in the Notes, which are arranged by chapter following the last page of the text.

The purpose of this book is to provide inspiration, information, and opinions on the topics covered. It is sold with the understanding that neither the publisher nor the author is engaged in rendering psychological, medical, sociological, legal, or other professional services.

The number of people I wish to thank for helping to make this book a reality includes those who completed my surveys and allowed me to interview them—those who are anonymous, those who are named, those who shared their stories, and experts who shared their knowledge. I also want to thank my dedicated, kind, thorough, and hard-working editor at Simon & Schuster, Caroline Sutton, and her conscientious assistant, Nicole Diamond, for their guidance and enthusiasm since I first proposed this book in December 1999. I also want to thank Trish Todd, vice president and editor-in-chief of the Trade Paperback Group at Simon & Schuster, who shared my previous book on friendship, *Friendshifts: The Power of Friendship and How It Shapes Our Lives,* with Caroline Sutton, which eventually led to my writing a proposal for a new book on friendship, which was the basis for *When Friendship Hurts: How to Deal With Friends Who Betray, Abandon, or Wound You.* Thanks also to Simon & Schuster's Marie Florio, Christine Lloreda, Laurie Cotumaccio, Marcia Burch, and Loretta Denner, among others.

There have been others who have cheered me on through the demanding research and writing stages of this new book—sociologists, psychologists, writers, foreign literary agents, and my dear friends—and I want to name them, asking forgiveness in advance if I have inadvertently left anyone out: Joyce Guy-Patton, Mary Tierney, Sharon Fisher, Suzanne Vaughan, Judy Cohn, Pat Agostino, Nona Aguilar, Illa Howe, Jennifer Ash, Ginny Mugavero, Gail Tuchman, Pramilla Poddar, Elia Schneider, Jose Ramon, Susanne Sinclair, Rhonda Ginsberg, Amy Frishberg, Ruth Winter, Arlynn Greenbaum, Charlotte Libov, Abra Anderson, Mitzi Lyman, Art and Sheila Kriemelman,

Lil Schaeffer, Cathy Sebor, Marcia Hoffenberg, Judy Hottenson, Duffy Spencer, Jane Resnick, Janice Papolos, Vicki Secunda, Fran Dorf, Joanne Kabek, Elizabeth Lewin, Phyllis Henkel Silver, Jeanne Muratore, Emily Rock, Linda Blatt, Dottie Berman, Milt Haynes, Laurie Smith, Val Smith, Charlotte Greene, Eddie and Candy Craven, Jon Chakoff, the webmaster of my web site www.janyager, and his wife Lana Chakoff, who put the friendship and betrayal survey on my web site, Nancy Creshkoff, the late Dr. David Leeds, Scott Mendel, Jane Jordan Browne, Evelyn Lee, Ib and Bebbe Lauritzen, Lora Fountain, Michael Meller, Bob Tanner, Elfriede Pexa, Antonia Kerrigan, Kiyoshi Asano, Asli Karasuil, Helene Raude, Lorna Soifer, Shoshi Grajower, Jane Grossinger, Anita Walsh, Sarah Gallick, Julian Padowicz, Jim Cox, Jan Nathan, Terry Nathan, Marilyn Ross, the late Alfred McClung Lee, J. Barry Gurdin, D. Schroder, Norio Irie, Nancy Trent, Nanette Thylan, Brian Bigalow, Rosemary Blieszner, Rebecca G. Adams, the late C. H. Rolph, Judy Kaufmann, Christine Hartline, Gerald R. Baron, Albert Ellis, Kate Cohen-Posey, Betsy Lampe, Bruce Serlin, Laura Lorber, Lillian Vernon, David Hochberg, David and Michelle Riklan, Peggy Stautberg, Andrew M. Greeley, Lucy Hedrick, Fran Pastore, Mark Sanborn, Don Gabor, Jim Donovan, Irwin Zucker, Patricia Gottlieb Shapiro, Nancy Samalin, Diane DiResta, Marsha Snaider, David Carradine, Susie Glennan, Caryl Frawley, Kathy Lindberg, John Dutrow, Marilynn Smith, Bronwyn Polson, Anette Moos, Emma Samuel Etuk, Mae Woods, Lelia Taylor, Leslie Banks, Beth Kalish, Robert and Rande Davis Gedaliah, and Pat Schroeder. I also want to express my appreciation to my sister, Eileen Hoffman, who generously shared her expertise about conflict resolution with me. The section on "Handling Conflict with Friends," as well as the sections on friendship and conflict resolution at work, were greatly enhanced by the information she so graciously contributed.

I also want to thank my wonderful husband, Fred, and our two sons, Scott and Jeffrey. I am fortunate to have such a devoted family, and I thank them for their sacrifices so I could complete this project. I can, of course, never make up for the time I took away from our family to finish this book, but I can at least say, "Thank you."

Researching and writing a book is the crucial first step; the next step is getting it published; and the third step is helping people know about the book so the fourth step can be reached: readers actually reading it. There are numerous ways that readers learn about books, from book reviews and "word of mouth" to discovering it on the shelves of a local library. I would like to thank all the book reviewers who have written about my friendship research and writings, librarians who have bought copies to place in their collections, as well as all those producers, hosts, interviewers, reviewers, reporters, and business and feature writers who helped me to get the word out through television, radio, and Internet programs, as well as in newspapers, magazines, and newsletters. By discussing my book *Friendshifts* and my friendship research and writing on scores of television and radio shows throughout the United States, including radio and phone interviews nationally and for Taiwanese and British radio broadcasts, I was able to share my expertise as well as learn about the friendship concerns of those who watched or listened to those programs and then contacted me by e-mail or letter. I want to especially thank the producers, hosts, and support staff, including Oprah Winfrey, Katie Couric, Meredith Vieira, Bill O'Reilly, Gayle King, Montel Williams, Jenny Jones, Tammy Filler, Paul and Sarah Edwards, Ilana Arazie, Dianne Atkinson Hudson, Amy Craig, Kati Davis, Dana Brooks, Jack Mori, Angie Kraus, Ray Dotch, Donna Bass, Rachel Chamberlin, Dana Glaser, Jim Blasingame, Jessica Stedman-Guff, Star Jones, Joy Behar, Bill Geddie, Ann-Marie Wiliams-Gray, Patricia Raskin, Kelly Gratke, Ruth Koscielak, and so many others at television and radio shows, as well as the dozens of journalists and feature writers who interviewed me for newspaper, magazine, and web site articles about friendship, including Sue Shellenbarger, Nancy Ann Jeffrey, Rita Papazian, Caroline Palmer, Sara Eckel, Theresa Churchill, Anne Fisher, Marguerite Kelly, Laura Gilbert, and Megan Rutherford.

Because anonymity was requested or required by so many of those who provided the examples and anecdotes in *When Friendship Hurts,* I want to thank those who have filled out surveys or allowed me to interview them— who gave of themselves in the interest of research and helping others (although numerous respondents noted that sharing about friendship and betrayal helped them as well).

Jan Yager, Ph.D.

Dedicated to my loving husband, Fred, our sons, Scott and Jeffrey, my mother, my sister, my extended family, the memory of my late father and brother, and my devoted friends.

Contents

When

Friendship

Hurts

When Friendship Turns Unfriendly

For some, "friends for life" seems to have replaced the ideal of a lifelong marital relationship. Of course, there are positive, wonderful friendships that are mutually beneficial to both friends that *should* last a lifetime. But there are other friendships that are negative, destructive, or unhealthy that should end. There may also be friendships that you thought were going well but, alas, all of a sudden, your friend stops returning your phone calls and won't answer your letters, and the friendship ends. Years later you still don't know what happened, and it haunts you.

In the two decades during which I have been researching and writing about friendship, I have seen the interest in learning about friendship soar. From a topic that was addressed infrequently by psychologists, psychiatrists, and sociologists (who tended to focus on parent-child or husband-wife relationships), articles about friendship are now a staple in popular magazines and daily newspapers, and also on web sites; and there are many books about this glorious relationship between peers that we call friendship.

Friendship has certainly been "discovered." Its benefits have been extolled by numerous researchers through anecdotes and examples, as well as through quantitative (or qualitative) studies by epidemiologists, sociologists, and psychologists, who have found a correlation between having even one close friend and an increased life expectancy, as well as better mental health and a greater chance of surviving breast cancer or a heart attack.[1]

So why is there a need for a book like *When Friendship Hurts*? Because in all the excitement about getting the word out about the importance of friendship in our lives, too little attention has been paid to the notion that negative friendships can wreak havoc. Another reason is to have a forum to explore the possible causes of finding yourself in such a relationship, and how to best rid yourself of a noxious friend. Furthermore, if your friendships are consistently less than what you had hoped they would be, a Band-Aid approach to changing that situation is doomed to long-term failure. You need to look at the underlying causes of the negative friendships in your life; you need to go back to their roots in your parent-child and sibling relationships.

This book offers help and hope in understanding the complexities of friendships, as well as advice on how you can turn around your life—not just your friendships—by understanding why you have negative friendships and by finding and cultivating positive friendships. Having positive friendships—and that may not mean finding new friends, just interacting differently with the ones that you already have—can help turn around your career. For example, not only do friends help friends get jobs, but once you land a job, how quickly you rise at a company or in a career could depend as much on who your friends are at work and in your professional field as on your talents. By the same token, a friend can derail your career or get you fired. That's what happened with Marjorie (not her real name), a 23-year-old single female working as a teacher's assistant. Marjorie explains:

> My best friend told my boss that she feared for her life after we got into an argument and I wrote her a nasty note, even though we had been friends for six years and she knew I would never hurt her. Because she went to my boss, I was fired after working there for a year and a half. She [my best friend] even went to the police but was told that nothing in the note was threatening. The reason for all of this had to do with the fact that she was highly competitive and felt this was a way of winning.

Unfortunately Marjorie's experience is more typical than you'd think. A 45-year-old married speechwriter at an Illinois corporation was fired because a single female friend at work, fearing that she herself might be fired after a poor performance review, blamed her unsatisfactory behavior on her boss, the head speechwriter, who was also her friend, alleging that his sexual attraction to her, which she called sexual harassment, made it difficult for her to concentrate. (Her claims were unsubstantiated but her boss/friend was fired anyway for failing to properly supervise his friend/employee.) Carol, a 39-year-old married woman, after finally landing her dream job as a florist, was betrayed so badly at work by three casual friends that she "had to take a three-week medical leave."

Losing a job or having a reputation damaged beyond repair is bad enough, but friendship has been partly to blame for even darker situations. An infamous example is the friendship of the two teenagers who perpetrated the horrific murders of 12 of their classmates and one teacher, and injured 20 more, at Columbine High School in Columbine, Colorado, in April 1999, before committing suicide. Those boys, allegedly bullied and not part of the "in" crowd, seemed to act together, getting the strength to commit mass murder and suicide *from* their friendship.[2]

Then in March 2001 it happened again. A 15-year-old boy in Santee, California, again the alleged victim of bullies, supposedly shared with four friends and one adult that he planned to shoot his classmates, but then reassured them that he was only kidding. The next day he *did* carry out his threats when he allegedly shot and killed two classmates. Three families were destroyed, a school was branded, and a community was shocked and grief-stricken. The boy's friends, believing him when he guaranteed that he was just kidding, were transferred to other schools. The authorities feared retaliation by their classmates for failing to report their friend's macabre bragging to the proper authorities.[3]

But we don't need tales of murder and mayhem to find value in examining negative friendships and the consequences of betrayal. Over the two decades I have been researching friendship and friendship patterns, I have interviewed people who were betrayed when a "friend" seduced their romantic partner. Others ended a friendship because of a betrayal that, at the very least, stopped a pivotal work project in its tracks. I've interviewed men and women who told me that a friend had derailed their career by sharing privileged information that was supposed to be just "between friends." Others reported that a friend had stolen money from them. Here are other examples of betrayal that I have observed or heard about through interviews in the course of my friendship research:

- "One of my best friends romantically pursued every woman in which I expressed interest." (24-year-old single male)
- "She told me she was sleeping with my boyfriend and tried to convince me we should 'share.'" (37-year-old divorced mother)
- "[My close friend at work] went to our mutual boss and described something we were either both working on or that I had taken the initiative to set up and talked about how he had handled it." (55-year-old, twice-divorced woman)
- "A close female friend is jealous of me being married." (44-year-old married man)
- "A best friend I grew up with attacked me [physically] for no reason." (23-year-old married female)
- "A casual friend started a rumor about me at work." (50-year-old divorced mother)

- "My maid of honor stole money from me on the night of my bachelorette party." (30-year-old married teacher)
- "I'm not as open as I had been, [I'm] more reserved, because of what happened." [She was devastated when her best friend referred to her by a derogatory name when they were both 11.] (32-year-old married mother)

Jealousy can hurt someone's self-esteem and may also end a friendship, as Brenda, a 40-year-old homemaker and musician from Michigan, found out. "I used to weigh two hundred pounds," she notes. "I now weigh one hundred twenty-five pounds. My friend was two hundred and fifty pounds. When I lost the first few pounds, she backed as far away as possible."

Cheating with a romantic partner or spouse may end a friendship. A 31-year-old art instructor let her "really close friend" and co-worker live with her and her husband when her friend couldn't find an apartment. During that time, the friend "flirted or even had a relationship" with her husband. The friend also undermined her at work, spreading untrue rumors that she was being physically abusive to her art students. The marriage is on the rocks, and the friendship is over.

But some potentially destructive or harmful friendships may be difficult to spot. That's because when a friendship is forming, during the "courtship" phase, your friend may be charming, polite, and completely appropriate. Once your friendship is well underway, a friend may change. The very act of becoming friends may send someone with intimacy problems into an emotional tailspin, changing those involved as well as their behavior toward each other. As friends become closer and more intimate, expectations also may rise so that disappointments become more likely, and painful, than during the early stage of the evolving friendship.

Furthermore, as a friendship that formed within a certain context, such as at school or at work, expands to include a multiplicity of situations and even other relationships, conflicts may arise that may derail the friendship. In addition, the longer you remain friends, the greater your investment in maintaining the friendship; you are more likely to ignore or try to explain away negative behaviors. But you (or your friend) will be able to put up with only so much, and the friendship may last only until such an act of betrayal occurs that the situation has to be addressed and resolved or the friendship will end.

Friendships can certainly change in the level of intimacy, and expectations can be lowered about a friend, even if the friendship does not end completely, over betrayals, disappointments, or unmet expectations. That's what a 43-year-old market researcher found out when he gave a friend $150 to conduct interviews for a project on the researcher's behalf. Instead his best friend pocketed the money and never made good on his promise to do the work. Although the friendship hasn't ended, one wonders how close it is if they haven't seen each other "in many years."

Betrayal by a friend can even lead to the ultimate betrayal: murder. Twenty-six-year-old Don is married and a father. He is also serving 15 years to life for killing his best friend in an argument over Don's wife. "He had been dating my wife while I was out of town, and finally she ran away with him," Don notes.

Although not as drastic as murder, feeling miffed by a friend, even if it is a misunderstanding, can lead to extreme and even criminal acts. That's what seems to have happened to a 38-year-old married nurse whose friend at work "stabbed me in the back by spreading a false rumor about me which ingratiated her to the head nurse and which caused the head nurse to dislike me." Or the 49-year-old single woman whose jealous and angry friend "stole my jewelry."

Because of my extensive friendship research, writings, and expertise, as well as the workshops I facilitate and the lectures I deliver on friendship, I am often asked to appear on talk shows to discuss friendship. Journalists who are writing about the topic frequently interview me, and their many questions about recognizing, and coping with, negative friendships helped me to realize there was a need for this book. But I wanted to go even further: I wanted to help people to understand *why* they might select friends who eventually betray them, to reverse that pattern, and to address social trends that could be behind the fact that friendship betrayal seems to be more widespread than ever before.

I also wrote this book to help dispel the embarrassment and shame that too often accompany failed friendships. For some, admitting to a broken friendship has become like admitting to a failed marriage. It seems that, inspired by the very "pro-friendship" tone in writings and discussions about the topic over the last two decades, a myth of lifelong friendship has emerged, even as the ideal of a lifelong marriage has, sadly, become an unrealistic reality for many people.

The romanticized ideal that friendships should *not* end or fail may create unnecessary distress in those who should end a friendship but hold on, no matter what. They are clinging to the myth rather than understanding the relationship. But if neither all friendships nor all marriages last a lifetime, what's left to believe in that does?

The goal of *When Friendship Hurts* is to give you the tools to detect, and cope with, friendships that are destructive or harmful. I hope that reading it will give you greater insight into why friendships, especially your own or those of people close to you, may have ended or should have ended, and how to cope with these endings. Furthermore, if you have a habit of forming negative friendships, this book will help you to start choosing positive and healthy friends who will enrich your personal life and help you succeed faster and go further in your career.

There may even be current or past friendships in which, unwittingly or on purpose, you betrayed a friend. Understanding the impact of betrayal on the one who betrays, as well as on the one who is betrayed, can free up important emotional energy that otherwise may be drained by feelings of guilt, remorse, sadness, or associated emotions related to the betrayal. You can learn to forgive yourself, if you betrayed a friend; or if you were the betrayed one, you might consider how forgiving your betrayer might help *you*.

Most of us are blessed with supportive, caring, trustworthy friends. There are plenty of books available today that describe the process of forming and maintaining positive friendships, as well as extolling the benefits of friendship, including my own popular book, which takes an interdisciplinary approach that draws from sociology and psychology, *Friendshifts®: The Power of Friendship and How It Shapes Our Lives.*

But where can you turn for help if you feel a friend has betrayed you? Betrayal is when a friend, whom you counted on for support, love, affection, trust, loyalty, camaraderie, or respect, has somehow destroyed your trust. She may have violated a confidence or told a lie about you, harmed your other personal relationships, or even cost you your job. He may have failed to come through for you in your hour of emotional need, taken your money, stolen the affections of your romantic partner or your spouse, or, in the worst-case scenario, physically harmed you or even caused someone's death. Were these "friends" ever really friends? How could a "friend" commit such treacherous acts? Did this friendship start out as a destructive or harmful one, or become that way over time? Where did it take a wrong turn, and what do you do to end it, if ending is the best way of coping? If it started out that way, how can you learn to be a better judge of character early on so that you avoid befriending those who end up harming or betraying you?

In addition to answering those questions, another goal of this book is to help you to start asking your own questions about these issues, and finding your own answers. Some of you may be able to make this journey completely on your own; others may wish to get help along the way. If you do wish to seek outside help, in addition to asking others for referrals to professionals for one-on-one counseling or to self-help or professionally led groups, you can consult the Resources section in the back of this book, which provides a list of associations that offer referrals to local organizations or affiliated professionals.

Betrayal in friendship is a subject few people want to talk about openly, but one to which all of us can relate. But by offering anonymity and confidentiality, if necessary, I found men and women, boys and girls, who not only wanted to talk about betrayal but actually *needed* to talk about it as a necessary catharsis. In my most recent friendship survey, of the 171 people (out of 180) who responded to the question "Has a casual, close, or best friend ever betrayed you?" 116 (68 percent) answered "yes" and only 55 (32 percent) replied "no."

Betrayal can be defined as when a friend lets you down and is not there for you emotionally, or even literally: when a friend ends your friendship but you still want it to continue (and you sometimes may never find out why it ended). That is what happened to a young married woman from Colorado who wrote to me soon after watching an interview with me about friendship on a network morning talk show. I was discussing how friendships sometimes end, and that it's okay and normal for some friendships to end, especially if it's through no fault of your own. She was so moved that she sent me a "thank you" card, saying how much the point of view I had shared on the show had meant to her. She had been haunted by a friendship that ended although she never knew why. It actually kept her up at night.

If a friend ends a friendship and you are obsessed with not knowing why, you will probably have to deal with the reason for your obsession. In other words, you may never know the answer. (There is a discussion later in the book about how to get over obsessing about a failed friendship.)

But if it is you who decides to end a friendship, even a negative one, you should be careful to avoid possible vendettas. Remember that *how* you end a friendship may be as important as your decision to end it. That person who used to be your friend may at some point be in the position of deciding whether you get a raise, a major contract for your company, or a promotion at work.

Certainly, over the years, I have experienced the ending of several friendships that were extremely close. If I was the one to end it, I wondered if there was another way of handling the situation. If I was not, I felt confused, angry, and betrayed. So I have wanted to find answers to my own questions about betrayal in friendship, as well as evaluating the preferred way to deal with negative friendships that should end, if there is one.

I researched and wrote this book to answer my own questions as well as the ones that I am so frequently asked, through letters, e-mail, and even in the question-and-answer sessions following the talks I give on friendship: Why do friends do hurtful things to their friends? Why do friends betray each other? Why would someone get into a negative friendship? How do you get out of a destructive friendship? How do you find and cultivate positive friendships in your personal life and career?

How I attained my own metamorphosis to becoming a better friend, as well as all the original research and observations I have done over the last two decades, form the basis of this book. Just as my life—including my career, and all the relationships in my life, including friendship—has been enriched by what I have learned along the way about friendship, I hope to help you to reap the joys that healthy friendships will bring you. As you will see in reading *When Friendship Hurts,* sometimes the changes must start within us before we can expect anyone else, or our friendships, to change.

Part 1

Friendship: The Basics

Chapter 1

What Is a Friend?

Although there may be as many definitions of friendship as there are friends, it's a relationship that has four basic elements:

- It is between at least two persons who are unrelated by blood.
- It is optional or voluntary.
- It is not based on a legal contract.
- It is reciprocal.

There seems to be an informal consensus that friends should not be lovers or sexually intimate or the relationship becomes something more than friendship.

Beyond those basic tenets, there is a wide range of opinion about what a friendship should entail, including trust, empathy, honesty, confidentiality, commonality, care, love, being soulmates or kindred spirits, having someone to talk to, do things with, and confide in—someone who will be there and not just make idle promises. Most intangible but perhaps most crucial of all, a friend is someone you like who likes you, and with whom you share a positive chemical reaction.

It is useful to divide the general term *friend* into three categories based on the level of intimacy: casual, close, and best.

A *casual friend* is a giant step above an acquaintance. There is a bond between casual friends, although it is not as intimate or exclusive as a close or best friend. Although a casual friendship may deepen in time to a close or best friendship, there are also friendships that remain indefinitely at the casual level. In business, especially, casual friendship may be more common than, and even preferred over, a close or best friendship.

Although less intimate than close or best friendships, a sense of trust and "liking each other" that is genuine and shared should be present in a healthy and positive casual friendship.

"I really enjoy casual friends," says Penny, a 65-year-old, twice-divorced financial consultant. Penny, who has a boyfriend but lives alone, goes out to dinner on Wednesday nights with a friend who is her age but is married and generally unavailable for socializing in the evenings. But her husband, who served in the Vietnam War, has a meeting for veterans every Wednesday night. Over dinner, Penny and her friend talk about their children and grandchildren. They also talk about their shared interest in antiques; Penny's friend writes a newsletter on antique collecting. Penny, who also travels extensively abroad, has little time or emotion available in her hectic life right now for a close or best friend; casual friendship suits her just fine.

With a *close friend,* it is assumed that you could also feel comfortable sharing your deepest, most intimate thoughts or secrets, if you wish to. Most find that the competing demands of other roles—worker, romantic partner, sibling, parent—make it possible to have only a handful of close friends at any one time. If some close friends live far away, there may be time and energy for additional close friends nearby as well. But few are able to comfortably handle 10 or 20 close friends—4 to 6 is more typical—whereas 10, 20, or more casual friends is not an unusual number, especially for students, workers, or business owners. (In analyzing the 180 friendship surveys for this book, the average number of close, best, and casual friends was 6 close, 2 best, and 26 casual friends.)[1]

Here are typical expectations about a close friend:

- "A close friend is someone with whom you can be yourself." (45-year-old married male staff writer for a magazine)
- "A close friend is someone who can be turned to in a time of special need." (36-year-old married male college professor)
- "A close friend is one who listens closely without judging, who does not interrupt to recount her problems when you're telling her yours. She or he is 'unmistakably' unselfish." (44-year-old divorced female entrepreneur)

A *best friend* ideally will have all the criteria required to be a close friend, but with the additional distinction of being, by definition, *the* premier friend. I've often heard married couples, especially men, refer to their spouse as "my best friend," but technically a spouse cannot be a best friend but only "like" a best friend. (Just how universal this mislabeling of a wife as a "best friend" is shows up in the book *A Woman's Guide to Being a Man's Best Friend,* by Michael Levin, which is really about how to be a better mate.)[2] Over and over again, married men have been quick to point out in interviews or in surveys that they consider their wife their best "friend." For example, 31-year-old Gregory, who heads a publishing company with eight employees, answered the question on my friendship survey "How did you meet your closest or best friend?" with the qualification "other than my wife," followed by "right now my best friend is my business partner."

Throughout history, the pulls and pushes of having more than one best friend have created problems. The immortal words of the French essayist Michel de Montaigne immediately come to mind. In his famous essay "Of Friendship," he wrote: "If two called for help at the same time, which one would you run to? If they demanded conflicting services of you, how would you arrange it? If one confided to your silence a thing that would be useful for the other to know, how would you extricate yourself? A single dominant friendship dissolves all other obligations."[3]

Vikki, a single working woman in her late twenties who lives in western Europe, shared with me her vision of what a best friend should be, an ideal that many seem to share. She told me how much she longed for a best friendship like the one that was the cornerstone of the television sitcom *Cybil*, which was still being broadcast in Europe. Vikki notes:

> One of the big story lines is Cybil's friendship with her best friend Marian. Their relationship and their adventures are especially heart-warming for me. I sometimes think: Oh, how wonderful would this be to have a BEST BEST friend who comes to your house every day and who shares everything with you.

Alas, at what stage in life are you most likely to be when that best friendship occurs? For most, it will be during the early years, during school as well as the years of being single, before or after marriage. At some periods in most lives, especially if work, dependent children, and a romantic relationship compete for primary emotional attention, best friendship is hard to maintain.

Vikki duly notes that there are circumstances that foster the best friendship between Cybil and her best friend Marian:

> These two women do of course have great prerequisites for such a close bond: They are both in their late forties, and their children are grown up and out of the house. They are both divorced, and Marian is the very rich, independent ex-wife of a plastic surgeon, so she does not have to work to support herself. It is, of course, all fun fiction!

Well, I don't know what life will bring me. Maybe someday I will find such a person again! Never give up hope, right? Yes, wouldn't it be great fun to have a best [friend] in your life?

Trust

In order to have friendship, most agree that there has to be trust. But being open to sharing with a friend and entrusting her with your thoughts or privileged information needs to be a two-way exchange. Don't just ask yourself if you would tell your friend your deepest secrets; ask yourself if you wish to be entrusted with hers.

Trust also sets the stage for possible betrayal. Jill, a 47-year-old married entrepreneur with five grown children, explained that her early-childhood experiences, including the abrupt, inexplicable ending of her one close friendship, have made it difficult for her to trust anyone except her husband. Jill admits: "You have to trust people." But right now Jill cannot. She is working on her distrust with the therapist she has been consulting since 1990 when she began dealing with her abusive childhood and how it has restricted her ability to have friends. "What is a friend?" Jill asks, rhetorically, as she quickly answers, "See, I don't know. I envision a friend as someone you can tell anything to, and I can't do that."

Some of the fear of betrayal could actually be avoided if friends would think carefully about what they confide in their friends. Unless you have tested a friendship and are absolutely sure that this is a close or best friend whom you can completely trust, avoid sharing with friends who are not yet tried-and-true any of the following:

- Business confidences that would be a violation of trust and ethics if revealed
- Details about the sexual performance of a romantic partner
- Secrets that put someone else in jeopardy
- Anything you would not feel comfortable having repeated on the six o'clock news or published in a national newspaper or on the Internet

If this sounds harsh, it is because it is meant to be a wake-up call. Especially in America, we are quick to call someone a "friend." Men and women share business and personal confidences, even creative ideas and projects that, if given to the competition, could ruin or derail a career, all in the context of "friendship." But how often has that person proven herself to be a trusted friend?

There are expectations and assumptions about being able to trust a tried-and-true, long-standing, close, and best friend with whom you have a history, as opposed to an untested, relatively new friend about whom you are still learning crucial information about the friend's character and values.

Empathy

Empathy is the ability to understand another's point of view, to have feelings, to care, and to show sympathy for someone—all traits that are eagerly sought after in a friend, especially a close or best friend. The feeling of empathy for a friend, of course, stems from a deep-rooted emotion toward that friend, but it also reflects a basic ability to listen to others and truly care about what they are going through. When asked what is the one thing he wants to learn about having friends, one middle-aged man responded: "How to find one who listens as well as talks."

Honesty

Honesty is a controversial topic. When I speak about friendship, I like to share this concept: A close or best friend is someone you feel you *can* share anything with, but you decide whether or not you really want to. Here is an example: Your friend, wearing an outfit that you don't like, asks you, "How do I look?" Now it might be honest to say, "So-so," or "I hate that outfit," but is it tactful? Is it what will be most beneficial for your friendship or your friend?

Telling the truth is, of course, the cornerstone of a close or best friendship and even a reliable casual one. But when is omission of certain facts or information being tactful, and when is it dishonest?

When I discussed friendship with three women in their late twenties and early thirties, they shared with me three key issues that they wanted to learn about friendship: two had to do with honesty: "how honest to be with each other" and "learning to be more honest." (The third issue had to do with how to handle problems within a friendship.)

One woman in that group, a 33-year-old personnel counselor at a fashion company, married for 10 years, explained: "I ask my friends 'What do you want to hear?' I have a hard time lying. I try to be tactful."

Honesty in friendship runs a lot deeper than just commenting on an outfit or a hairdo. It has to do with whether or not you and your friend can share your feelings with each other, including your thoughts, opinions, and dreams. There has to be an assumption that you can speak openly and honestly without being laughed at or fearing repercussions, such as having what you have shared passed along to others without your permission.

Confidentiality

If trust and honesty are the two most important factors in a close friendship, being able to keep secrets is next. Being able to maintain the confidentiality of self-disclosures, entrusted by a friend as a way of sharing private and privileged information, is not the same thing as keeping a dangerous secret that puts that friend or others in jeopardy. Communities and police departments, especially in response to the growth of school violence, have in place hotlines that enable someone to share information, anonymously if necessary, that a crime or life-threatening action has taken place or is about to happen.[4]

That is not the kind of secret I'm addressing here. The type of self-disclosure I'm referring to, by contrast, is quite innocuous, even meaningless or inconsequential, to practically everyone else besides the one who is sharing the secret. The "getting off the chest" that a person accomplishes by sharing a secret may even have a beneficial cathartic effect.

Unfortunately, the friend who hears the secret may then feel burdened by the information that he or she has learned. Hence, the "hot potato" effect of telling someone else may come into play, more as a way to get rid of the burden of the secret than as a malicious way of spreading the secret or betraying the friend.

But the secret that was shared is sacred and meaningful to the friend. The act of sharing that secret with others, without permission, violates the loyalty and respect for privacy that is traditionally a cornerstone of a close or best friendship. As a 47-year-old single film director from the Netherlands notes: "I told my friend of a faux pas [I had committed] and made him promise not to tell anyone. I was not feeling good about the incident. My friend spilled the beans immediately."

Confessing, or self-disclosing, may also be done as a way of bonding with a friend more closely. "I'm going to tell you something I've never told anyone else," especially if it is true, certainly helps to elevate a friendship to an exclusive you-and-me-against-the-world pact, at least in regard to this one secret. It could be anything from a deep-seated feeling ("I'm in love with so-and-so, but I don't know how to tell her") to an embarrassment ("I completely forgot about a dental appointment I had today and it's never happened to me before") or a dream or goal ("I'd really like to be a rock star"). A close or best friend will keep those self-disclosures confidential and will not belittle a friend for sharing those innermost thoughts, however inconsequential they may seem.

Of course, there are also certain caveats that friends may need to observe when hearing a secret. If a friend says, "I'm going to tell you something, but you have to promise not to tell anyone else" and you have a policy of "no secrets" from your spouse, you may need to declare that to your friend in advance of hearing the secret. "I won't tell anyone else but my spouse because we simply do not keep secrets, but my spouse will be bound to secrecy." If your friend is still unwilling to share the secret with that caveat, that may be just fine, since you need to be careful about letting a friend put the friendship, and a secret, between you and your spouse or romantic partner (or parent or child, or from whomever else you are unwilling to withhold a secret).

Sharing a secret, and having a friend accept the information without laughing, belittling, judging, or criticizing, can be one of the most enriching and cementing aspects of a long-lasting friendship. Sharing a secret and keeping one can further strengthen a friendship. This is one reason that friendships encompassing more than two people are so much harder to maintain on an intimate level. Sharing a secret but not sharing it with everyone can create factions and conflicts. That is why, as friendship groups grow in numbers, the information shared tends to become more superficial, and less intimate, and what friends do together tends to become more focused on shared activities and conversation rather than intimate exchanges and emotional support.

Commonality

The broad term *commonality* covers another key ingredient in a positive or healthy friendship: the feeling that you and your friend have feelings, experiences, ideas, or beliefs in common. There is no need to be completely alike. However, there has to be enough that is in common that a bond develops and strengthens through sharing interests, activities, and conversation.

An extension of commonality is one cornerstone of friendship that is too often taken for granted because it is so hard to articulate. It is the feeling that you and your friend like or even love each other. Forty-nine-year-old Bonnie, who is single, met her close friend Regina, who is married with two grown children, 30 years ago, when they lived in the same dorm at college. Regina lives in a distant state, and they haven't seen each other since Bonnie turned 35, but they keep in touch with weekly phone calls. Bonnie expresses the powerful bond she feels with Regina, based on mutual liking:

> If she's not [my] best [friend] she's one of the best. I feel very distant from her in a certain way because I haven't seen her in so long, but I also feel a very strong connection to her because we have [had] a very strong connection [since] the beginning.

How Much Jealousy Is Too Much?

Almost always you are genuinely happy for your friends when they achieve something, whether it's losing 25 pounds, winning an award, being promoted, having a baby, getting married, or going on a dream vacation to Spain. Yes, there may be a twinge of jealousy, envy, or competitiveness, but it does not get in the way of your genuine joy for your friend. For some, the ability to contain jealousy when a friend succeeds is part of being a good friend. As 36-year-old Patricia, a married vice president of sales for a cosmetics corporation, notes, "A good friend won't desert you when you are down. Nor will she turn away in jealousy when you succeed."

Of course, there will be some envy or jealousy, as well as competitiveness, in every healthy friendship. But just a small amount. These emotions, even toward family members or romantic partners, are normal and natural. Jealousy, envy, and competitiveness help to spur individuals on to get for themselves what those they care about are getting for themselves. What distinguishes a healthy friendship is the level and degree: how much envy, jealousy, or competitiveness occurs, and how often? Is it occasional, or is there a consistent, mean-spirited element to it?

Writer Mary Alice Kellogg notes in her article, "When True-Blue Turns Green":

> For me, true friendship depends on the mutual ability to rejoice over life's triumphs together. But if, because of my own troubles, joy isn't exactly what I'm feeling at the moment, I should at least find the strength to push envy aside and not louse up the relationship entirely. This isn't an easy thing to do, but trying to keep a perspective on what the friendship means (and, more important, what would happen if that friendship suddenly were not in my life) can go a long way toward putting the what-about-me demon in its proper place.[5]

Pseudo-friends: Fair Weather and Foul Weather

In addition to categorizing friends as casual, close, or best, you may want to learn to recognize and rule out "pseudo-friends." These are relationships that have characteristics that ultimately prove they were not friendships at all.

As pointed out earlier in this chapter, defining a relationship as a friendship needs to be reciprocal. *The wish to become and remain friends needs to be shared* (even if the specifics of what is shared by the friends is not equal). By contrast, pseudo (or false) friendships are not equal or shared; pseudo-friendships are one-sided.

The two basic types of pseudo-friendships are the fair-weather friend and the foul-weather friend.

The fair-weather friend is the most common type of destructive or harmful "friend": one who is there for you when all is well, but who vanishes when times get tough. How do you recognize a fair-weather "friend"? When do you know that questionable behavior is a sign of a pseudo-friendship or when something else is going on that might cause you to cut this friend some slack?

First, you need to see if there is a pattern: Your friend is there for you, but when you need your friend, she consistently disappears or says, "Sorry, not this time, but next time I can help you out." Next time it's always the same story.

Before you decide that your friend is really a pseudo-friend and therefore no friend at all, you have to ask yourself some questions, and answer as honestly as you can: Are you too demanding? Are you unrealistic about what your friend is capable of offering you? Are you expecting your friend to be there for you in a way that is more reasonable to expect from a family member or spouse? Are you misusing your friend as a bank, therapist, doctor, or caregiver? Are there very real challenges and demands on your friend that offer a reasonable excuse for the disappearing act?

If you are being realistic in your expectations of your friend, as well as what to expect from friendship in general, and your friend is still not there for you, then you need to consider that this person might be a fair-weather friend. This type of situation is actually far easier to deal with than more complicated and convoluted betrayal situations in which one or numerous acts of deception or disloyalty put your friendship and even your personal relationships or career in jeopardy.

The best way to guard against getting in too deep with a fair-weather friend is to be very observant about the way she responds to your simpler requests for attention or help. Does she listen when you speak, or is your friend more concerned with what she has to say? Are small requests heeded or ignored? Does this friend have one excuse too many about why, yet again, she is disappointing you?

Even more insidious than the fair-weather friend is the less well known but potentially more damaging foul-weather friend. This friend plays such mind games that, unheeded, he could hamper your self-development, to say nothing of your self-esteem. This friend needs you to have problems and foul weather. Especially if you met and became friends at a problematic time in your life, this friend gives you clear as well as subtle messages that he will not be there for you when things go well. This friend may also directly or indirectly try to make your relationships or career go bad. Foul-weather pseudo-friends may set you up for personal or professional embarrassment or disaster by providing you with misinformation, inappropriate leads for new business, or recommendations or referrals that are offered with an undertone of negativity or ambivalence.

Here are some questions to ask yourself to determine if a friend is really a foul-weather friend:

- Have this friend's suggestions led more than once to embarrassment for you in a personal or business situation?
- Does this friend seem to be more available for you when things are going badly or when things are going well?

- Do you detect excessive jealousy or even rage when you share good news, in contrast to backslapping and support when you're down in the doldrums?

How a Stranger Becomes a Friend

The process of moving from being a stranger to an acquaintance to a friend has been described by social scientists as well as by writers, such as Mary Kay Shanley, who depicts the process so simply and beautifully in her book *She Taught Me to Eat Artichokes.*[6]

In my book *Friendshifts®*, I shared a chart I developed that shows how a friendship evolves from a shared situation (such as living nearby, working together, going to school together, volunteering on the same committee) to an acquaintanceship.[7] From there, a friendship may—or may not—start to develop. If there are structural changes to the situation, such as one friend relocating to a new neighborhood or a different job, those changes will test the emerging friendship. Will it survive, even though it may no longer be convenient? Will it maintain its current level? Will it dissolve into "no contact" and the end of the relationship? Or will it continue to flourish, as it becomes a casual, close, or best friendship?

Why is a friend chosen? A connection has to occur, almost like a chemical reaction. It is the friendship version of that feeling, in your heart and your entire being, that there is something about this person that clicks with you, whether you're similar or opposite, whether you share the same interests or have contrasting interests. My research into friendship has shown another key factor: The strongest predictor of longevity in a friendship is shared values.[8] Therefore, what may initially also draw you together is the realization that you and the potential friend share the same beliefs and basic orientation to the world and relationships. (For further discussion of how friendship blossoms, see Chapter 8, "Finding Good Friends.")

Twosomes, Threesomes, and Groups

Often you find yourself becoming friends with not just one new person but two, three, or more. A two-person friendship (a dyad, or a twosome) is the kind of friendship we most often think of. But each type of friendship pattern has considerations unique to the number of friends in the group. The two-person friendship is most likely to involve a friend with whom you can become close or best friends. It has the greatest potential for intimacy and trust, but since it depends upon each of its participants for its existence, it is also the friendship that is most likely to dissolve if there are conflicts or separations.

The three-person friendship (triad) is easier to maintain than the two-person friendship since the friends can share information about each other and they have the triad in common. ("I spoke to so-and-so and she told me to tell you that . . ." or "X and I got together, and we reminisced about the time you and X went to . . .") But it is also more challenging in terms of intimacy than a two-way friendship since information has to be shared equally with both friends; there may be jealousy or competition among the friends. Furthermore, it is said that there is no such thing as a friendship that is equal among all three participants; instead it is a friendship pair plus one. Who the pair is, and who the "extra" friend is, may shift around because of a friend's availability, in terms of time or emotion.

Rosalie, a 34-year-old married public relations manager, had a three-way friendship that ended. Rosalie explains:

> It was a triangle situation. I found that another friend and I were excluding the third. When I realized that it was really my friend that was the ringleader and consciously keeping this third friend out, I began to feel I couldn't trust her. That feeling of distrust was what eventually made me end the friendship. I felt as though if she could be this unkind to our third friend, what was to stop her from treating me like that one day?

Friendship groups of four or more offer many benefits: the feeling of camaraderie, of being part of a friendship group, even of being part of an exclusive circle. The advantages in numbers, especially having more choices for companionship since you could get together with one of the friends if the others are busy, are offset by the diminishing intimacy or feeling of uniqueness about the bond, which is more typical with a friendship twosome or even a triad.

Cliques

At certain times, such as when you're in high school or when you work with many colleagues, being part of a clique may seem to be the most important way, the only way, to feel liked and validated. Being part of the "in" crowd, at least on the surface, makes someone feel accepted and important. Quite often, the superficial reason given when teen or elementary school violence breaks out is that the perpetrators were not part of the "right" clique at school, and that enraged them. Of course, we all know that the causes for such horrific violent acts run much deeper, but it does reflect how high emotions run if you are outside of "the" clique.[9]

Beginning in middle school, I preferred to have one or two close or best friends rather than being part of a group of friends or a clique. By high school, there was a distinctive clique, the "in" crowd. It seems practically everyone acknowledged that these were the half-dozen elite, an amazing accomplishment in a senior class with more than 1,500 students. Failing to be in "the clique" definitely made me feel rejected and like a second-class citizen.

At my twenty-fifth high school reunion, I ran into a man who had been in "the clique." I said hello, and he replied, "I was hoping you'd be here." I was stunned. He was hoping I'd be at the reunion? I didn't even know that he knew I existed. Then he shared with me that he had always wanted to talk to me, but that I had never seemed to notice him.

Cliques, I realized, and those who are part of them, may be as much of a mystery to those who are in them as to those who are left out of them.

Unlike friendship networks or groups, which can be productive and beneficial, cliques tend to be restrictive. The key difference between a friendship network or group and a clique is that a network is not exclusive; it allows members to enter and leave without a stigma or fanfare. By contrast, a clique is inclusive and limiting. Not only is it difficult or impossible to break through or get into a clique, once one is formed and operating, there are emotional and social ramifications if someone decides to opt out.

Cyberspace Friendships

Until recently, except for the occasional pen pal, almost all friendships began in a predictable pattern, with both friends interacting in the same space, most frequently through living nearby, going to school together, attending camp, participating in a shared community or volunteer activity, working together, or being introduced to one another through shared friends or romantic partners.

In the last five years, however, a new category of friendship has arisen: cyberspace friends. Just when everyone thought friendship was on the decline for busy students, workers, and parents, Internet friendships have emerged.

But are these relationships, which are started and often maintained on-line without the benefit of face-to-face meetings, really friendship as we define and know it? Is e-mail really helping traditional friends to stay connected?

Friendships that start on-line have the Internet as the shared place for their initial meeting. It may be that two potential friends are brought together within the context of participating in an on-line chat or being part of the same Internet list.

There are three basic kinds of Internet friendships: friendships that begin on-line and are maintained as strictly on-line friendships; friendships that begin on-line but in which the two friends eventually meet, continuing the friendship through a combination of on-line and face-to-face meetings; and pre-existing friends who now use e-mail as another convenient and cost-effective way to help maintain their relationship, especially if they live at a distance.

Within these three types of Internet friendships are the categories of casual, close, or best friendships, based on intimacy, as previously described. Whether you meet in cyberspace or standing in line at the post office, it is still going to take time to gain each other's trust and to move the relationship along from acquaintanceship to a casual, close, or best friendship. You will therefore want to be careful about what information you give out; you should observe how it is used and guard yourself against its misuse, just as you would with a relationship that begins in a more traditional way.

It is meaningful to spend some time looking at the evolution of cyberspace friendships, and the special challenges they pose, because the potential for friendship betrayal exists with these new types of friendships even more than with traditional ones.

Why Has Internet Friendship Evolved?

One reason for the evolution of Internet friendship is the technology itself. The Internet has opened up the potential for connecting beyond the geographic boundaries of time and space that in the past limited access to potential friends.

Another reason is lack of time. Those who are busy juggling career and family, who were putting their traditional friendships on the back burner, are now connecting through Internet friendships that are available at any time of day or night.

Nowadays parents are less available to children because both parents often work and teens may return home from school to empty apartments or houses. The Internet has become a convenient and accessible way to connect with friends across town or around the world. A parent is unnecessary to shuffle a child or teen to or from his or her cyberspace friend.

A fourth reason is immediacy. You don't have to wait for your phone call to be returned or to make the time to have lunch together. "The allure of the on-line relationship, for me, is that it is instant," says Suzanne Boyd, owner and general manager of Kindercloset.com, located in the Seattle, Washington, area. Suzanne, 34, is married and the mother of two children, ages five and four. "If I have something I want to celebrate, or need a 'cybershoulder' to cry on, I can do so almost immediately with confidence that I will be heard."

A fifth reason is that Internet friendship affords an opportunity to share with others who may reflect your own diverse interests. Thirty-year-old Kimberly Kurpgeweit has three children, ages 8, 10, and 12, lives in Colorado, and is editor-in-chief of FamilyFusion.com, an on-line community for stepfamilies. She notes: "E-mail friendships allow me to connect with people who share the same interests as myself. Many of my other friends are stay-at-home mothers who have no interest in running a business because they don't need to or want to. E-mail friendships are extremely valuable to me right now. . . . I have found support, advice, information, and education by connecting with others who are either in the same situation as myself or are more experienced at all of this."

For adults who may want relationships outside the narrow boundaries of their towns or cities, cyberspace friendship allows an international connection with friends. When these friends live hundreds and sometimes thousands of miles away, even communicating by phone, because of a large time difference, might be difficult or impossible.

Internet friendships also provide an opportunity to have friends who are dissimilar in age, gender, socioeconomic status, and career, marital, or family situation.

Still another appeal of cyberspace friendships is the particular communication style that it offers. As Suzanne Vaughan, a Colorado-based motivational speaker and the author of *Potholes & Parachutes,*[10] observes:

It has been my experience that these cyber-friendships are established more rapidly than through conventional methods. I think one of the reasons is that we do not have the physical image of the other person to distract us from getting to know them. . . . We communicate much more openly and with more truth, which helps us to establish trust between one another quickly and easily. I believe that is because we don't see this person on a day-to-day basis or interact with them in a professional or personal environment. Therefore, we open up to them and share parts of our lives we wouldn't ordinarily share that soon in a one-on-one relationship. We cut to the chase. We say it like it is as there is less fear of judgment. There can be tremendous support in this kind of relationship, support that helps us deal with problems or challenges we don't feel safe in sharing with any other friend.

Finally, Internet friendships enable those who are embarrassed about their appearance, or even housebound because of a disability, to connect without the pressure, terror, discomfort, or inconvenience that they may associate with traditional face-to-face friendships. I described Jill previously in relation to the early childhood abuse that she has struggled to overcome as the reason behind her fear of friendship; she is also extremely overweight. Jill admits that her embarrassment about her appearance is one reason on-line friendships are so much better for her right now. "It's easier for me to meet people on the Internet," Jill explains. "There's that anonymity. They can't see you. I would like to learn how to be friends in person [but] I have trouble even talking to the neighbor next door. When people start getting close, I start backing away. I think there's that fear of being hurt." For Jill and countless others, the Internet seems emotionally safer and, as long as the friendship remains on-line, less risky. "Because I'm overweight, there's an embarrassment and shame there, so I don't like people seeing me."

But for those who thought they would save time by having cyberspace friendships, quite often the opposite is occurring. Without strict guidelines about how long to stay on-line or how lengthy to make a typical e-mail, what may begin as a time-saver can quickly become a time drain. Internet friendship, like traditional face-to-face friendship, takes time. A 45-year-old married, home-based business owner in Virginia with two children, ages 10 and 14, who wants to be referred to by her screen name of Zannrose, points out: "Cyber-relationships take time like regular friendships. It takes time to communicate, for instance, in instant messaging, chat rooms, e-mails. . . . At first, I was on the Internet late at night, and this did not help my sleep needs or my family life. I am getting better at this, at finding time needed for my family and outside activities and still creating people relationships with my cyber-friends and business associates."

But a friendship that has only the Internet as its foundation may not evolve into the nurturing, dependable relationship that we have come to associate with face-to-face friendships. First, the cues we all need for interpreting communication and nuance are lacking. Second, it is too easy to pull away, disappear, or unwittingly offend a cyberspace friend by a change in the frequency of the exchange or the misinterpretation of language.

Nancy, a 55-year-old writer who lives in Europe but is originally from Massachusetts, finds e-mail an essential way to keep up with her close and best friends, who live far away:

> To many people, communicating by e-mail may seem superficial, but since so many people who are important to me are scattered all over the world, it is a real blessing. I am in contact much more often with friends now, even if it's only to say, "Hi, I miss being able to see you regularly." Through e-mail, I've been able to renew contacts with friends whom I have not seen for over twenty years. I stay in touch at least every few weeks with my two best friends, one of whom is in Oklahoma and the other in Illinois, and both of whom are just as busy as I am. Before e-mail, we were lucky to be able to write to each other more than once every three to four months.

But e-mail can also damage a friendship, if misused. Fifty-year-old Linda, a respiratory therapist in Texas, explains how e-mail sabotaged her friendship with a co-worker:

> I've known her for ten years and she seemed to be of great character and integrity. [She seemed] to have the same ethics I did. We got along very well. Not an intimate relationship but a good relationship.
>
> I was working on a project and thought I might be making a mistake. So I consulted an expert and found out that I was indeed wrong. But my friend immediately e-mailed me *and* 15 people that it was unacceptable and that it was definitely wrong and I should be aware that I was making a huge mistake.

Why didn't she e-mail only me? Why didn't she come to me first [and say something like] I don't agree with this? She didn't come to me at all. It should have involved myself, her, and one other person in the end. It should have involved only three people total, but she felt this need to tell 15. So I e-mailed a response back to her and to the 15 people to set the record straight.

What could have caused Linda's friend to do this? Says Linda: "Since she was new to the department, I really think it was a power play, a staff play, a way to make a stand in her position."

Internet Friendship Tips

How can you protect yourself from some of the potential pitfalls of on-line friendships? Here are six suggestions:

1. Let the friendship evolve at a pace that is comfortable for you. Don't be pressured into sharing thoughts or information on-line with one person, a list, or in a chat room that is intimate or confidential before it feels right.
2. Remember that it is almost impossible to protect information that is shared on-line; nothing is really "confidential," especially if shared in a group situation.
3. Be careful not to let your face-to-face friendships suffer or to become too addicted to the immediacy of e-mail friendship or the short time it takes to send and answer e-mails.
4. If you get to the point of feeling a face-to-face meeting is mutually agreeable, take all the precautions about protecting yourself that have traditionally been suggested for those answering a "personals" ad. These include meeting in a public place, and not giving out any personal information until you are absolutely sure whom you are dealing with.
5. Follow the rule that I advocate in my book *Business Protocol:* Praise in writing, criticize verbally. Avoid writing anything in an e-mail to an individual or to a list that could defame, slander, or negatively criticize someone or her business.[11]
6. In general, avoid putting anything in an e-mail that you wouldn't feel comfortable reading about the next morning in the newspaper.

Used wisely, and not misused, the Internet can open up a world of new casual, close, or best friends, as well as functioning as a time-saving tool for keeping up with the friends you already have. Thirty-five-year-old Kevin, a single college professor, credits e-mail with helping him to stay connected with friends who, once they married and had additional time and relationship constraints, might have fallen by the wayside: "I once heard someone older than I am say that friends come and go, and in twenty years, all of mine will be different. [But] it seems the Internet has preserved many of my friendships by allowing me to keep in touch." Similarly, a 48-year-old educator notes that "e-mail has been the best thing that ever happened to friendship. Through e-mail I am now back in contact with high school friends, friends I made when I lived in Europe, and college friends. Instead of the yearly Christmas letter to keep up to date, now we e-mail [and] we keep truly up to date."

Chapter 2

Detecting Harmful People *Before* They're Friends: 21 Types of Potentially Negative Friends

There is no crystal ball to predict that a particular friend will turn out to be a reliable, positive relationship in your life or, by contrast, a negative association that will cause you emotional distress, or worse. Since destructive or negative friends are not always that easy to spot, being forewarned is forearmed, as the saying goes. Recognizing the 21 types that I have observed and studied and that I describe in this chapter may help you to reevaluate your current friends, as well as to reassess past or potential friendships. Some may have more than one of the traits that follow; you may even recognize yourself in one or more of these types.

The following 21 distinctive friendship types, which revolve around seven central issues—trust, empathy, honesty, confidentiality, competitiveness, acceptance, and the existence of appropriate boundaries—are likely to be negative or destructive:

1. The Promise Breaker (constantly disappoints you or breaks promises)
2. The Taker (borrows and fails to return something precious or valuable to you)
3. The Double-crosser (betrays you big-time)
4. The Risk-taker (puts you in harm's way because of illegal or dangerous behavior)
5. The Self-absorbed (never has time to listen to you)
6. The Cheat (lies or steals your romantic partner)
7. The Discloser (betrays your confidence)
8. The Competitor (excessively combative with you and wants what you have—relationships, job, possessions)
9. The One-upper (always one up on you)
10. The Rival (desires whatever you possess and may try to take it from you)

11. The Fault-finder (overly critical)
12. The Downer (always negative, critical, and sad, and makes you feel that way, too)
13. The Rejecter (dislikes you and lets you know it)
14. The Abuser (verbally, physically, or sexually abuses you)
15. The Loner (would rather be alone than with a friend)
16. The Blood-sucker (overly dependent)
17. The Therapist (needs to analyze everything and give advice)
18. The Interloper (overly involved in your life)
19. The Copycat (imitates you)
20. The Controller (needs to dominate you or the friendship)
21. The Caretaker (needs to be a friend's keeper, parent, or nursemaid, rather than an equal)

Recognizing what might be causing these behaviors and learning how to cope with them may give you peace of mind. But there is always the question of degree. You may recognize some of the 21 traits in yourself or in a friend, but the occurrence may be so rare or so minute that it does not pose a problem.

Some friends may be betrayers from the start; others may turn into betrayers because of what's going on in their lives or because of changes in their personality. Sometimes you need to consider what your friend is really like within the context of all the behaviors. I can't emphasize enough that you need to consider the root cause.

In this chapter you will also find a profile of the "ideal" friend, followed by a self-quiz to help you deal with negative friendships and a checklist of factors that distinguish positive from negative friendships.

1. The Promise Breaker

This friend constantly disappoints you or breaks promises, most likely because she herself was probably constantly disappointed during her formative years. Your friend is unable to stop herself or himself from repeating that pattern. It is an annoying but comfortable pattern for your friend, and without psychological help, it may be hard for him or her to alter this pattern. You could abandon the friend and the friendship, or you could find a way to detach yourself by lowering your expectations for this friendship. If she promises to do something for you, even to meet you for a cup of coffee, you can say, "Sure," but protect yourself by knowing, in the back of your mind, that this friend "nine times out of ten" is going to cancel out on you.

Although your friend may always have been this way, she may have also recently acquired this trait because of something she is going through right now. If a friend who has always been there for you, through thick and thin, has only recently become less reliable, you might want to cut her some slack. You have to decide if this is a lifelong trait that will be hard or impossible to change, a temporary condition that will be short-lived, or something, if it does continue indefinitely, that you are willing to accept and handle.

One way to try to change the Promise Breaker is to help her to understand the consequences of your ignored pledges. Perhaps you have been keeping your disappointments about this to yourself. Try telling her how it makes you feel. "Of course, I'll understand that you're not in the mood to drive over, but I was really looking forward to our visit." Perhaps she is unaware that this is a pattern rather than an isolated incident. "Yes, of course, I understand, but do you realize this is the fourth time in as many weeks that you've backed out on something you promised to do with me?"

If you want to continue your friendship with the Promise Breaker, make sure you reconfirm any plans at least once or even right before you are supposed to meet. If you have a cell phone or beeper, make sure your friend is able to contact you so at least you won't be left waiting if, once again, he cancels a meeting. Have "back-up" for any promises your friend makes; at least if the Promise Breaker disappoints you again, you won't be as inconvenienced by it.

The next time he promises something, try saying, "Yeah, right." When he gets angry at your sarcasm, explain that you are simply pointing out his habit of breaking his promises. Then reframe it in a more positive vein by saying, "Prove me wrong. This time, keep your promise."

2. The Taker

If it wasn't so annoying when a friend keeps something you have loaned him, you might be downright flattered. After all, this type of friend has a need to keep a piece of you, as symbolized by whatever object you have loaned, whether it's a sweater, a book, or even money.

The Taker has such low self-esteem that it is emotionally too difficult for him to return something to you, even though it's rightfully yours, whether it's a magazine or a compliment. Keeping what you have shared helps the Taker to feel as if the scales are tipped in his favor; he actually feels you have much more than he has, whether it's wealth, attractiveness, accomplishments, or relationships.

A possible cause for the Taker's behavior is a childhood characterized by nothing ever being enough. Whether or not her parents actually had money or were destitute, they conveyed a sense of material or even emotional deprivation to your friend, so now the Taker needs to take, rather than give. The Taker may not be impoverished; she could be a millionaire, but she feels poor.

Avoid the unpleasant feelings that such withholding is bound to cause by avoiding this trap in the first place. Or if you do loan something to a friend who is a Taker, emotionally and financially wash your hands of it. If you get it back, it's gravy. But you're not disappointed, angry, or surprised if the Taker keeps it.

Your friendship may help the Taker to develop a more positive self-image so that she can more readily return feelings, compliments, favors, or material goods to you and to others. The Taker has to develop a self-awareness about her tendency to keep things as well as the possible root causes.

You might also help a friend who has this tendency by concretizing the loan: Any money that exchanges hands, especially if it is a large sum, has a formal loan letter or agreement attached to it, including a date and terms for repayment, with interest, if any. A book or article of clothing that is borrowed has a fixed return policy and even a written notation as to expectations for its return.

Of course, when the Taker is a thief, that may be a betrayal without any recourse but ending the friendship. For example, one woman's former friend stole her jewelry; another's maid of honor stole money from her at her bachelorette party. The Taker might also take something less tangible than jewelry or money, but it is a theft nonetheless. For example, Lillian's workplace friend "took a recruit lead from me, which is just not done."

3. The Double-crosser
This negative friend betrays you big-time. It could happen when someone does something to hurt you, such as spreading a malicious rumor about you. Or it could be an emotional double-cross—for example, when a close or best friend stops speaking to you and you never find out why. That's what happened to Jill, who is now 47. Although angry words were never exchanged between Jill and her friend, the silence, the betrayal of their commitment to be friends and to share, was just as real as any harmful action. Jill explains:

> She was the only real friend I ever had. I didn't make friends easily. I wasn't allowed to have friends. When I got to high school, I met Dale, and we became very close. The one time I ran away, I ran to her house. It was a very special friendship. We went to nursing school together. [Then] one day she met another girl. . . . About a week later, she stopped speaking to me. I'd call her; she'd hang up on me. I'd write to her; she'd return the letters, unopened.

Ten years later, they resumed their friendship, although they still have never discussed why Dale stopped calling. The wounds from her friend's emotional double-crossing are there, however. "We're close, but not as close," Jill explains. But then she qualifies her description of her friendship with Dale as "close." "For me, for the type of person I am, it's close. For somebody like my sister, it's not close."

The double-cross could be something even more concrete, like the betrayal experienced by 43-year-old Susan, a homemaker. Susan was betrayed by a married close family friend who was attracted to her sister:

> He continued to express his desire and love for her, and when she insisted that he put an end to the numerous phone messages at her office, [and] she told him of her disgust at this attitude, he turned around and told his wife that my sister was coming on to him. It was a real fatal attraction. I personally phoned [him] and ended [our] friendship. I'm talking real betrayal. Our family felt totally betrayed by this man, whom we had all known since childhood.

Susan shares other betrayals, by another friend: "One of my girlfriends is now using my sister and myself as an alibi while she carries on extramarital affairs. This is very upsetting. She has also repeated some things to another friend which were said to her in confidence." This second friend is putting Susan in a compromising position, and possibly even an ethical bind, over the cover-up of her extramarital affairs. By blabbing privileged information, she is also acting like the Discloser, described below.

The Double-crosser may have some real emotional issues that need to be addressed if you are to continue a friendship with him. If your friend was betrayed by a parent or sibling during his formative years, he may have a need to repeat that behavior with his friends. The betrayal could have been as subtle as being disappointed by his parents or as blatant as being the victim of emotional, physical, or sexual abuse. Your friend may need outside help to reverse the cycle he is in, of doing to others what was done to him.

If you have been double-crossed by a particular friend, you may want to consider ending the friendship. If you have not been directly harmed by this friend but have evidence that she has hurt others, you have to decide if you are risking too much by maintaining the friendship.

If you do decide to walk away from this friendship, do it in a low-key way that avoids incurring the wrath of the Double-crosser. You do not want to be her next victim.

(For more insight into the Double-crosser, see the discussion of depression and other mental disorders in Chapter 3.)

4. The Risk-taker

This friend, by putting you in harm's way because of dangerous or illegal behavior, can be destructive and harmful even to the point of being pathological. At what point do you need to get "un-involved" in your friend's illegal or dangerous behavior? Should you just walk away? Should you first advise your friend that he or she needs to get help before it's too late? Should you tell the authorities?

These are complex questions, and the answers have to be tailored to each situation. It will, of course, depend upon the intimacy of the friendship, your history with your friend, your instinctive or acquired knowledge of just how far you can comfortably go in getting into a dialogue about these issues with your friend, as well as whether you perceive a real threat to you, your friend, your friend's family, your co-workers, or the community. You may decide that your friend's problems need to be dealt with by a professional therapist and that you are ill-advised to try to change his behavior yourself.

Therefore, you may decide that the ideal course of action is to stay far away from the Risk-taker, or you may find yourself arrested, imprisoned, or worse. The Risk-taker may drive excessively fast, put you in harm's way, or ask you to accompany her as she climbs a mountain that is exceedingly dangerous. Some people shoplift because they enjoy the thrill of taking a risk and seeing if they will get caught, but unconsciously they want to get caught. If you get mixed up with a Risk-taker, you could find yourself caught as well. The causes of this friend's behavior are psychological, pathological, and even sociopathic. You are not your friend's therapist or guidance counselor.

5. The Self-absorbed
Certainly the Self-absorbed is a tamer type of negative friend than the Risk-taker. Still, especially over the long haul, a friend who does not make the time to listen to you will eat away at your self-esteem. For you to feel good about yourself, and for your friendship to thrive, you have to be more than a sounding board. The Self-absorbed does not care; she listens to you only because she is waiting to speak.

Self-absorbed chatter is a way of covering up an inability to tolerate silence, which some, especially those who have intimacy problems, may find excruciating. You may ask your friend to try to become more aware that he is talking non-stop, and about himself, when it's really a nervous habit designed to fill up the time and space. Can your friend learn to relax more? Enjoy silence? Learn how to ask questions so that you don't feel like a dumping ground?

Once again, is this a trait your friend is aware of and choosing to ignore, or is he unaware of it and incapable of changing it? If change is not possible, is there enough that is positive about this friendship that you are willing to continue it even if it is decidedly lopsided?

Perhaps, in a gentle and non-offensive way, you could ask the Self-absorbed friend if she seems to notice that the give-and-take is unequal, that she shares more about her life than you get to share about yours.

With the Self-absorbed friend, you might want to plan an activity to share that minimizes this problem, such as playing tennis, going to the movies, or taking a class. You might want to avoid sitting next to each other on an eight-hour plane ride or having lengthy meals alone together. As with the One-upper, whose profile revolves around excessive jealousy, involving more friends with the Self-absorbed might help to offset her nervousness as well as create some "air time" that will even out the balance of power.

6. The Cheat
Next to the Abuser and the Risk-taker, the Cheat is the most heinous kind of "friend." The Cheat lies to you. The Cheat may lie to others. She may lie once or may show a pattern of lying. Since friendship, by definition, is a bond based on trust and honesty, lying should not be tolerated. This is a destruc-

tive behavior that you have to address directly or seriously consider as justification for ending the friendship.

Lying is a form of cheating; you are cheating someone out of the truth. People lie because they're afraid of the truth; they're afraid the truth will hurt them. So they lie. If your single girlfriend tells everyone she's forty, and you know she's fifty, you may feel sad that she has a need to lie about her age, but you might not want to end the friendship if she's honest about everything else. (She may have even shared with you her fears, however ungrounded, that her career or her social life will suffer if she reveals the truth.)

What should you do about lying? You can try to set an example of telling the truth so your friends will know it is something that you value.

Be aware if a friend lies, and try to see if there is a pattern to it. Is it something relatively harmless, like lying about age, or something more heinous, like falsifying credentials on a resumé?

If it's something inconsequential, try not to overreact. No one's perfect.

You will also want to be clear about whether something has been said in the interest of tact and diplomacy rather than being an outright lie.

You might also want to help your friend feel better about herself so that lying eventually becomes less of an option. If you witness your friend lying about her age, for example, you might want to mention it to her when you are in private by noting, "You know, you're so vital and talented that there's no reason for you to have to shave ten years off your age. You're successful and attractive, whatever your age."

But whether you should say something to a friend if you catch her in a lie definitely depends on the lie and the circumstances. It also depends on whether or not it's important that your friend knows that you know the truth. If your friendship is more important than lying about some little thing, you might want to ignore it. But what if it's a big thing? If you feel you are being compromised or that the lie is an ethical breach that cannot be ignored, you might have to speak up or end the friendship.

Of course, every situation is unique, and some circumstances are complex and complicated. For example, if you know your friend's dying of cancer and you ask him how he feels and he says, "I'm okay," you don't have to say, " Hey, I know you're lying. I know you're feeling terrible and you've got just a few days to live." Or if your friend just spent thousands of dollars on a new car and you hate the color but you tell your friend it's a nice car, did you just "lie"? Is that a permissible white lie or a tactful omission of an opinion that had not even been solicited?

So use your judgment. If someone has a reputation for spreading malicious lies about you at work or in social situations, that is certainly a negative trait that you need to consider very carefully.

The Cheat also includes someone who commits one of the greatest betrayals by a friend: cheating on a friend with the friend's spouse. Despite idealized tales of two friends who still maintain their friendship even after one cheats with the other's romantic partner, this is a betrayal that is hard to overcome or forget. If you do maintain your friendship, you have to ask yourself how and why the betrayal happened, and whether you can really forgive your friend and your significant other. Who is to be blamed, the friend or the romantic partner? Tempers run high, and anger and rage can get out of hand in these situations, so it's necessary to keep a cool head. It is also important to look at yourself and seriously consider if you did anything, consciously or unconsciously, to set up the situation. I am reminded of a woman I interviewed and wrote about in *Friendshifts*®. She often worked late at the office, so she asked her husband to take her friend, who was also her next-door neighbor, in her place, to the theater and other events. In time, her husband left her and went off with her friend.[1]

Of course, some friendships can survive cheating with a friend's romantic partner, as can romances or marriages. But if you and your friend, and your romantic partner, value monogamy, you will probably have to deal with this situation and the betrayal if there is a chance of putting it behind you.

7. The Discloser

When you say to this friend, "This is just between us," she nods her head but unfortunately that promise will last only as long as it takes her to get to her phone or e-mail. Although there should be an assumption of confidentiality and trust between friends, this friend can't help herself. Telling this person a secret makes her feel vulnerable and uncomfortable. Like the game "hot potato," she has to pass the hot secret along to someone else in order to relieve the anxiety knowing the secret made her feel. There are also some disclosers who simply have a big mouth. If someone you know has this personality trait, avoid telling her your innermost secret—unless, of course, you don't mind if it's shared with the world.

This friend quickly gets a reputation for being a gossip. Unfortunately, there may be some secondary gains to having that distinction. Maybe the primary friend is annoyed by the betrayal and the secret sharing, but everyone else, including other friends, may be delighted by the confidential information that is being shared.

You also have to be sure that your friend understands that you consider the information that you share to be confidential or secret. Spreading the news that you just got a raise or are expecting a child may seem like information that is fair game for retelling. If it is something you do not want retold, or if you want to be the one retelling it, let your friend know before you mislabel her the Discloser.

How do you know if someone will betray your confidence? If you suspect someone has this trait, share an unimportant secret that you could live with her spreading and see how fast or widespread the confidence is shared.

If you suspect that your friend is unaware that he discloses secrets, start by bringing this behavior out in the open. Pick a specific instance when your friend revealed a confidence, and see if he acknowledges his transgression. Does he apologize? Does he deny doing it? Does he ask your forgiveness, explaining that he was unaware the information was privileged?

If you suspect your friend is incapable of changing this pattern and you want to maintain the friendship, protect yourself by being more careful about exactly what information you share. You might also want to reconsider the level of intimacy for this friendship; if you want to maintain your relationship, perhaps it should be on a less frequent or less confidential basis.

8. The Competitor

A little bit of competition is healthy and to be expected. An appropriate amount of competition will motivate and stimulate. But too much competition between friends starts to destroy the friendship. One of the primary ingredients in a positive friendship is that one or both friends feel that they can be "themselves," and that they don't have to put on airs or impress one another. Competition implies a race in which one wins and the other loses; those conditions are quite the opposite of what someone typically expects in a positive friendship, especially a close or best one.

Friends who are competitors probably compete in every area of their lives and find it difficult or impossible to ease up even when it comes to close or best friends. They may compete at work, at school, and even in community affairs. They may be in competition with their spouses or romantic partners, or even with their parents or their children. The Competitor may find this distinctive personality trait hard or impossible to change or eradicate.

You can help the situation, however, by trying to avoid setting up overly competitive situations. For instance, if you share about a success in your life or career, especially if you ease into bragging, you may unwittingly be setting off an "I'll show you" reaction.

Helping to heighten the Competitor's awareness about this tendency might help her to deal with this proclivity. If you do want to share something that you think will propel her into a "me too" reaction, you could preface your comments with, "Let me just share something without it having anything to do with you, okay?"

The onus for changing the Competitor's behavior, however, is on her; developing a better self-image will diminish her need to compete with everything you say or do.

If you wish to stay friends with the Competitor, you may have to be willing to listen to his brags and boasts far more often than you can share your own.

9. The One-upper

No matter what you say or do, the One-upper has said or done it better. Her children are better, smarter, and more attractive than yours are. The One-upper makes you feel belittled and less significant than you want to feel. She is excessively competitive and jealous; but on the positive side, this friend may be very caring, devoted, and attentive. The One-upper may not have shown her true colors early on in the friendship because at that beginning stage you were both sharing brags back and forth. But in time the tendency becomes more and more annoying.

The One-upper has low self-esteem; if he were self-confident, the need to always be "one-up" would diminish or disappear. The formative years for the One-upper may have involved a parent who excessively compared him to his siblings, cousins, neighbors, or classmates. "Why can't you be more like . . . ?" or "Did you see what so-and-so just did?" At the opposite end of the spectrum, a parent who went overboard praising a child might have raised the One-upper. On his own or with professional help, the One-upper needs to see that he is neither lacking by comparison nor "the best" or "the one." Developing a realistic self-assessment that is neither grandiose nor self-deprecating will help your friend to accept what you share without having to always one-up you.

But while your friend is still the One-upper, do you continue the friendship, while dwelling on the positives? Do you ask your friend to minimize the one-ups, if she is able to? Or do you try to "one-up" the one-ups, beating her at her own game? You must decide if the friendship is close and valuable enough to justify the mental gymnastics. You might also consider including this friend in a larger friendship group of three or more. Keep the discussion to something less personal than individual or family achievements so the one-ups are minimized.

A group friendship may also help for another reason. It's just possible that the one-on-one intimacy may be causing some distress and anxiety in your friend, causing him to try (and succeed!) to create distance through one-upmanship. You can decide not to play into the trap of pushing the One-upper away, or at least realize that he or she is unwittingly trying to maintain distance, ignore his or her excessively competitive ways, and enjoy the friendship anyway.

10. The Rival

The Rival goes beyond the competitive instinct into the realm of green envy, jealousy, and even malice. This friend's desire for what you have—relationships, job, possessions—can be so severe that she actually tries to take them from you.

If you have a friendship with the Rival, be careful. If you think your friend has this tendency under control, fine. But if not, you need to protect your property and your relationships as much as possible. You have a terrific car? If your friend doesn't go out and buy the same car, or a nicer one, be careful that he doesn't ask to borrow yours (only to return it in less than optimum condition). Be careful and be forewarned; it might not be the best idea to ask this friend to take your romantic partner to a party if you have to go out of town on a business trip and don't want your mate to have to stay home alone. Bottom line: If you choose to continue the friendship, minimize situations where jealousy and envy could get out of hand.

The suggestions for how to deal with a friend who is the Rival are similar to dealing with the Competitor: Keep your bragging and boasting to a minimum.

Jealousy, however, is sometimes a two-way street, and seeing that you are as jealous of your friend as your friend is of you may help to keep this trait in perspective. For example, 55-year-old Michael, a divorced, self-employed consultant, talks about the jealousy that his closest friend, Larry, a former co-worker whom he met ten years ago at a manufacturing company, seemed to have toward him when they worked together:

The manager we had at the time was pretty much taken up with me. I had the right [Ivy League] credentials, and Larry, my buddy, didn't. I think he was very much put off [by the fact that] this woman preferred me and seemed to rate my skills above his.

I asked if his friend's jealousy for him had ended their friendship. Michael thought for a moment and then related that he also had been envious of his friend when they worked together:

I was actually a little jealous of him, too. I felt he had more street savvy and some additional computer skills. He probably had a deeper technical background than I did. I felt he had the smarts that fit him [better] into the situation for the kind of work [we were] doing.

Michael and Larry have never spoken about the jealousy they had for each other and probably never will. The friendship persists, even though they no longer work together. They have not seen each other since Michael left the company six months ago, but they do speak on the phone a couple of times a week. The envy is something Michael is willing to accept as part of their friendship. He says that Larry now seems jealous of Michael's freedom from the day-to-day corporate job. "I haven't set up a revenue stream, though, so what's there to be jealous of?" he adds, self-mockingly.

11. The Fault-finder

Nothing you do, say, or wear is good enough for this overly critical friend. The Fault-finder was probably raised by extremely judgmental parents who were also rearing equally hypercritical siblings. Being criticized during her formative years laid the groundwork for an overly critical adult. It's a hard trait to reverse, and your friend may even be unaware that she is so critical or that it annoys and upsets you so much. Before labeling this type of friendship as hopelessly destructive, you might want to see if your friend can recognize this excessively derogatory behavior and, with time and help, change that orientation. Otherwise, you may decide that you just have to accept this trait in your friend and realize that it reflects on her, not on you or your friendship.

If you value this friend and want to try to maintain the friendship despite the Fault-finder's criticisms, try sharing with him how his behavior makes you feel. "I know you like me, and I know you may not even mean to make me feel bad, but when you find fault in everything I say or do, it makes me feel bad about myself." He might get defensive, even saying it's "your problem," not his. But if you emphasize how the Fault-finder's behavior impacts on *you*, it may help him to reassess what he is saying or doing without having to be "right." Furthermore, by sharing how it makes you feel, you may feel less resentful if you decide you are willing to put up with it.

However, if you are at your wit's end and willing to try one more thing before calling it quits, try finding fault in the Fault-finder. Those who criticize and find fault are often unable to take it from others. If you do criticize the Fault-finder, it may break the spell of negativity that is now allowing this friend to say and do anything toward you. When the shoe is on the other foot, she may suddenly have an "ah-ha" awareness of what it feels like to others. But beware: The Fault-finder might cut off your friendship forever rather than deal with your criticisms or even try to understand the larger message you were trying to convey.

12. The Downer

This friend has a problem with being negative, critical, and sad. In severe cases, she may be clinically depressed and in need of professional help. Unfortunately, until your friend gets help, or even while she is getting counseling, her depression may affect your friendship.

Parents who were depressed or sad may have raised the Downer, or she could be married to a negative person or working in a contradictory environment and, by association, has become depressed. The Downer may be depressed or negative as a permanent or a temporary trait. Your friend may be going through rough times, including depression related to job pressures or even job loss, health concerns, family problems, divorce, or grief related to the loss of a loved one.

To survive a friendship with the Downer, you have to separate your own personality, attitudes, and relationships from your friend's negativity and related depression. If listening to your friend complaining or being blue is just too much, perhaps you can limit the amount of time you spend together, rather than cut him off completely. Obviously the Downer needs help, and if this is a friendship that you want to salvage, you may not want to end the friendship just because your friend has become excessively depressed and needy.

On the other hand, if this is a long-standing character trait, you may want to think again. If you are just now realizing that your friend is the Downer, you may want to reevaluate whether this friendship will work for you in the long run.

While you're deciding what to do, try to use this situation as a learning experience: What was it about your friend that attracted you to him, despite his negative outlook? Have you changed, or has your friend changed? Is the depression a temporary or chronic condition? Is your friend getting professional help? Are you also a depressed person, and is this a case of "like attracts like," or is this an example of "opposites attract"? Try to see how having a friend who is the Downer will help you understand how you deal with your own world and perhaps how your friends are labeling you.

13. The Rejecter

Why would someone who seems to dislike you, and tells you so every chance he gets, still want to be your friend? The Rejecter is motivated by sadism, cruelty, and a need to control and conquer. The Rejecter may have been all sweetness and light while you were first getting to know one another. But once you became friends, and as the intimacy of your relationship has escalated from casual or close to even best friendship, the negativity and the dislike seem to have escalated as well.

On the surface, it makes no sense. Your friend should like you more now that you're closer friends. But, alas, the Rejecter has a very low opinion of herself. Like the woman who, once married, starts finding fault with her spouse on every big or small matter because she has an intimacy problem, the Rejecter is set off by the very act of getting more intimate and committed. This type of destructive friendship is reminiscent of the old Groucho Marx joke, "Why would I want to join a club that would have me as a member?" Instead of seeing that this is a problem within herself, the Rejecter can't believe anyone worthwhile would want to be her friend, and thus puts the friend down.

You could try pointing out this pattern and motivation to the Rejecter and see if he wants to change his behavior or prefers to deny the validity of your insights.

If you have a thick skin, you could use it to tell yourself, "It's him, not me," as you patiently wait for your friend, on his own or through therapy, to get a grip on this behavior.

You could even try confronting this friend head on by asking, "If I'm such

a loser, why do you want to be my friend?" and see what she says. By bringing the behavior to the surface, and letting the Rejecter see how ludicrous
her put-downs are, you might be able to get your friend to change this unacceptable approach to you and your relationship.

Sometimes the Rejecter is a friend who is really angry with you because
of something you're doing. Unable to confront you or her feelings, the Rejecter turns on you and your friendship. This is what happened to Debbie,
who had been best friends with Samantha from fifth grade through high
school graduation. All that changed three years later, when Debbie made a
career decision that would leave Samantha behind. Debbie explains:

> I thought we were the best friends ever, until two or three years after
> school, right before I joined the U.S. Navy. She and I went to a party and she
> told me that she hated me, that she always had and that all the guys she
> went out with had used her to get to me. She [really] hated me for joining
> the Navy and leaving her to her miserable life. I felt betrayed. I left her to
> her miserable life and went on with mine.

14. The Abuser

This destructive friend may be abusing drugs or alcohol, or she may be abusing a child, spouse, or another friend through emotional, physical, or sexual
behavior.

There are countless books written about the causes of abusive behavior,
and each type of abuse has familial as well as psychological causes. For
some, however, being exposed to abuse during the formative years sets up a
cycle of abuse. The child who has been exposed to abuse or who has been the
victim of abuse may, in his adult years, replicate the very behavior that he
consciously despised when he was little.[2]

If your friend is the Abuser, he probably needs professional help or, at the
very least, to be part of a self-help program. (Having a past history of abuse
does not excuse becoming the Abuser.) You may also have to consider seriously whether or not you want to remain in a friendship with the Abuser.
You may see yourself as a savior to your friend or her family members. You
need to figure out why you would get involved with a friend who is the
Abuser or who has serious abuse tendencies. But you also need to think long
and hard about what you know about this friend. Of course, no one wants to
be a tattletale, but if you feel that there is a real risk of injury to your friend

or others, then you must act. Your local police, counseling centers, victims programs, addiction programs, and emergency hotlines all have procedures in place to deal with such situations. If your friend is a minor, you need to consider discussing your concerns with her parent or guardian, as long as you are sure the adult is not the perpetrator of the abuse.

The Abuser represents the extreme situation, if possible, that you want to avoid in the future. One way to reduce the likelihood that this will happen again is to take the Friendship Attunement Quiz in Chapter 8, "Finding Good Friends," and ask yourself those questions about the next person you want to befriend—especially if there's anything about him that makes you a bit uneasy.

15. The Loner

Loners have deep emotional wounds from childhood or failed friendships that make them afraid of new relationships. The Loner may be reclusive and anti-social, or she may sublimate the need for peer relations into her work or into such all-consuming creative outlets as music, art, writing, or even computers and technology.

Though the Loner may not seem interested in friendship, he may have positive and healthy romantic or family relationships, with or without par- enting responsibilities. As long as the absence of peer relationships in his life is not a problem, the Loner may have little motivation to look at the deep-seated issues that cause him to be so afraid of platonic relationships. But if a change occurs, such as retirement from work or physical problems that prohibit pursuing creative activities, or relationship changes such as divorce, the death of a spouse, or an "empty nest" at home, a loneliness may develop that propels the Loner to seek out friendship.

There are numerous reasons that the Loner is reluctant to have any kind of close or best friend, even if he tolerates casual ones. He may have been a victim of emotional, physical, or sexual abuse during his formative years; a parent, sibling, another relative, family friend, trusted caregiver or author- ity figure, or even a stranger could have been the perpetrator. For example, 30-year-old Brendan, a single executive assistant living in Las Vegas, is an example. As a child he was beaten, fondled by his father and, between the ages of seven and nine, repeatedly raped by his older brother and by his brother's friend. His mother stared at him inappropriately throughout his teen years as well. Brendan, who even describes himself as a Loner, writes about how his abusive childhood still affects him:

All of the abuse has carved notches in every area of my life. I was told non-stop how ugly, stupid, sissy, and moronic I was by all family members. Mother often said I ruined her life. . . . I have lived alone for most of the last five years. I would like to have a healthy relationship. But I have big problems with trusting anybody.

Negative sibling relations or harmful friendships during the childhood or teen years could make the adult Loner fearful of friendships. Or if the Loner was an only child and lacked playtime with peers in which to develop friendship skills, she may be unfamiliar with the process of forming and maintaining friendships.

If you want to befriend the Loner, you have to be willing to show patience as he becomes more comfortable with you and what friendship entails. You may even want to ask the Loner, "I want to be your friend, and I don't know if your reluctance to pursue a friendship is that you don't like me or that you don't want a friendship. Can you set the record straight?" In that way, you might be able to begin a dialogue with the Loner that will help him let you know if he wants to pursue a friendship with you and deal with his friendship fears.

To avoid diminishing your own feelings of self-worth, you may not be able to show patience. Instead you may want to pursue other friends who are more accessible to you. In time, the Loner may open up to you and become a cherished friend, either through being exposed to you and positive friendships, or through professional counseling or participation in a support group.

Until that occurs, if it does, you need to make sure that others address your friendship needs so that you do not recreate in yourself the same isolation that the Loner feels. The isolation may be familiar and comfortable to the Loner; you may find it frustrating and counterproductive. (For a further discussion of the motives you might have in wanting to befriend the Loner, see in Chapter 3 the section entitled, "The 'I Can Save You' Motivation.")

16. The Blood-sucker

The overly dependent friend, the Blood-sucker, expects you to be there every waking minute. She has an excessive need for help and comforting, to the point that it interferes with your own needs, your work or school commitments, and your other relationships. Perhaps this friend was not allowed to spend time alone as a child; she might have been one of many siblings and thus shared a room with a sibling or two, so that acting independently never became comfortable. The overly dependent friend might have lacked the attention she needed during childhood or adolescence, and now compensates by being overly dependent on friends for approval, companionship, or emotional satisfaction. The Blood-sucker may have been the victim of emotional, physical, or sexual abuse, causing her to have excessive separation anxiety in adulthood. As Carol, a 45-year-old married secretary who was sexually abused by her older brother when she was 10, notes:

> Separation anxiety is more of a problem for me today than when I was a child. When I was a child I wanted to be separated from my family. All they ever did was hurt me. Today I find it hard to leave people I become friendly with or even people who hurt me, but I feel an obligation not to separate from them. There is something strange inside of me that makes it hard to separate, even if I am in a bad situation.

The Blood-sucker needs you to set limits. If you do not give this friend limits, she will take over your life, your time, your thoughts, and your energy. If you have a loose arrangement, this friend may expect you to always make time for her. Instead you may want to have a specific time that you get together. The clearly defined boundaries associated with "Let's have coffee every Friday" or, "I'll give you a call after I finish this project" will benefit both you and your friend. Your friend is actually asking someone to set limits on her behavior.

As long as you give the Blood-sucker limits and recognize his need to make excessive demands on you, you can keep this friend in your life, in moderation. The positive side of having this type of friend is that if you are ever in need, he will be there for you because he has such empathy for that neediness. The Blood-sucker has a genuine need to be needed, not just to demand from others.

17. The Therapist

Sometimes you just want to vent or share, but the Therapist always has to make suggestions that he wants you to follow to make your situation better. He may also constantly analyze and try to find psychological explanations for everything you say or do. This can become annoying and unacceptable if you really just want a friend to listen and be there for you, but not give interpretations or opinions. The Therapist is not trained in psychology, psychiatry, social work, or psychiatric nursing, so in most situations his pronouncements are only as valid as anyone else's.

The Therapist may have a need for order in her world. When you share feelings or experiences that are stressful or unresolved, it creates anxiety in your friend. She wants a resolution *now* and offers suggestions in the hope that you will follow them and dispel her discomfort about your situation. The Therapist also needs to explain everything as a way of helping you to avoid problems now or in the future. "That's why this happened" or "This will help you feel better" is this friend's approach.

If the excessive analyzing annoys you, be clear with the Therapist. State quite bluntly, "You know, I'm not asking you to analyze or interpret what I'm sharing with you. I just want to let you know what's going on with me."

If that reaction does not curb the Therapist's need to analyze and you want to maintain the friendship, try listening patiently and, instead of reacting to specific suggestions or interpretations or getting agitated by your friend's advice, simply say, "Thank you for your comments, but I prefer to interpret or work this through in my own way."

18. The Interloper

A friend who is the Interloper starts off as someone who seems interested in your life, your ideas, and your career. Initially you're flattered by his concern and attention. But then one day or in one conversation, you start to feel that your friend's interest is becoming excessive, intense, and smothering. He is crossing the line from "interested friend" to the Interloper.

Perhaps you are venting about a problem at work. The interloper not only sympathizes with you and offers some suggestions but, in an extreme case, might call your boss or send an e-mail to the co-worker you've been complaining about, telling him or her to leave you alone.

Recognizing that someone is an interloper is the first step. You need to have clear, definite boundaries if you are dealing with an interloper so she will understand, quite clearly, that those relationships, topics, or situations are "off limits" for her discussion, opinion, or action.

You might consider cutting off the friendship if you detect that someone is an interloper. If you feel that a new friend is starting to seriously manipulate your life, it may be wiser to walk away than to allow such a devious friend into your life, because of the mayhem that may ensue.

But if you feel that your friend is wonderful and has just a slight or rare tendency to be an interloper, establishing clear boundaries and avoiding discussions that get too specific or too personal may help salvage the friendship. If your friend makes statements or declarations that are off base or out of line, you could say, quite clearly, "I know you care, but that's none of your business" or, "Thanks for your advice, but it's my life and I'd like to handle this in my own way."

The Interloper probably had an unhappy childhood and was also made to feel inadequate and helpless. Because of that, he or she wants to become over-involved in your life so he or she can feel some power and purpose. Furthermore, he or she probably looks up to you in some way; this hero worship causes him or her to want to make your life "right" all the time. There may even have been some overt or latent sexual abuse when this type of friend was growing up, blurring the boundaries between the abuser and the abused.

Obviously, if your attempts to keep the Interloper out of your life fail, you have to decide whether to end the friendship, particularly if the friend fails to get professional help to deal with the root cause of the behavior.

19. The Copycat

John Lutz's page-turner thriller *Single White Female,* which was made into a movie staring Bridget Fonda and Jennifer Jason Leigh, is a fictional depiction of the Copycat. In this type of negative friendship one friend copies the other.[3] Of course, some copying by friends goes on all the time and could be seen as flattering; a good friend may want to wear a similar shade of lipstick, to work in the same industry, live in the same community, read the same books, go to the same movies, or attend the same school as her friend. However, it is necessary for both friends to feel that this copying is mutually acceptable; if one friend does not welcome that kind of flattering imitation of her appearance, career, or life decisions, the other friend should back off.

In *Single White Female,* Lutz shows what happens when Allie Jones, after throwing out her boyfriend, takes on a roommate, Hedra Carlson, who soon goes from envying Allie's life to imitating it. The situation begins with Hedra copying Allie's wardrobe and hairdo but escalates to murder and bedlam, with Allie fighting not just to get back her apartment but to save her own life.

The Copycat, like the Interloper, initially makes you feel liked and admired. If imitation is the highest form of flattery, then there must be something to the flattery that often accompanies being copied. But soon the flattery becomes annoyance, followed by a sense of betrayal. Everyone wants to be unique, so trying to become the exact duplicate of someone you admire, rather than taking her as an inspiration to do your own thing, diminishes her uniqueness.

With the Copycat, as with the Interloper, you need to set limits and be clear about when the copying is acceptable and flattering and when it has started to become annoying and excessive.

Lacking a strong ego or a developed sense of self, the Copycat gains his strength from imitating what someone else is doing, wearing, or even thinking. He needs to have his own sense of self bolstered up and reinforced so that he can cultivate and feel more confident about his decisions and choices.

If you like your friend but not this tendency, you can try to keep the friendship going by at least not fueling the Copycat's over-involvement by providing too much information. If the Copycat likes your new hairstyle, you can withhold the name of the hairdresser or salon you went to. If you fear the Copycat will go on the same vacation you have planned, don't provide all the details until you return.

Consider confronting the Copycat if you think he or she has the capacity for self-help. You may find that, once confronted, the Copycat shows hopeful signs that she will stop or get help to overcome this annoying trait.

20. The Controller

This type of friend probably experienced a rigid childhood where everything had to be a certain way, so he now feels the need to control everyone in his personal or work life. This trait can persist in a friendship without any problems until there is a confrontation, at which point the Controller disapproves of what a friend is doing and says so. This is different from the Interloper, who gets over-involved in a friend's life or work. The Controller needs to impose her will or unique point of view on her friend. This could range from everyday issues, such as where to meet for coffee or what movie to see, to bigger concerns, such as whom to date or what career to pursue.

Issues of control were behind the two break-ups that Bonnie had with her very close friend Regina. As noted in the first chapter, they met 30 years ago, when they were both living in the same college dormitory. After three years, their college friendship came to an abrupt halt because Bonnie was dating someone and there was a suspicion that he might be married. Regina disapproved of her friend dating a married man, even if he had initially concealed the truth, so she ended the friendship.

They had not spoken for a year when they ran into each other at a student activity, Regina apologized, and their close friendship resumed. When Regina ended the friendship a second time, a decade later, it was again over her disapproval of something that Bonnie had said or done. (Bonnie couldn't recall the exact circumstances behind the second break-up, five years ago.) About nine months later Regina called her, once again she apologized, and they reinitiated the friendship.

Bonnie explains how her friend behaved in a controlling way throughout their friendship, but she is willing to accept her that way since she cares so much about her friend. As a 49-year-old single woman whose parents and only sibling are deceased, and who is not romantically involved with anyone right now, Bonnie finds that Regina provides an intimacy and a shared history that is crucial to Bonnie's emotional well-being:

> Regina made the major decisions. Basically, from the very beginning, she wanted to be the leader or the controller or something. So when I did something, whatever it was, that didn't fit the way she thought was right, I was out. [Regina was the one who decided] whether or not to reinstate the friendship [both times]. The whole thing is based on her being in charge. I think her family had very rigid rules, and anybody that broke the rules was considered not a good person to be friends with. With my personality, I said things that didn't always come out right.

The cooling-off periods enabled Regina to decide that she did not want to lose Bonnie's friendship. Regina has also seemed to mellow and become less of the Controller. Bonnie explains:

> I think maybe she was asking for too much, but as time went by, she got more generous with her feelings. I think that she was judgmental and when we first met, I didn't mind having someone leading me along. I think now she is more accepting of other people's flaws.

21. The Caretaker
Debbie is the oldest of six sisters and brothers. Although 41 years old and single, she has been the Caretaker with all her friends from her youngest days. This type of friend may be resentful if you do not share her need to

take care of others, if you do not return her nurturing, or, just as annoying, if you refuse or resist her concern and parenting.

Like Debbie, the Caretaker may have been the oldest of numerous siblings that she was expected to parent, or she may have had a disabled parent or sibling for whom she was responsible, whatever his or her age.

The Caretaker may be so busy taking care of others—children, parents, spouse, siblings, friends, pets—that even though giving is what she needs to do, she may not have the time or emotional resources to give anything to *you.*

You may also like your independence and find that the excessive parenting the Caretaker is compelled to give gets in the way of the friendship of equals that you wish to have.

If your friend is the Caretaker, and she is willing to be open about this trait, and even lighthearted, it may be possible to continue the friendship anyway. When you find your friend launching into the Caretaker role, you could say, whimsically, "Okay, I know you have a need to take care of everyone, but you're not my mother and I'm not your child. You're my friend and we're supposed to be equals. So don't waste all that good catering that you can spend on the parents, children, spouse, or other friends who want it from you. I can take care of myself, thank you very much."

We've looked at 21 types of potentially negative friends, but what about the Ideal Friend? What are the personality traits of the Ideal Friend, the traits you want to look for in a friend?

The Ideal Friend

Although everyone may, to some degree, possess a bit of each of the 21 traits described above, an ideal friend will not possess any of those traits to the point that it represents a dominant negative force in the relationship. From time to time, there may be moments of self-absorption or a need to be alone, but overall an ideal friend has her issues in check enough to be a positive person in your life, and in her own. Your friend can call into play the ability to take care of you, if you're sick, distraught over a romantic break-up or a death in the family, or dealing with a career high or low. But her caretaking is appropriate and based on your need for it, not on her compulsive need to always be that way in every situation.

An ideal friend combines the right amounts of neediness and dependency with the ability to be alone and self-sufficient. Friendship is a welcome relationship in his life but he does not make you or his other friends feel excessively burdened. He is either self-nurturing or connected enough to others—whether other friends, family members, or romantic partners—that the friendship is a positive additional relationship in both your lives.

Unlike the child or teen who was raised in a home with overly critical, distant, or even abusive parents or siblings, an ideal friend had a positive childhood from which she draws her current emotional strength and health. If she was abused, neglected, or criticized, she has worked these issues through in therapy or resolved them enough on her own that she is not acting out those negative patterns in her friendships.

The ideal friend probably was loved, appreciated, and cared for by parents and siblings, yet there were clear and appropriate boundaries between "me" and "you." (Even if the ideal friend had negative parents or siblings, or a troubled childhood, he has dealt with it so that those harmful early experiences do not prevent him from being a positive friend.) Respect for feelings, possessions, and relationships helped him to develop the ability to be there for his friends, but not to be overly involved in his friends' lives, decisions, or other relationships. A realistic but loving appreciation of your friend's talents, abilities, and accomplishments also helps your friend to keep his competitive and jealous feelings under control. He was not praised so much that he fears others who may distinguish themselves and have a realistic right to do so. Nor were his abilities ignored and minimized so that he responds with jealous or envious feelings that are disproportionate to a situation, because of childhood wounds that are stirred up.

This ideal friend has confidence in her opinions but does not inflict those personal insights, especially about relationships, school, work, or parenting issues, unless specifically asked for advice.

Respecting the difference of a friend is a pivotal trait of an ideal friend; secure enough in who she is, she has no need for a friend to be a carbon copy of anyone else's looks, goals, ideas, or preferences.

This ideal friend is usually "low maintenance." You, of course, try to tell your friend if you are going away, and you always try to return phone calls, e-mails, or letters promptly. But if you or your friend take longer than usual to get back to one another, there is enough trust and security in the relationship to assume that all is fine and that eventually one of you will contact the other.

Your ideal friend keeps your confidences and does not gossip about you. Your friend is honest with you, and you are able to be the same way with her.

Gloria, who is 42 and single, has had a best friend for the last two decades. Suzie, 43, who is married, has three young schoolage children, and lives in another country, seems to personify the traits many are looking for in an ideal friend. Gloria and Suzie met when they both worked at the same company. As Gloria notes:

> Suzie is my friend for ALL occasions. You know that it is said that we all look for our Mr. Right? Well, while I'm still looking for him, I have found my "Ms. Right," and we both agree on this.
>
> We hit it off from the time we met 24 years ago, and though our friendship lasted only two years before she moved [to another country], we really bonded, and through the years, in spite of the friendship somewhat drifting because of factors in our lives, we religiously sent birthday cards no matter what. We guaranteed that.
>
> We are always on the same wavelength, no doubt about it, and we know it's the "little" things (like sending a spontaneous "thinking of you" card) that count. We both love music and so we share music files on-line (how's that for being close?). We both enjoy having our late-night chats (when I'm there) and discussing what we admire about each other or what troubles us or just rummaging through old music.
>
> How do we stay in touch? Well, via daily e-mail, but we also telephone one another every few months, because we just have the urge to—or if we know there's a crisis and we know that it's important to hear the voice of someone who cares. I hope to see her very soon, because I really enjoy her and her family.
>
> If you were to ask me what I appreciate about her, one thing would be that in spite of her very busy life, she can still find time to correspond with me and in such a genuine and consistent way. . . . The great thing is that Suzie has remained the same warm, loving, giving, selfless person I have known and loved. Isn't that great? I often think I'm so lucky to have met her.

Are you still unsure if you are in one or more destructive or harmful friendships? If so, take the following self-quiz. Answer *no, sometimes, most of the time,* or *yes* to the questions that follow. At the end are some guidelines for analyzing what your answers may be telling you about a specific friend or friendship.

Quiz: Recognizing a Harmful Friendship

1. Is your friend trustworthy?
2. Does your friend return your phone calls?
3. Does your friend always keep appointments or meetings and promises?
4. Do other friends praise this friend?
5. Do you enjoy listening to your friend?
6. If you have an opposite-sex friend, and you're both romantically involved with others or married, does your friend's romantic partner know about your friendship?
7. Is your friend someone you're proud of?
8. Is your friendship based on who you both are now, rather than on what you were when you first became friends?
9. After you see your friend, do you find yourself thinking, "Wow, I'm glad we're friends?"
10. Does your friend respect your boundaries and your privacy?

The above questions are all posed in a positive way; ideally, your healthy friendship should enable you to answer *yes* or *most of the time* to most or all of the above questions. If you answer *yes* or *most of the time* to most or all of the above questions, your friendship is based in the here and now, not just coasting on an old tie. You and your friend mutually respect each other's needs for intimacy, as well as your need for privacy and, when needed, emotional or physical distance. You and your friend do not make idle promises; you make and keep appointments and meetings, and follow through on whatever offer is extended by you or your friend.

If you found you answered *sometimes* or *no* to two or three questions, you need to seriously consider this friend and friendship. Look over the questions that received a *sometimes* or a *no* answer. How pivotal is that trait or condition to the health of this friendship? If you answered *no* to question #4, "Do other friends praise this friend?" it may be less of a concern than if you answered *no* to question #1, "Is your friend trustworthy?" Take some time to look over your answers and consider what your *no, sometimes,* or *most of the time* answers are telling you about this friendship. Are these answers based on a new situation that is causing your friend to act differently—such as his upcoming marriage in four months, which leaves him little time for you or his other friends, or a major emotional upheaval, like the loss of a loved one, that is causing your friend to temporarily withdraw from you and become self-absorbed?

If you answered *sometimes* or *no* to four or more questions, you need to immediately reevaluate this friend and friendship and whether it is in your best interest to continue it. The negatives of this particular friendship may be outweighing the benefits of having a friend; you deserve to have your boundaries and privacy respected, to be listened to, to have promises kept and appointments honored. Your romantic partner or spouse should know about this friendship if it's on the up-and-up, and your friendship needs to be based on today, not just old memories. You want to be proud of your friend, to be glad you're friends, to have your phone calls returned, and, most important, to feel deep down that your friend is a trustworthy person.

In summary, here are two checklists, one for positive friendships, and one for negative or destructive friendships:

Positive Friendship

- You like (or love) each other.
- You have fun together.
- You share confidences, activities, talking, and/or emotional support.
- Trust, honesty, and loyalty are expected.
- There is little or no jealousy.
- Competitiveness is minimal and healthy.
- Contact is as frequent as both need and want.
- Confidences are kept.
- Gossip is nonexistent or extremely rare.
- Friends are not used or put in compromising positions.
- Promises are kept.
- Borrowed items are returned.
- Tact is practiced.
- Honesty is essential but not misused for hurtful reasons.
- The friendship is flexible, changing as situations or needs change or shift for one or both friends because of school, career, or personal reasons.

- No matter how busy each friend gets, the friendship is still a priority concern.
- Each friend is there for the other, in fair or foul weather.
- You have a lot in common but enough that is different to make the relationship interesting.
- The relationship is equal.

Negative or Destructive Friendship

- Jealousy is rampant.
- Competitiveness is excessive.
- Secrets are shared without permission outside of the friendship.
- Borrowed money or items are not returned.
- Promises are broken.
- Poor excuses are offered for failing to get together.
- One or both friends brag to others about the friendship for opportunistic reasons.
- The friendship is rigid and inflexible, with attempts to maintain the status quo despite predictable and normal shifts or changes that make new demands on each friend.
- The friendship is a low priority.
- Conversations are strained or unpleasant.
- Even if you once had fun with your friend, it's now a relationship of duty rather than enjoyment.
- The sharing of activities, emotional support, or confidences is rare or one-sided.
- The relationship is unequal.

Part 2

Why Do Friends Hurt Friends?

Chapter 3

What's *Really* Going On?

What causes one person to betray another? A vicious personality? Jealousy? Rage? Revenge? Depression? Those are possible reasons that come to mind. But there are other reasons that betrayal occurs in a friendship that you may not have considered, such as the need to retaliate when the wish to remain friends is not shared. Poor self-esteem. The inability to deal with change. Those are just some of the possible causes of betrayal in friendship. Some are easier to detect, handle, or even reverse than others.

Trying to Understand the Betrayal

When is betrayal more likely to occur in a friendship? If a friendship evolved too quickly, if not enough information was exchanged, or if you failed to experience enough shared situations that also acted as tests on the friendship, you may have misjudged your friend from the get-go.

Since friendships tend, on average, to involve those who are similar in background and values, betrayal is more likely if the friendship involves those of disparate status, abilities, or values. Perhaps one has romantic feelings about the other (or the other's partner or spouse). Perhaps both want the same thing, but there's room for only one to get it. Betrayal in friendship can thus occur surrounding promotions or jobs. One professor has shared with me how sad he felt that he was the only one of his four friends (who worked in the same department and college) who was able to get tenure. The close friendships did not survive even though the "betrayal" was not his fault. A friend may betray a friend because there is the perception that she has already been betrayed by that friend. In that case, the betrayal is actually in retaliation for the first one.

Remember that if you and your friend have different values, what she sees as a positive act, even an act to save you, you may see as betrayal. This seems to be the view proposed by Linda Tripp about her former friend Monica Lewinsky, one of the most famous cases of alleged friendship betrayal in the twentieth century. In 1997, Linda Tripp, thinking that her action was in the best interest of her friend and the country, taped her conversations with

Monica Lewinsky, telephone chats in which Lewinsky detailed her romantic involvement with then-president Bill Clinton. In an interview by Nancy Collins published in *George* magazine, Tripp explained her view of the betrayal:

> *By talking, didn't you betray a friend?*
>
> I didn't betray Monica Lewinsky. I figured that whatever happened would be better for her than the callous abuse she was suffering at the hands of the president. Getting the truth out would end her obsession. Besides, privacy wasn't Monica's concern; she had already told 14 people.[1]

Nancy Collins's interview with Linda Tripp is a fascinating one, definitely required reading for anyone who wants to understand that there are always two sides to betrayal in a friendship. Here is the last question in the interview with Linda Tripp:

> *How do you respond when people ask, "How do you sleep at night?"*
>
> I sleep well. I look in the mirror without a problem. I have absolutely no regrets about what I did. I would do it all over again, only better and sooner.[2]

Revenge and Vindictiveness

Betrayal, such as saying or doing something that you or your friend considers counterproductive to the betterment of your friendship, may occur because of a perceived wrongdoing. If an assumed or real wrong has transpired between you and your friend, a betrayal may occur as a form of retaliation—a version of "tit for tat." This reinforces one of the meanings of the adage "Do unto others as you want them to do unto you." If you wish to avoid betrayal, do not betray. If you don't want to be bad-mouthed, do not bad-mouth others.

A key here is this: Are there friendship conflicts that, unresolved, have led to this need to betray as a way of getting revenge? You may not be able to stop the progression that is occurring, if this is what is behind an act of betrayal in a friendship, but if you wish to try to salvage this friendship, you might want to consider the suggestions for handling conflict in a friendship, as discussed in Chapter 5, "Can This Friendship Be Saved?"

There are, of course, countless reasons one could feel rage toward a friend, and many of those reasons are discussed throughout this chapter. They include jealousy, envy, excessive competitiveness, depression, and anger, which, if not dealt with, turns to rage.

Of course, this overly simplistic view has to be cushioned with the caveat that you can do everything right—your behavior can be laudatory—and still a friend may act vindictively and vengefully. (For a discussion of those deep-seated reasons that often have nothing to do with you, see Chapters 4, "It's All in the Family," on parent and sibling roots of betrayal in friendship.)

As with most of the causes discussed in this chapter, the motivations to betray, abandon, or hurt arise from one's background. Although you may not be able to change what a friend does to you, understanding it may at least give you a better way of coping with the feelings of shock, denial, anger, and even the wish for revenge and vindictiveness that the betrayal makes you feel.

Although in *Love and Betrayal* Dr. John Amodeo is referring to romantic couples more than friends in his comments about the roots of revenge, the insights can be applied to possible causes of friendship betrayal as well:

> Rage and revenge are often reactions to feeling powerless to affect others' predilection for caring about us, wanting us, and validating us. Such rage is a vehicle through which we try to control others by demanding that they value us. If we are snubbed, our vengeful actions will ensure that our presence will be felt in one way or another, such as by making life as miserable as possible for our ungrateful partner. If we can't make this person feel love for us, we can make him or her feel something else—pain and misery. Then our ex-partner will suffer just the way we have—by stripping him or her of value and dignity. Then we'll know that we've had an impact, even if it isn't the one we preferred. But at least we will be back in control—we will feel significant—although in a most temporary and twisted way.[3]

Flirting or Having Sex with a Friend's Romantic Partner

One of the major reasons for blind rage—the kind of rage that is so over-whelming that men and women have been known to kill because of it—is the rage caused by a friend's real or perceived sexual dalliance with a romantic partner or spouse. This kind of rage is legendary for the angry words or violent actions that it usually provokes. You may recall the example of Don in the first chapter; he is serving 15 years to life for killing his friend, who was having an affair with his wife.

I have studied crime and crime victims, taught criminology and victimology, and written a book about crime victims entitled *Victims.* Based on that research, I do not in general agree with the theory of victim precipitation, whereby the victim is seen as acting in a way that caused the crime to occur. The wronged friend who assaults or kills his or her friend, as Don did, or her romantic partner, for alleged infidelity is still legally, morally, and ethically responsible for his criminal actions. The reason for the betrayal of a friend or for violence may seem to have a clear connection to the victim's behavior. However, there are more acceptable and less drastic reactions to this ultimate betrayal, such as separation or divorce from the romantic partner or spouse who strayed, ending the friendship, working it through with conflict-resolution techniques, or letting it work itself out through a cooling-off period.

But a cooling-off period was not going to work for Jessica and her long-standing close friendship, which ended over a romantic triangle. Jessica and Barbara, now 43, had known each other since they were 20. Several years after Barbara divorced her husband, she began a lesbian relationship with her business partner. Her partner-and-lover was extremely jealous of any other relationships in Barbara's life, especially her close female friendships. Although the precipitating cause for the end of the friendship was that Jessica, who was also financially strapped, turned down Barbara's request for a business loan of $5,000, Jessica's underlying fear for her safety—fear that Barbara's lover might harm Jessica out of jealousy—was the real reason for the rupture of their 20-year friendship.

Sexual jealousy also ended another 20-year friendship. A woman I met and interviewed when I was on a business trip to Europe shared this story:

> I have one girlfriend—I guess now she's an ex-girlfriend—we had a long history. I've known her since we were in our early twenties. She was in law school. We used to hang out, and back then it was party-party-party. Another girlfriend sang in a band, and we'd go to all the gigs. We were having a great time hanging out. But Brenda was always jealous of my boyfriends because she had a thing for me. I used to tell her, "I love you, but I like boys." Still, I guess she always held it against me that I wouldn't have an affair with her.
>
> So I had this one boyfriend. Carl was the most unattractive man you would ever meet. He was fat, bald, not good-looking. He had a sort of an abrasive personality until you got to know him, but when you got to know him, you realized the guy was brilliant. Total intellectual. All we did was have these great arguments. Great arguments. All the time. I was crazy

about Carl. He was the best lover I ever had. He was so totally sensuous—maybe it had to do with [the fact that] he was zaftig and really into food. I went out with him probably for about a year, and Brenda, of course, hated him because I still wouldn't sleep with her. So she told this other friend that I was sleeping with Carl for money. And then, of course, when something like that goes out, it goes out and it goes farther and farther and farther. I didn't know for the longest time until it finally got back to me.

This was a friend that I finally, I just thought to myself, "Well, she's not my friend, she's my enemy."

Conflicts over Money

Writer Lois Duncan shares, in her article on friends and money, how being stiffed by a friend for even a small amount of money has bothered her for years:

> When I was in the third grade, a girl named Olivia borrowed money from me to buy a Coke. She never paid it back. I was too embarrassed to ask for it. I didn't want my friend to think I didn't trust her.
>
> One day Olivia was absent from school. She had moved to Philadelphia, and my money had gone with her. I was outraged!
>
> Many years later, I am still outraged.[4]

Why would a friend betray you over money? Especially if it is a small amount of money, it may not be the money per se but what the money represents: status, power, success, connection, wealth, or love.

If you want one surefire way to minimize the likelihood of betrayal in friendship, avoid loaning your friends money. Again and again, perfectly sound friendships turn sour when money is borrowed and not returned. Included in this prohibition against loaning money is the lending of treasured or valuable items, especially such high-ticket items as a car, a computer, or a cherished or hard-to-replace book, CD, or video. Harold, a 42-year-old executive, was betrayed by a friend who "did not repay loans of money." In answer to the question, "Has a friend ever done something really terrible to you?" Harold referred a second time to that same friend, when he noted, "Yes," then explaining that his friend "Promised yet [did] not deliver [on] payments for loans."

Unfortunately, if you do loan money or valued goods, you unwittingly put yourself, your money or goods, and your friendship into the grip of the unconscious associations that your friend has to money or valued belongings that may have nothing to do with you. If your friend was raised with "checkbook love," she may need to hold on to your money or possession as an extension of that early childhood relationship. Simplistically put, your friend's dad or mom was distant or unloving but tried to make up for it with money or presents. In time, the money or gifts became associated with love, so that keeping the money or the gifts is not even a choice. To return the money or to return the borrowed object is to give back the love, which your friend cannot or will not do.

If you do loan money or goods, or borrow any yourself, you and your friend should have some ground rules in advance to minimize the likelihood that your friendship may fall apart over material goods. First of all, there should be something in writing. Second, you should loan your friend money only if you are able to afford to do it, knowing you might not be repaid, and if you agree you will not let the money situation color your friendship.

Gloria, whose ideal friendship to Suzie was described previously, has another friendship that turned into something quite the opposite. Of course, there is usually a multiplicity of reasons that a friendship sours, but in this case the reason was clear: money. Although Gloria had a full-time job, her friend talked her into becoming a partner in a joint venture. Gloria, who is single and self-supporting, signed for loans for the business. The new business venture floundered, then it failed, and Gloria was out $10,000. The money was gone, and so was the friendship. Gloria explains:

> I met her in a class and struck up a friendship. I talk to people very easily. That's how it started. We had been friends for six or seven years when she came to me and said she thought I would be a good business partner. She saw how I operated at work. She had a certain amount of faith and confidence. She kept telling me that I would be a very good business partner. . . . That friend had a lot of influence on me at the time.
>
> It's a long story. She needed money and I signed some over. It cost me dearly. I have realized never, never money and friends. A very difficult situation to deal with.
>
> I'm never, ever loaning anyone any more money. I was making money in one business and losing it in another one. I don't know where my mind was, but I'm very aware of it now.

> Sometimes I'm told I sweep things under the carpet. I'm very aware of what problems I have. In my office, I'm very confident about these things. In my personal life, it's difficult for me to confront.

It is also important to remember that sometimes a friend might be asked for money but that decision is not the friend's to make. Spouses, other family members, or business partners may have to be involved in the decision as well.

Try to avoid asking a friend to loan something that you may wish to use for pleasure or fun when that item is fundamental to your friend's income or career, such as a writer's computer (or typewriter) or a musician's guitar.

If you are the one who asked a friend for money and you were turned down, before you write off any friend for turning you down, see if she can be there for you in other non-monetary ways, such as providing emotional support. Perhaps that friend cannot loan you the $5,000 that you need to buy the car you have your heart set on, but maybe your friend can help you in other ways. Maybe your friend could go car shopping with you for a new car that is within your budget. Or your friend could offer to help you find loan options that you might be eligible for, or to give you a lift from time to time if you are currently without a vehicle.

Jealousy and Envy

The German word *Schadenfreude* is the combination of two words: *Schaden* (damage) and *Freude* (joy). I first came across the term in a Liz Smith column. She defined it as "the thrill of seeing your friends and acquaintances fail. It exists throughout society."[5]

Few like to admit to it, but jealousy is a key factor behind friendships that are seen as destructive or negative, yet most friendships have some degree of jealousy in them. When is jealousy excessive? What causes jealousy in a friendship, especially a negative or destructive one? If your friend is jealous of your success, is she really a friend? Are there cures for jealous friends besides just ending the friendship? Are there any behaviors you could adopt or adapt that might help minimize jealousy in a friendship?

Just because a friend is jealous of you, or you are jealous of a friend, you need not automatically dismiss that friendship. Even very close friends may be jealous at times. The fact that the jealousy rarely occurs helps define them as friends rather than "everyone else." As the director of human resource development at a manufacturing corporation says, "Understand that everybody is going to have feelings of anger and jealousy, no matter how much they care for you or like you. You've got to realize it's their agenda, not your agenda."

Consider where the jealousy is coming from—what in your friend's life is causing the jealous feelings—and try to understand that those jealous feelings say something about your *friend,* not about the *friendship.*

As hard as it is, remember that jealousy is not about *you.* Jealousy is about what your success or example stirs up in someone else that causes her to have the need to make you feel bad. The other person feels inadequate and threatened by you so she does the only thing she, sadly, is capable of doing to retaliate. She criticizes you, pulls away from you, withholds praise, ignores you, or devalues your accomplishment, to try to make you feel as bad about yourself as she feels about herself.

You cannot change your friend's jealous or envious rage toward you. If the friend is only a casual one, you may be better off dealing with the feelings arising within you rather than confronting that person. Confrontations can backfire and inspire a wish for retaliation.

If it is a close or best friend—that is, if it is worth the time and effort to consider confrontation as a way of trying to work through these jealousy outbursts—you could engage your friend in a dialogue about what is happening as it relates to a particular situation. For example, you share the fact that you have just gotten a raise or won an award, and your close or best friend either ignores what you have said or fails to show the enthusiasm you would expect.

"Has what I just said brought up feelings in you about your situation that you'd like to share? Could that be why you're not giving me the enthusiastic praise and accolades that I hoped to hear from you since you are one of my cherished close [or best] friends?"

Hopefully this will help your friend to talk about what she is feeling. Perhaps she will reply, "Of course, I'm happy for you, but it makes me wonder, 'What have I done with *my* life?'"

The benefit of engaging in this kind of dialogue is that your good fortune, and your close or best friend's unsatisfactory reaction to it, no longer becomes a "me versus you" conflict. If left unattended, that conflict could escalate into a full-blown argument or, even worse, a pulling away from each other as the friendship starts to come apart and, eventually, to end.

"I'm so glad you said something," your close or best friend might then respond. "I've been wanting to talk to you about how I've been feeling about my own situation, but I didn't think you cared or noticed since everything's been going so well for you lately. I was afraid to burst your bubble and bring you down by talking about my frustrations."

By discussing the situation, you facilitate a possible change in your friend's attitude and behavior by making the unconscious conscious so you can both look at it, analyze it, learn from it, and try to modify a pattern. But what if you say to your friend, "You're jealous," and she answers, "Don't be ridiculous!" You can't make someone else want to look at her own unconscious behavior if she is not ready to do so. Denial is a strong defense mechanism. You have to decide if you are able to continue your friendship, ignoring your friend's jealousy as something that has nothing to do with you, especially if it's something that is a temporary situation.

Thirty-two-year-old Miranda, a married librarian with an eight-year-old son, has a "lifelong friend," someone she grew up with, who is "still jealous to this day." She maintains their friendship, despite her friend's professed jealousy. As Miranda explains: "She tells me every so often. She told me she was always jealous of me, of what I had and she didn't."

Twenty-five-year-old Dale has also chosen to ignore her lifelong best friend's jealousy. Dale grew up with her best friend, whom she describes as "more like a sister." Dale notes: "We never let [her jealousy] impact our relationship." What did her best friend do? Especially from the ages of fifteen to twenty-two, "she would always make rude comments about whoever I was going out with. Then she would later tell me that she was sorry and admit that she was just jealous."

It might have been her friend's ability to admit to the jealousy, or Dale's forgiving nature, or a little of both that has enabled this best friendship to persist and thrive. Says Dale, "I learned to ignore the bad things about her and only focus on the good things. That is why we have been best friends for twenty-five years."

Just how common is jealousy? Of the 136 people (out of 180) who answered the question "Has a casual, close, or best friend ever been jealous of you?" in my most recent friendship survey, 85 (62 percent) answered in the affirmative, and 51 (38 percent) answered "no." Of those who answered "yes," 56 provided what they felt was the reason for their friend's jealousy. The reasons given seemed to fall into four categories:

- Jealousy based on something material or tangible that they had but that the friend lacked, such as money, career success, marital status, or the ability to travel: 22
- Being jealous of another relationship or spending time with someone else (a romantic partner or other friends): 16
- Jealousy based on being seen as more attractive than the friend, including three with weight-related reasons: 9
- Jealousy based on a personality attribute, such as the ability to meet people with ease, having a talent, or having a "social and friendly" personality: 9

These four groups of reasons provided for a friend's jealousy make clear how much of the jealousy related to friendship revolves around the perception, however unfounded in reality, of one friend feeling lesser than the other or of one friend having something that the other wants. Unfortunately, I did not ask the question, "Have *you* been jealous of a casual, close, or best friend?" so I could compare and contrast whether their response about a friend being jealous toward them matched the presence or absence of their own feelings of jealousy.

Family- or Romantic Relationship–related Resentfulness

When I was conducting interviews for my book *Single in America,* single men and women often confided how much they envied their married friends' romantic relationship as well as the children that they were raising. But I also had many married women and men confess that they envied the freedom that their single friends seemed to have.[6]

The envy and jealousy that friends harbor for a friend's family status or romantic relationships has more to do with how happy they are with their own situation than it does with the reality of what their envied friend possesses.

What is the friend who expresses resentment toward another friend's relationships really saying? It falls into two basic categories. The first is the envy for the relationships of one friend that another friend wants. Although the envy is most often associated with romantic relationships or children, it could be any intimate relationship that one friend sees as lacking in her or his life. For example, my mother and I have become close over the years, but in my early twenties we were quite distant and I found it very painful. During my twenties, if I saw a young girl and her mother shopping together in a department store, it would make me jealous; if a friend shared how she and her mother spent quality time together or were especially close, I was envious.

Linda is a married respiratory therapist and parent to a college-age son and a 14-year-old daughter. (In Chapter 2, Linda discussed how e-mail sabotaged one of her work friendships.) Linda spoke about the jealousy her friend, who is single and childless, feels about the relationship Linda has with her daughter:

> This has been a very good friend of mine for 30 years. She's single, never married. No kids. She called and asked me to go see a show with her. I'm her best friend. [I told her] I wasn't interested in going. She went into this big thing. "We never do anything anymore. All we do is go out and eat."
>
> [But] I've been doing that with my friends for 35 years. That's all I want to do. If I want to go to the movies, I'll go alone. If I exercise, I want to go alone. The only thing I like to do with my friends is have conversation, food, or coffee.
>
> "You've known this all these years. Why are you so upset?"
>
> "You do everything with your daughter."
>
> "My mother was my best friend. [Linda's mother died two years ago.] My daughter is my best friend. Yes, I go shopping with my daughter. Any activity I do with my daughter is different."
>
> "I feel that the time you spend with your daughter is taking away time from our friendship."
>
> I was dumbfounded.
>
> "You know how much I adore and love my daughter. It has no reflection on our friendship whatsoever. You're saying that you're jealous of my daughter?"
>
> "I just want us to go out and do something."
>
> "I do not have to prove to you that I value our friendship after thirty years. You don't know that I value our friendship? If I have to prove it , the friendship is over. If you can't leave it the way it's always been, I'm very sorry you feel this way. I was trying to be tactful, [but] then you attack my time with my kids, my time with my daughter."
>
> So she started to cry. I just went on consoling her.
>
> "You know I love you. You're my good friend. I can't prove that I love you. It's like my husband saying, 'You don't love me because you don't want to go to the fights with me.'"

So that changed the relationship forever with me.

"She'll ask me, 'Can we meet for lunch or coffee?' I'll say, 'Yes,' which I do rarely partly because I did resent what she said and [partly] because of time constraints. I stuck to my guns—coffee or lunch. It hasn't seemed to diminish the friendship except that I feel a little bit more distant. I feel a difference. I don't know if she does. I don't think she does. [But] I do have a certain love for her. . . . I do have a strong affection for her even though our relationship is not the same.

I wondered how the friendship started. Linda explained that they had met 30 years ago when they worked together. Her friend was also a respiratory therapist at the time, although a few years later she left to go back to school to become a librarian. Linda had a very big friendship network, unlike her friend, who weighed 350 pounds and was "very quiet, very shy, depressed, and alone." Linda explains: "I had so many friends I took her into my group and that made her have friends. People figured if I liked her, there must be something to her."

The way the friendship started does have a bearing on why Linda was so shocked by her friend's jealousy of her time with her daughter. Linda explains: "I felt, 'I did you a big favor and here you are jealous of my daughter.' Now she has friends where she lives, she has more friends now, why is she demanding more of me?"

I asked Linda what her friend could have done differently so that it wouldn't have been so upsetting to her:

To not make me feel guilty about the close relationship I have with my daughter and to not make me feel she was jealous of her. To say, "I understand that you have so many family obligations. I understand that you miss your daughter and our time is less, but I understand." She didn't say, "I understand how much you adore your daughter and how close you are." She didn't say that, she just said, "I resent it. I feel like your daughter is taking you away from me."

Hello, go anywhere, but don't touch my kids.

A 30-year-old anthropology graduate student ended a best friendship over jealousy. First, her "past best friend was very jealous" that she was married and her friend could not find a date. Then her friend "threw a huge fit [when] I told her I was initiating a divorce after ten years of marriage." She continues: "She couldn't understand why in the world I wanted to end something so precious and blessed (never mind the big problems and unhappiness in the marriage for me and my ex). She gave me a preachy religious lecture for an hour, and things have never been the same since." She refers to this former best friend as "now only an acquaintance."

Competitiveness

Unlike jealousy and envy that gets out of hand, some competitiveness is normal and to be expected in all relationships. Competitiveness is a natural outgrowth of what sociologists call a *reference group,* the group or category that you use to judge yourself.[7] The reference group could be a group that someone is already in, such as a friend comparing himself or herself to other friends in the friendship network, or a group someone aspires to be in, such as business majors comparing themselves to corporate CEOs.

In small doses, and as long as it is not vicious, malicious, or out of hand, a little competition can be a motivator. Wanting what you want for yourself, as long as you or your friend do not begrudge the other's achievements, does not need to lead to betrayal. But if the competitiveness gets out of hand, it could lead to attempts to sabotage a friend's continued success or more subtle ways of betraying a friend's deserved achievements, such as ignoring a success or minimizing or putting down the source of the competition. Statements such as "Who wants a big house anyway? It's just more rooms to clean!" or "Anyone could do that if she really wanted to" are actually sour grapes, competitiveness run amok.

Hubris

The previous discussion of jealousy and envy mainly involved the jealous or envious friend who must be dealt with, understood, or forgiven. But hubris, whether in yourself or others, can inspire jealousy and envy in others, as well as the impulse for betrayal and retaliation. Hubris is excessive ego and boasting; it sets someone up for betrayal because it makes him a likely target for contempt. In the scores of interviews I have done over the years with celebrities and highly successful men and women, I have found that the ones who still have friends, even when they are very powerful, are the ones who are humble and accepting, not boastful.

By contrast, once hubris is detected, friends will often desert in droves rather than stay around a puffed-up friend. Of course, the difficulty in noticing or dealing with one's own hubris is that it often occurs when one is at the height of fame and success. In the midst of all the excitement and adulation, it is hard to remember that it may not last forever. Once all the phone calls stop and the fan mail dwindles, it's those tried-and-true friends who were always there for you, and who you were there for when you were so in demand, who will make all your days—not just the ones in the limelight—more joyful and connected.

If you or someone you know is showing hubris, you may want to consider whether this is a temporary trait, a reaction to a sudden change in circumstances, such as winning a prize or getting a big bonus, that just needs to be played out. In a few days or weeks, if you or your friend have not gone back to your formerly humble selves, a reassessment of someone's basic personality may be necessary.

Anger

Jealousy and envy are tied to anger. Behind those powerful emotions, which often cause betrayal in friendship, is the anger that a friend, through no fault of his own, has made someone feel less than he or she wants to feel. Rather than directing the anger at oneself, and then redirecting the anger into positive actions that could bring about growth and change, the anger is directed at the friend. You could be the one who has caused your friend to feel jealousy and envy and the residual anger, or you could be the one who is feeling anger toward a friend.

Thirty of the 180 surveys that I analyzed for this book were expanded questionnaires with 104 questions; those extended surveys posed this intriguing question: "What was the worst thing *you* ever did to a friend?"

Reading over the answers those 30 respondents supplied, I found myself sensing their relief in finally being able to share, in confidence, some or all of the injustices that they had done *to* friends. With the survey, they had a chance to show that they had committed unfriendly acts that may have bothered them for years. Some of those replies to the question "What was the worst thing *you* ever did to a friend?" are:

- "Taking a bunch of pills knowing I had had too many (understatement) and left him wondering whether I would wake up or not in the morning." (46-year-old married mother)

- "Flirted with a girl he was interested in." (28-year-old single male truck driver)
- "Publicly made fun of them." (42-year-old married teacher)
- "I was confused about my feelings, but was not honest about my confusion, and so, in trying to do what would make anyone and everyone happy, 'fooled' some people, and usually myself at the same time, that there was a close friendship. If confronted, I said, 'Of course, we're friends. I want to be your friend.' Later I wondered if that were true; it didn't seem so anymore. I hurt a few people this way, years back. . . . I bet I've done worse things, but I can't think of anything else now." (47-year-old single nurse)

Answering the question "What was the worst thing *you* ever did to a friend" is an exercise you might want to undertake as a way of getting in touch with the anger you have felt toward your friends, but also the anger you may have made your friends feel.

It is also vital to assess if what you feel is betrayal in your friendship, or even if the act of betrayal that you have endured is a misguided attempt to show anger. Few of us are taught how to express anger directly and simply. We are instead "taught" that anger is to be avoided, pushed down, swallowed, denied, projected, and ignored. Instead of saying, "I'm angry," instead of owning the anger and working it out with the people with whom one is angry, betrayal occurs. The action then becomes a substitute for the anger; it is still not a direct expression of the anger but the substitute for it.

Why does someone avoid expressing anger? Because she is afraid that to express anger will make others disappear, evaporate, reject her, and not wish to be around her any longer. Ironically, committing angry acts of betrayal results in rejection, the very situation that was most feared in the first place.

How to get out of this doomed cycle? Embrace feeling the emotion and the verbal expression of anger as a healthy, positive behavior, as psychiatrist Theodore Isaac Rubin advocates in *The Angry Book.* In the last part of the book, Dr. Rubin shares 103 rhetorical questions about anger that provide insight into this powerful but misunderstood emotion. Here are a few:

[15.] Are you aware that anger is closely linked to love and that you can and usually do get angry at people you love? Love and anger are not mutually exclusive. You can get deeply angry at people and love them enough so that you want the very best of all things for them.

[16.] Are you aware that the biggest dangers are not feeling and not knowing what we feel? Accepting anger equals feeling equals knowing who and what we are.[8]

But what if someone is angry at you? Anger makes us feel uncomfortable; the first instinct is to take the anger personally. Before you do that, you need to ask yourself: Is my friend really angry at me, or is he angry at someone else and displacing his anger onto me? Unfortunately, when someone is angry at you, rather than calmly and carefully sorting out the real source of the anger, the tendency is to get angry back, often resulting in a shouting match, name-calling, the spouting of insults, hanging up the phone or—the more acceptable response—tuning out or even cutting off the relationship.

Very few grow up learning how to appropriately handle either the anger directed at them or the anger they feel toward others. Denying the anger and trying to get rid of the relationship that is originating the angry feelings toward you are quick fixes to a more fundamental challenge. By separating the anger from the person who is expressing the anger, by trying to hear the words behind the anger, rather than just the overwhelming emotion that can be so frightening, you expose yourself to information that is potentially beneficial to you and to your relationship in the short and long term.

Therefore, if someone is angry with you, ask yourself the following questions as a way of gauging what will be your ideal response:

1. Is the anger warranted?
2. Is the anger directly at me or am I a substitute for the person my friend is really angry at?
3. Is this an occasional or a persistent behavior that I am able to cope with?
4. Can I help my friend to cool down so we can deal with her anger in a calmer frame of mind?
5. Do we need someone else to intervene and help us deal with the cause of my friend's anger?

6. If I choose to ignore the situation, because I think my friend just had to vent, will that help or hinder our friendship or me?

How you and your friend deal with anger in your relationship, when or if it does occur, may be as pivotal a predictor of how dependable your friendship is as how you cope with conflict when and if it arises. (See also the section "Handling Conflict with Friends," in Chapter 5, "Can This Friendship Be Saved?")

Change

Structural changes, such as getting a new job (if your friendship began when you worked together) and moving (if you used to live nearby) are major challenges to friendships. My studies about this have led me to believe that feelings of betrayal may result because the one who did not change things often assumes that it is the responsibility of the one who changed to make the overture in the friendship. Whether it is out of jealousy or a fear of looking too desperate, the one left behind expects the one in the new circumstance to reach out, as if that is the test that the friendship still matters. The one who has changed or is in the changed circumstance may also think that she should be the one to be contacted because, after all, her life is in flux; let the friend whose situation is more stable be the one to reach out and connect.

These tests, however, are faulty, and many friendships will unfortunately fail them. For example, when someone moves, too often a year or two later he will comment, "I just don't have any friends from before." Why did that happen? Usually the reason is that the person who moved left it up to the old friends to contact him after the move. But it is a fact of life that it is often up to the person who moved away to reach out to his old friends.

Why? Because it is easier to be the one moving away than it is to be the one left behind. For whatever rational reason the move occurred—a better job, a marriage that necessitated moving to live with the spouse, a dependent child forced to move by her parents, a wish for a dissimilar situation for raising a family—the one left behind experiences the change as a rejection. After all, she is still in the old situation. Why wasn't that—the status quo—good enough? Certainly if the move is to a bigger and better lifestyle or a dramatically different one, the person left behind may feel that as friends the two do not have that much in common anymore. There can even be competitiveness and territoriality, as when someone who relocates to California feels she has to negate her former New York lifestyle, or when someone who moves to a new community justifies the expense, inconvenience, and upset of moving by proclaiming it was the "right" decision.

Change stirs up jealousy. Deviation may threaten intimate friendships, as those who allowed themselves to become close now have to deal with the perceived or real feelings of abandonment and separation stirred up by change. If only one changes, unless you and your friend deal with the feelings that the change has brought up, resentments and bitterness may build up that could sabotage your friendship.

If someone gets a promotion, for instance, instead of calling to say "congratulations," a friend may feel that the promoted friend needs to "prove" her friendship by taking the time, in the midst of all the excitement surrounding the promotion, to call her friend and say "hi." Be careful about saying things to your friend who did not get a promotion or some other goal that she is aiming for but that you just achieved, in the guise of making your friend feel better. Such comments such as, "You deserved the promotion more than me" or, "I'm sure you'll find Mr. Right very soon as well" may be taken the wrong way. Instead of building up your friend's self-esteem, the comments unwittingly focus on her unfulfilled dreams and goals. If possible, keep what you have achieved separate from what your friend is still striving for.

Bring your old friends into your new life as much as possible. Everyone will probably be aware that you all have to find other, more convenient friendships, but that does not diminish what you once had or can still have, though perhaps with an altered frequency. Telephone as often as possible, invite them for intimate brunches or dinners, as well as those "big" occasions that make you feel good about your network but at which it is often hard to talk or connect intimately with each guest. Be willing to go back to your old neighborhood to see your old friends. The invitations should be a two-way street, sharing the burden of the time, effort, and expense of getting together.

Also remember that change takes time to incorporate: weeks, months, even years. If you are working on certain behavior patterns that are negatively affecting how good a friend you can be right now, let your friends know. By the same token, if your friends are in the throes of changes that are causing them to be less than ideal friends, see if you can discuss these changes, how they are affecting your friendship and how they make you feel. There may be nothing your friend can do about them, at least temporarily, since the causes of the changes are beyond her control, such as the chaos caused by a different job, a new baby, relocation to another country, a marriage, a divorce, or returning full-time to school.

Another concern about change has to do with friends who, once they pair off, are saddened or annoyed that the combination of boy plus girl plus friend or friends seems strained, forced, or downright negative. Friendship, like romance, is, after all the analysis is over, based on a feeling, a strong feeling that arises because of that inexplicable element known as chemistry. So there is absolutely no reason to assume that just because you like Friend A, your romantic partner or spouse is going to like Friend A, or that Friend A is going to like your spouse. Add in Friend A's romantic partner or spouse and the number of possible combinations explains why finding two couples where all four people like one another is challenging and rare.

Sometimes, however, it may be easier to start anew as a couple, seeking out other couples that you meet from that point on, rather than trying to reshape old relationships in the image of the new couple identity. Furthermore, since it may be difficult for some friends who related to you as a single person to adapt to your couple status, it might work out better in the long run to invest the time and energy in also cultivating new friends who see you from the get-go as a couple.

There are no hard and fast rules about this, but it is clear that it is unfair and unfortunate to stay stuck in a situation whereby you and your spouse only have friends independent of your relationship instead of also venturing forward as a couple to form fresh friendship bonds together.

That is just one of the many changes that impacts on current friendships and could account for the acting-out that is often an expression of frustration, feelings of abandonment, confusion, and hurt caused by that much-feared but universal phenomenon known as change.

Weight-related Changes. Another change that can effect friendships is weight loss or weight gain. Weight loss may be a challenge to a friendship if one person loses a noticeable amount of weight and the friend, especially if he or she is still overweight, resents it or is jealous. As noted in the introduction, jealousy over weight loss ended 40-year-old Brenda's friendship. When Brenda weighed 200 pounds and went on a diet, her friend, who weighed 250 pounds, withdrew as soon as Brenda lost several pounds.

However, it is possible that this friendship might have been salvaged if Brenda had realized that her friend's jealousy was probably not vicious or malicious. It shows that an accomplishment has touched a nerve: What you now have is what your friend values (and wants for himself or herself). Wanting for yourself what someone else has does not mean you wish someone else did not have it.

Joel Yager, M.D., editor-in-chief of *Eating Disorders Review* and professor of psychiatry at the University of New Mexico, shared these insights about weight issues and friendship:

> Friendship plays a central role in how we judge our weights and our eating behavior, and what we do—or don't do—about our weight-related issues. For those with weight issues, true friendships should be helpful, and certainly not harmful. The secret ingredients are compassion, understanding, acceptance, and gentle encouragement. Fair-weather friends, and those whose friendships are based on competitiveness and status, sabotage or poison friendships through comparisons, teasing, envy, undermining, backstabbing, colluding and enabling.
>
> If you can speak to a friend about your weight issues and feel better about yourself at the end of the conversation, that's good. If your friend has sincerely confronted and challenged you to do better when you need that sort of push, that's good, too.
>
> But if your friend leaves you feeling that you're just being put down, disparaged and devalued, and you just simply feel worse about yourself without constructive and supportive guidance, consider the possibility that your so-called friend has issues about his or her own weight, his or her own narcissism, or is in competition with you.
>
> When you find friends disparaging you because of your weight issues, point their behaviors out to them, and ask them to think through their attitudes. If they seem to take pleasure in subtly humiliating you, call them on it. If they're envious of your successes at weight control and seem to want to see you fail, call them on it. If they're unable to stop acting destructively, it may be time to trade them in for a better set of friends.

If you feel jealous about a friend's weight loss or you feel others are jealous of you, face these feelings. Give them time. Especially if friends have not seen you in a long time—unlike the friends nearby who may have been getting used to the "new" you—part of the problem is the newness of the change and the shock of seeing someone you defined in one way looking quite different. Thinner people often dress and carry themselves differently than overweight people (or people displeased with their size, whatever their weight). A friend who has lost (or gained, if too thin) weight may start wearing flashier clothes—and getting more attention when you walk down the street together—which may be a change for you both.

Gaining a lot of weight may also have an impact on some friendships. For example, if you have friends who measure their attractiveness by the company they keep, having a friend who is severely overweight may challenge their own sense of self-worth. They may start avoiding an overweight friend without even knowing why. They may make snide comments because of their own feelings about being overweight, which has little to do with your specific weight gain. They may be afraid: If *she* could gain weight, maybe it could happen to me. Bring their reactions out in the open. You can initiate a dialogue with your friend by explaining, "I'm not saying this is right or wrong, I just feel as if you're judging me because I've gained weight. Are you aware that you are treating me differently and that it's hard for me to be around you now?"

Career-related Changes. Switching jobs or even careers is a change that may cause jealousy and envy; it could be the end of a friendship. However, it need not be. Indeed career-related changes may actually help friendships that involve excessive competition; being in different jobs or professions may make comparisons and competition less likely, or even non-existent. The friendship could survive because of the feelings between the two friends, rather than the career-related "shop talk" upon which the friendship seemed to be based. Of course, this necessitates having enough in common beyond the work so that the friendship can change, and even deepen and flourish.

If your friend cannot relate to you because of your new career, it is probably your friend's problem, more than your own. Once again, at least try to emphasize what you have in common and what remains unchanged. (Don't you both still like to read novels, eat out, go to baseball games, or play tennis?)

"I don't feel comfortable with the old gang since my promotion," says a man in his late twenties. He is more honest than most that his advancement has caused him to prefer new friends at his higher level. Unless he finds a way to integrate his old and new friends, he will be continually moving from friend to friend as he moves up the ladder, without the foundation of long-term friends who "knew him when." In that way, he will miss one of the best reasons for maintaining a friendship over time, namely, having a shared history.

Income-related Changes. Betrayal by a friend could be caused by income changes. Whether it is a friend who suddenly inherits wealth and can now go to expensive restaurants way out of reach of his other friends, or a reversal of fortune that causes a friend to sell the house and move into a rental or to a less expensive community, income changes can throw all but the most secure and stable friendships into a state of confusion and flux.

As with all the changes that have been noted, the key to help avoid betrayals based on these changes is to emphasize what is still similar between friends—what has not changed. Maybe incomes are widely disparate now, but everyone pays the same price when they go to a movie together. You may want to meet at the movie and go out for coffee afterward, keeping the interactions on neutral territory. In that way, if you and your friend are now living in situations that are dramatically different, the friendship can get past those materialistic trappings and stay focused on the interaction and shared experiences that bond you.

If you are the one whose income has suddenly soared, you want to avoid being accused of hubris. If it is your friend who has just gotten a half-million-dollar bonus and told you and everyone else he or she knows about it, you might want to point out to your friend, gently, that hubris is rearing its ugly head. Your friend may be unaware that he or she is bragging about the income shifts that others envy.

By contrast, if your friend has an income shift downward, be careful not to offer money because of all the reasons noted in this book that money often destroys friendship. Furthermore, you do not want to unwittingly insult your friend if her standard of living is fine despite the income decline. Be careful of projecting onto your friend what you might want someone to do for you if the situations were reversed. You and your friend are separate and unique individuals. Take the time to find out what your friend wants you to do to help her, even if the request is to "do nothing."

Marital Status or Romantic Relationship Changes. Over and over again, while researching my books *Single in America* and *Friendshifts®: The Power of Friendship and How It Shapes Our Lives,* I heard the same complaint: My friends were always there for me, but then my spouse died and they don't seem to be comfortable around me anymore, especially those who are still married or in a relationship. The same is true for those who get divorced: "They've chosen sides," I'm often told, usually by the one who is on the side that is being ignored and not chosen for continued socializing.

Yes, this is a betrayal of years, even decades, of friendship.

Yes, it is annoying and unfair.

But it is important not to take it personally. Friendship is an optional role, so if your friendship now makes your former friend uncomfortable, either because your partner died or you and your partner split up, you have to respect that that is the way he or she feels, and move on. Of course, you could try to confront every friend who has mistreated you by summarily dumping you after you are "suddenly single." They may actually agree with you that their behavior is hideous and unacceptable. They may even agree to get together, as a threesome—or as a foursome, with you bringing along a new intimate relationship in your life.

That's all fine and dandy, and your friend is trying to do the right thing, but how does it feel when you all get together? Are you comfortable and relaxed, or tense and annoyed?

Your friend may be trying not to betray you and the friendship you once had, but with the change in relationship circumstances, feelings cannot be ignored. If the comfort and familiarity is no longer there, it cannot be faked or forced. Just as "birds of a feather flock together" is the cornerstone of one-to-one friendships, so too couples need to have that feeling about others they befriend, whether couples or single people. In most cases, couples simply have an easier time relating to the world of a couple, contrasted to a single's life.

Rather than forcing a couple situation where your friends have to "choose" between you and your ex, or, if you've been widowed, reminding them of their dearly beloved and missed friend, try to create new situations without as many memories. If you were closer to the same-sex friend in the intact couple, try getting together without his or her romantic partner or spouse, as long as it doesn't cause friction in their relationship. That might be a more comfortable compromise even if it is not the ideal of keeping it all going as a threesome the way it used to be as a foursome.

The more problematic situation in a threesome or foursome, however, may be when a spouse asks her partner to "choose" between their current relationship and maintaining past alliances that are no longer comfortable. This is what happened to 25-year-old Hillary, a stay-at-home mother with two young children, whose husband, George, has been cut off from Mark, his friend of 15 years. His friend married Hillary's former friend Jessica, and she is preventing the two old friends from communicating. Once again, it is important not to personalize what is going on but to instead look at what Hillary's former friend's behavior may be saying about her own marriage, which, Hillary points out, does not seem to be going that well. "Jessica won't let Mark call his former best friend of fifteen years. But George still tries."

In that instance, the disparity in happiness between the two couples might be the reason Jessica wants to curtail contact between the two old friends. Although there are numerous examples of opposite-sex friendships that persist even after one or both friends partner with others, there are times when the outcome is not as congenial. In those situations, when there is a pre-existing platonic friendship, or a romantic partner befriends someone of the opposite sex, a romantic partner may be jealous of her partner's opposite-sex friendship, even if all agree that it is based on friendship, not romance. Is it fair for a partner who is jealous of her spouse's platonic friend to ask, or even demand, that he curtail his opposite-sex friendship just to placate her? There are no hard and fast answers to this complex question. In some relationships, a spouse's jealousy of an opposite-sex friendship may be based on underlying insecurities that have nothing to do with the genuinely platonic basis of the relationship. In other cases, the spouse may be picking up on romantic feelings being showered on her mate that are not yet apparent to him. Before dismissing every opposite-sex friendship as unacceptable or suspicious, you might want to ask yourself the following questions:

- Is there any evidence of flirting?
- Are you opposed to your romantic partner having any opposite-sex friendships, or is it this particular friend that makes you uneasy?
- Has anyone else mentioned to you that this is a situation that you should be watching?
- How important is this friendship to you or to your romantic partner so that working through this issue is worth your collective efforts?
- Has your romantic partner left the decision about whether or not to pursue this platonic friendship up to you?
- Have you tried to become friends with your romantic partner's platonic friend and it has been unsuccessful?

Your answers to the above questions may help you and your romantic partner to determine the best way to deal with each situation if it raises any conflicts or strong feelings.

Growing Apart

- I've had this longstanding friendship and recently I realized we've grown apart and just aren't the same people we used to be. The friendship just isn't there anymore. Why did we ever want to be friends in the first place?"

- "We met when our children were toddlers. Her marriage was strained even then but eventually dissolved while my marriage, though not great, was intact. . . . I remained friends with her for many years, helping her through her separation. There were three things that ended the relationship. . . . I felt I had to choose between loyalty to her and her [distorted] perceptions and loyalty to him [my husband]. I chose him. . . . The [friendship had] lasted ten years."

Often long-standing friendships will persist for years, or decades, as long as there is little demand placed on either friend to maintain it: The pain and potential despair associated with ending the friendship are greater than the effort involved in maintaining it. But then something may happen that forces one or both friends to take a hard look at the friendship and decide, definitively, if it can be salvaged or needs to be shelved. That's what happened to Annie, a 58-year-old married entrepreneur, the mother of three grown children, who lives with her husband. They retired to the small Midwestern town where Annie grew up after living in a distant Western state for almost four decades.

During the years Annie lived in the West, it was easy enough for her to maintain her childhood friendship with Sally. She and Sally had met at church when they were both in high school. They kept up the friendship after high school even though Sally married an executive and had four children within eight years. By contrast, Annie moved to Los Angeles and had a career. When she married five years later, she gave up her career to go to school while raising three children.

Annie recalls that when she and her family would visit her hometown and stop by to see Sally and her husband, it was just "super uncomfortable." But living so far apart, and with so little contact with her friend, there was no need to do anything about their friendship.

Then, when Annie and her husband retired to her hometown, everything changed. Suddenly Annie found her old friend's materialism hard to stand, so up close. As Annie sums up why she ended the friendship, "I keep thinking there were things that meant something to her, that were important to her, that had no significance to me at all." Then she asks the question that almost everyone who has ever ended a long-standing friendship will ask, "How did we stay friends for so long?"

Interestingly, even if most people who question a long-standing friendship understand why they became friends in the first place, everyone wonders why or how the friendship persisted for so long. But growing apart is definitely a valid reason for letting a friendship fade or, in some cases, even end. You need not end it dramatically or "officially." You may wish to let it wane (as discussed in the chapter on ending friendships), but in your heart you need it to end. Why is it important to minimize or even end a friendship. when you have grown apart?

First, unless you let go of this friendship or friend with whom you have grown apart, you may be less likely to open up your heart to someone new with whom you could grow and remain close. There are only so many hours in the day, in the week, in a year. If you are spending all your time and energy on friends from whom you have grown apart, where are you getting your nurturing? How will you have time for the friends you truly need and want?

This is a very important concept because there are few rules about how many friends to keep close in your life. There are also individual differences. For example, there are working parents who can juggle career and family easily while still finding time for hobbies and friends, while others find it hard to manage child-care issues, let alone work, friendship, and outside interests. Similarly, there are those who can handle five, ten, even fifteen close or best friends and others who can handle only one or two. If you can only handle a couple of intimate friends and both are friends from whom you have grown apart, you are going to have to do something to free up your time and your emotions.

Second, betrayal is more likely to occur between close or best friends who have grown apart than between those who are still connected and concerned. On the surface, the betrayal may seem to be related to anything except one of the friends turning on the other. But it can be the very act of growing apart that so enrages the friend, who feels this pulling away that cannot be reversed or stopped. A betrayal brings the whole situation to a dramatic conclusion. You want to try to avoid betrayals, and one way is to avoid giving a friend, or former friend, emotional fuel for such an action. Growing apart may set the stage for a betrayal, even an unwitting one, as a former friend casually shares confidential information with others that he would earlier have kept secret. But now that the bond has been loosened between the two friends, the lips are looser as well. If "loose lips sink ships," as the adage goes, then growing apart loosens some lips, which sets the stage for potential betrayal.

You can reduce the likelihood of growing apart provoking a betrayal by not dragging out the feeling of rejection that sometimes arises when a friendship is no longer as intimate as it used to be. Hopefully, your friend will replace you with other friends with whom she does feel connected and validated so that no betrayal or dramatic ending to your friendship is necessary. If you wish to let the friendship fade, do it with tact and diplomacy. Avoid gossiping about your friend or your friendship to others since this may get back to your friend who, at the very least, may be hurt by your comments and even feel you have betrayed her by discussing the course of your relationship.

There is an art to pulling away and letting your friendship fade with such finesse that your friend "gets the hint" but does not feel it is vindictive or nasty. However, if you think the growing apart can be reversed, you can try to reconnect with your friend and see if putting more time and emotion into the friendship can rekindle the bond you once had.

How do you know that your friendship is growing apart? In most cases, it's a gut feeling. So many people are overly busy today that simply not having time to call, get together, or even write letters or e-mail, may not be an accurate criterion. The quality of the communication between friends is probably the best way of assessing if a friendship is still close and intimate or if it's fading and you and your friend are growing apart. One clue is whether or not you share intimacies or secrets, if that has been part of your friendship from the beginning. (It may not have been since some people do not share secrets with anyone, especially anyone outside of their immediate family.) Another clue is if one or both friends is now always bringing along a third or fourth friend, diminishing the intimacy and time alone between the original friendship pair.

Growing apart will be most painful when the pulling away is by just one friend and not the other, especially if one friend wishes to maintain the friendship at the level of intimacy and frequency that it has always been. What makes friendship such a precious but fragile relationship is that it takes two friends to agree to start and maintain a friendship, but only one to pull away or end it.

However, you most certainly can let this friendship fade; a confrontation may not be productive or desirable. A confrontation over why you want to end the friendship, or why your friend is pulling away from you, may also open up the greater possibility of betrayal. As noted in Chapter 6, "When and How to End It," simply not returning your friend's calls (or getting the hint if your friend stops returning yours) may be the best way to deal with friendships that have grown apart and are not salvageable.

Friendshifts

The way that friendships may shift or change as you move through life is distinct from simply growing apart. Friendshifts, a word I coined in 1985 that also became the title of my first book on friendship and friendship patterns (published in 1997), are expected and natural. In most cases, it just seems to happen. You move away and you notice after a while that you did not maintain the friendship you had with a neighbor who had become a casual friend. Or you and your close friend worked together, but since you both switched jobs and relocated you rarely call each other, let alone get together.

The word *friendshifts* emphasizes that shifts occur naturally, such as when the elderly have to keep expanding their friendship network or, as friends move or die, they will find themselves without any friends, especially friends nearby. Or the high school graduate who goes away to college on his own and must make additional friends at the new school to really enjoy the college experience. When students don't have current friends who share what is going on, symptoms associated with having few or no friends are more likely to occur, such as depression, poor class attendance, and even lower grades.

Growing apart, although it could be because of friendshifts, implies that one of the friends would prefer to keep the friendship the way it used to be. That is the source of the conflict and the way that growing apart, if not dealt with appropriately or effectively, can set the scene for betrayal.

The way that friendshifts could be a potential source of betrayal is if one or both friends are unaware of how normal and predictable friendshifts are. Failing to accept that friendshifts are part of life, rather than a reflection on friendship, could cause anger, rage, and the wish for revenge, vindictiveness, and betrayal. For example, if a friend marries and his single best friend sees a change in their original friendship as unacceptable and a reflection on their relationship, all sorts of unpleasantness, ranging from bad-mouthing of the new spouse to put-downs of the friend and possibly even betrayal, are possible.

Poor Self-esteem

How does your self-esteem factor into having negative or destructive friendships? It's not a simple cause-and-effect relationship, although, in general, the higher your self-esteem, the less likely you are to be involved in a destructive friendship. High self-esteem might also allow you to wait out a destructive or harmful phase in an otherwise positive friendship without over-reacting to a temporary setback that causes you to want to say or do something that cannot be undone.

If your friend's self-esteem is low, she may not feel worthy of friendship and, consciously or unconsciously, may do or say things to push you away. These "tests" on your friendship, unfortunately, are the hoops that some low self-esteem friends may put you through to force you to "prove" your friendship.

In order to like your friendship choices, you first have to like yourself. If someone has low self-esteem and low self-worth, so that he devalues who he is, he may devalue his friends, by association, as well. In that way, low self-esteem is a problem for the person who has it, and it can be an issue for her friend as well.

Those with poor self-esteem may also take on the problems of their friends as if they were their own problems. Conversely, they may reject friends who are going through hard times (or great times) because of how their friend's situation makes them feel. Those who have healthy self-esteem, by contrast, would be able to see a friend's good or bad points and triumphs or disappointments as distinctly their own, not reflecting on anyone else's worth.

Positive, healthy friendships that last can help raise someone's self-esteem. But poor self-esteem may cause some people to sabotage their friendships or avoid friendship all together, reinforcing their poor self-worth.

The Challenge of Intimacy

Be careful not to overreact if you, or a friend, find the intimacy of genuine friendship too much to handle. It could just be your friend's personality: Some people are less effusive in how they communicate or share feelings than others are; that's as close as they get with anyone.

Closeness makes you vulnerable. Being close opens you up to the potential for loss and pain. You have to connect before you can separate, as psychologist Dr. David Leeds has said. There are some friends who have never made the necessary early family connections to allow them as adults to connect with and separate from friends. You cannot solve that problem for them. They may change, through life experiences or therapy, but in the meantime, if you want to keep your friendship going, you have to accept your friend's emotional limitations.

Sometimes, however, the disappointment that emotional distance brings can just make it too difficult to put the time and energy into a friendship that does not provide an anticipated emotional payoff. You could end the friendship or just put it on the back burner until you are willing to invest in it, knowing full well that your friend lacks the ability to get close at this time and maybe indefinitely.

Ironically, if you are befriending someone with an intimacy problem, you may be frustrated to find that as your friendship gets closer, your friend starts backing off. Such friends actually thrive in less demanding or more superficial relationships. The problem is that as your relationship advances from acquaintance to close friendship, your realization that your friend is incapable of going the distance may make it just too hard to go backward. If you do choose to continue a friendship with someone who backs off, remember that it's their problem, not yours. As with jealousy, depersonalize what is happening so that you can preserve your self-esteem. You cannot force someone to get close to you if she won't or can't. Patience may have its payoff, or it may not. You may just continue this friendship at the level where your friend is comfortable, and get what you need from other friends who are more emotionally open to you.

Getting the Hint

Although it is well known that dating and courtship are sorting and sifting processes along the road to mating, some people fail to see that deciding whether or not someone should become or remain a friend is a similar pruning process. Some perceived betrayals may actually be desperate attempts to end a friendship that someone either did not want in the first place or has decided is not right to perpetuate.

What's so valuable, and also powerful, about friendship is that it is an optional role. You can decide you do not wish to continue a friendship, or a friend can make the same decision about you, and that's perfectly fine. There are no legal, ethical, or financial ties, in most cases, to force you to perpetuate the bond. Yet especially with close or best friendships, the emotional investment can be as intense as and sometimes longer-lasting than a romantic relationship, so that ending the friendship can be devastating, especially to the one who is abandoned without warning or seemingly without a valid "reason."

Friendships are ended for a host of reasons. But a refusal to take hints that a friendship is on the rocks or that someone wants to end it could provoke that friend to do something drastic to bring about the end in a more dramatic way. (This is in contrast to the "crossing the line" acts of betrayal that typically end a friendship, as discussed in Chapter 6, "When and How to End It.")

If you take the hint, or your friend takes your hint, and you can slow down or fade the friendship before a dramatic betrayal occurs, you might be able to revisit the friendship at a later date, when circumstances or personalities have changed or mellowed—you have more time, your friend is single and now has a need for friends, or you or your friend go through a life experience that changes you so your personalities mix better.

Depression and Other Mental Disorders

The irony about depression: Isolation may cause depression, but depression also may lead to isolation. So it can be a vicious cycle. If having a friend who is depressed or dealing with your own depression pushes the friendship to the point of emotional betrayal, outside intervention by a therapist may be necessary. Friends should not be misused as therapists. A close or best friend could be expected to listen to your complaints or deeper longings that emerge based on your depression, but if it is chronic depression, you or your friend needs to seek outside help. If someone is taking longer than a couple of months to a year to cope with the death of a loved one, grief counselors are available to deal with this issue. (How long it takes someone to deal with a major trauma or loss—such as losing a job, divorce, or the death of a spouse or parent—is highly individual and depends upon a range of factors, including the individual's coping skills; whether or not the current loss or trauma brings up unresolved previous losses; the strength of social, familial, or community ties, which can help during transition periods; personality; and whether the trauma was expected or sudden.) Some people resist going to a therapist because they are afraid they will find themselves in a 10- or 20-year plan. Others are afraid of what they may find out, period.

But there are as many types of therapists and styles of therapy as there are depressed patients needing help—everything from short-term, solution-oriented therapy to long-term insight therapy; group therapy; and therapy with a social worker, psychologist, psychiatrist, counselor, psychotherapist, art therapist, music therapist, behavior therapist, and others. There are pharmaceutical treatments for depression that may work in some cases, as well as hypnosis and cognitive therapy.

What is important to emphasize is that depression can undermine a friendship even with the closest and best of caring friends. Friends are not trained therapists or cures for depression. You or your friend need to deal with the depression as a separate issue and then reevaluate the friendship without that burden attached to it.

Those with serious mental disorders could betray a friend because they are unable to help themselves. If someone is a pathological liar, for instance, you could not expect him to tell the truth to you or to anyone else. That is a mental disorder that requires therapeutic intervention.

If you or your friend has a psychosis that causes mood disorders, hallucinations, or splits with reality, as may occur with schizophrenia, these conditions will almost certainly affect the friendship. You cannot separate the friendship from the person; if you or someone you are friends with should evidence a mental disorder, this is probably a condition that existed before the friendship.

The real roots of most instances of betrayal in friendship are set in early family life, as discussed in the next chapter. In all but the very extreme instance of, say, a friend being unfaithful with her friend's romantic partner or spouse, causing the betrayed or cheating friend to flip out, mood disorders have roots outside of friendship.

Unless a friendship is somehow unhealthy, it will be as beneficial to those who have mental disorders as to everyone else. But if you or your friend has a mental disorder, you need to reevaluate any behavior that you see as a betrayal in light of deeper problems. I am reminded, with embarrassment, of my insensitive reaction three decades ago when a woman I had befriended in college, whom I'll call Cindy, shared with me that she had tried to kill herself. I knew she had been raised by an extremely strict father who possessed exceedingly high academic standards for his daughter. And I had always wondered whether there might have been some father-daughter abuse, although I had no proof of such a thing, and I did not know if it might have been mental, physical, sexual, all three, or none of these. But *I* actually felt betrayed by her suicide attempt, as if it was a slap in the face of our friendship. Looking back, my thinking, however selfish and confused at the time, might not be that atypical. My first response was to wonder how much she cared about me as a friend if she was willing to cause me to suffer, as I would have if she had succeeded. The friendship fell apart over the next year or two. I knew it was not just because of the distance (we lived in different cities) since I kept up with another friend I had met around the same time despite the physical distance. The main reason was that Cindy's mental illness scared me.

From time to time over the years, I have thought of trying to find her again, to see if she got help and her life turned out okay, but I never make the call. With so many positive, healthy friendships and relationships in my life now, I take the coward's way out and do nothing, but every once in a great while I wonder, "Whatever happened to Cindy?"

Personality or Temperament

Unlike mental illness, which requires treatment and help, especially if it is severe enough to prohibit someone from functioning, there may be personality or temperament issues that cause someone to be more likely to betray or to be betrayed. You have to decide whether the need to betray friends is so much a part of a particular friend's personality that change is unlikely or impossible. You also have to consider whether or not you have a "betrayal detector" that is so sensitive that you are seeing acts of betrayal where none are intended. For example, your close friend fails to return your phone call for three days. By the time he calls, to share with you news of the wonderful vacation he just took, you're so worked up with rage at your sense of abandonment that it's hard to hear his words. He even apologizes for failing to call before he left on the trip, but he was running late to the airport and he decided not to check in for messages for a few days so he could really unwind. If your friend has a need to betray others, he needs to change. The fault is in his personality, not you. But if your own fear of being betrayed causes you to overact and misperceive a betrayal when none is intended, then you must change. Increasing your self-esteem and self-confidence will help you to give your friends the benefit of the doubt; you will not look for betrayal in every action, however innocent, such as the delayed return of a phone call or a comment that was meant facetiously or in jest.

Addiction

Some people betray because it's a habit they have gotten into. They have not developed the value of loyalty and trustworthiness; they are addicted to betraying others. Some stay in friendships that are characterized by betrayal or hurtful behavior because they have become addicted to being disappointed, angry, and betrayed by their friend or friends.

There are those who get addicted to a person just as others become addicted to a drug or even to work. Dr. Howard M. Halpern's emphasis in *How to Break Your Addiction to a Person* is on how to overcome being addicted to a partner in an unhealthy marriage or romantic relationship. The techniques he suggests for getting over this relationship addiction could be applied to friend addictions as well:

- Keep a relationship log in which you record the events related to the relationship, then use the log to find the patterns in your relationship.
- Turn to a supportive network for help in breaking your relationship addiction. Dr. Halpern suggests turning to a friendship network if you are trying to break an addiction to a romantic relationship. If you are trying to break your addiction to a particular friend, you could turn to a friendship network that does not include that friend, or turn to a romantic partner or family member.
- Psychotherapy can help you to break your addiction to a person.[9]

The "Mirror Image" Trap

Does your friend fall into the trap of assuming everyone should approach life the same way that she does? Instead of respecting your differences, does she try to change you or tell you that you are "wrong" even about issues or situations in which many opinions are equally valid? For example, you might go to a movie together and when you and your friend have opposing views about it, you're told that you're "wrong." Or you may, when asked, share your interpretation of a situation only to be told, "No, that's not it at all," even if the opinion expressed was a distinctively subjective one.

Having a "mirror image" approach to friendships will definitely make it challenging or difficult for a healthy, positive friendship to flourish. If you are willing to put up with your friend's "mirror image" trait, you may find yourself keeping your opinions to yourself or "lying" just to avoid a confrontation. In time, you will decide that you can no longer put up with the silence, or acquiescence, your friend has forced you into, or you will have a knock-down, drag-out argument when your views are in opposition but, for once, you refuse to give in.

Is It *Me*?

It's so easy to see the harmfulness or negative traits in others that make a friendship less than ideal. But could there possibly be just a little destructive or harmful behavior in you? Of course, it's threatening to see anything but good in oneself, but do at least consider that there might be something in you that is attracting destructive friends (who then betray and disappoint you). There's just too much evidence supporting the age-old concept that "like attracts like."[10]

So, if it is true that like attracts like, what does it say about you if you are attracting destructive or harmful friends?

Denial

Denial is a psychological defense mechanism that enables someone to perpetuate a self-defeating behavior by refusing to acknowledge either the behavior or its consequences. Someone may be unaware that a friend is betraying her; she denies the betrayal until she sees it for herself or until it is pointed out in clear and graphic terms. It is more likely that you will deny being in a negative friendship or that a friend is betraying you if you do not have other healthy friendships and other relationships to turn to as alternatives. The consequences of seeing the friendship for what it is, especially if ending it may be the recommended solution, would be too painful, so the negativity or betrayal is denied. Often it takes "crossing the line" acts of betrayal to make someone in denial see that a friendship is really not working.

Identification with the Aggressor

Friends who are insecure and scared may identify with the aggressor and, instead of being kind and caring, act tough, nasty, and negative. This goes back to their childhood models, which are explored in greater detail in the next chapter, "It's All in the Family": Were your friend's parents loving and positive? Were her siblings kind and supportive? Your friend may have been a shy, quiet, sweet, overly subservient, but abused child or teen, so having a friend who is self-centered, strong, demanding, and selfish may make your friend feel that she too has those aggressive traits. Someone's wish to be more aggressive may keep someone from seeing how a friend's behavior is actually undesirable.

The "I Can Save You" Motivation

If you feel your friend is really a nice person, deep down, and that you can help him to be the wonderful friend you know he could be, you might keep the friendship going so you can save your friend. There are a couple of issues that go along with this kind of altruism. First of all, this is a friend, not a family member or a dependent child. Although it is admirable to be loyal to a friend, you need time, energy, and resources for your job and primary responsibilities, especially if you are married, have dependent children, or have a job. Saving your friend is outside the expectations of a typical, healthy friendship. If your friend needs saving, a professional therapist or a 12-step recovery program may be what's needed.

Rationalization

By rationalizing or making up excuses for your friend's behavior, you may be perpetuating it. If you accept it and excuse it, you may eliminate your friend's motivation to change. Not only is your playing it safe unwittingly causing you to put up with traits and behaviors in your friend that should be unacceptable, but your friend is missing out on your sincere, heartfelt disapproval, which could be a helpful eye-opener to her. Your reaction could be a catalyst to change. Here are some typical rationalizations I've heard over the years:

- "I know Bob lies all the time, but his father was a liar, so we just have to expect that in Bob."
- "Sure, Melissa is very self-absorbed these last few months, but she got the lead in the class play, so what do you expect?"
- "Linda's boyfriend left her for someone else, so being an empathetic friend right now is the last thing she's concerned about," even though Linda is *never* empathetic.
- "Look, he's too busy right now with his job to worry about being a good friend," but you've known him since school and he has always been like this.

Masochism

Some people have a psychological need to be treated badly by someone else. We call those people masochists. (Sadists enjoy hurting other people. I'm reminded of the old joke in which the masochist says, "Hit me," and the sadist answers, "No.") So, in essence, behind every masochist there usually is a sadist. Do you fault the masochist for needing to suffer, or the sadist for needing to cause the suffering?

If you find yourself in a pattern of unsatisfactory friendships, of somehow picking friends who end up betraying you, you may have masochistic tendencies that need to be understood and overcome. Once you get to the bottom of the issue, you will be able to select friends who will treat you with love, respect, trust, and loyalty (and whose love, respect, trust, and loyalty you are able to accept and return).

Guilt

Masochism is tied to guilt: Most masochists feel guilty about something, and that is why they need to suffer. Did a family member abuse you but made you feel it was your fault? As a child, did you ever wish for something bad to happen to someone and then, if something bad did happen, did it leave you feeling guilty? We all know, rationally and consciously, that thoughts can't make an event happen. Still, thoughts that are seen to have "magically" caused harm to a loved one could be at the basis for someone failing to allow herself the joys and self-affirmation that come from a dear and healthy friendship.

Nothing's Enough

You may have the kind of personality, because of early childhood experiences that have left you feeling unloved, ignored, or unappreciated by your parents or siblings, that always feels "nothing's enough." Your friend may be the most loving, devoted, and trusting friend that anyone could wish for, but since nothing's enough for you, you dwell on every little perceived affront or disappointment. If "nothing's enough" typifies your personality, you may have to change that orientation if you are to find and keep the loving, caring friends whom you know you deserve but who so far have eluded you. (See the next chapter, "It's All in the Family," for further discussion of how your earliest childhood experiences factor into your current friendship patterns.)

Perfectionism

Tied to "nothing's enough" is the friend who seeks perfection in her friends as well as in herself. If that describes you or your friend, you may misperceive betrayal where none was intended or fail to forgive your friend for insignificant actions and comments that others would pass off but that, in your search for the perfect friend, you cannot take so lightly. Since there are no perfect people, there cannot be perfect friendships. Searching for such a perfect relationship will only set you up for failure and frustration, as well as foster an overreaction to a friend's unique approach to life and situations as a reflection on you or your friendship. If your friend is the one who is the perfectionist, you might try pointing out to her that "no one's perfect, not even you," although outside help may be necessary for a permanent cure for severe cases of perfectionism.

Being Overly Sensitive

If you are so sensitive that your friends feel as if they are walking on eggshells every time they say something to you, you may perceive betrayal in friendship where others would only see divergent opinions. If you are so overly sensitive to feedback or comments, you may find your friends withholding their opinions to avoid a confrontation. In time your friendships will seem artificial or phony because fear of offending you inhibits feelings and thoughts that could be shared.

An Inability to Take Criticism

Tied to being overly sensitive is an inability to take criticism. Such an inability can cause even the best of friends to see betrayal and animosity where none was intended. This is a tricky but important concept to understand as a possible explanation for why you see negativity where none was meant. We praise the virtues of honesty, truth, openness, and confidentiality as cornerstones of the ideal friendship. If you should be able to say anything to a friend, especially a close or best friend, why are you so upset if your friend says something that makes you feel criticized? Similarly, why does your friend act as if you've betrayed her just because you've voiced your honest opinion about something she said, did, wore, created, or even thought?

We have seen that it is human nature to get defensive, to dig in one's heels and try to prove that one is right. But that defensiveness can get in the way of friendship and cause someone to see betrayal or negativity where none was intended.

Was the criticism shared in such a way that it was really feedback? Was it even requested? Some ask for an honest reaction but balk at what they hear. Was a comment made in a malicious or a helpful way? Was it delivered with some wit and humor or in an angry, vengeful manner?

Is it possible for you to see criticism as feedback rather than criticism? That might help you at least to accurately perceive your overreactions to what your friend says or does.

I have observed that those who have a difficult time accepting criticism also have an extraordinarily rough time giving it as well. So start there. Find a way to give feedback to your friends in such a positive way that they actually thank you for it. Practice giving your friends feedback (criticism) without it having a negative impact on your friendship.

Go out of your way to encourage your friends to express their opinions, even if they say critical things to you, so that you can experiment and practice handling it better.

Being Overly Negative

If you approach every interaction with a negative point of view, you may also perceive betrayal in a friendship when none was intended. In this case, either you or your friend has to change how you process words and actions; objectively the events are not acts of betrayal. The friendship, if viewed by an outsider, is not negative or destructive; your definition and frame of reference (or your friend's) may need to change.

What do you say to yourself about a particular friend or friendship? Do you tell yourself that it's a wonderful friendship and you're lucky to have that friend in your life? Or are you dwelling on why it's a negative friendship and that you should get rid of it? How much is real and how much is a self-fulfilling prophecy? If you start viewing your friend or a particular friendship as positive, perhaps you will see the positive in it.

Projection or Displacement

You may be betraying your friend by what you say or do, but instead you accuse your innocent friend of doing to you the very thing you are doing to him. That is projection or displacement, a defense mechanism called into play when you have feelings so strong that, rather than own up to them, you displace them onto someone else. For example, your friend calls to ask what time the movie starts and you instead jump in and say, "Are you asking what time the movie starts because you are having second thoughts about going tonight?" Your friend really just wanted to know when to meet you at the movies; you're the one who's feeling guilty about going out because you have a report due the next day and you haven't completely finished it.

To see if projection or displacement is what's really going on with a particular friendship, take a long and hard look at what is causing you to think your friend has betrayed you. Be as objective as possible, creating a timeline of events, if necessary, to try to determine who is doing the abandoning, if anyone. Is your friend really hurting or betraying you, or are you the one inflicting harm on your friend or wanting to abandon her? Rather than taking responsibility for your own wish to fade or end a particular friendship, are you (falsely) accusing this friend of harming you?

Chapter 4

It's All in the Family

You may think you choose your friends because you want to have a wonderful, supportive relationship with someone with whom you share a lot. But if you have unresolved issues, your friends may be a manifestation of your unconscious conflicts. If your parents made you feel unloved and unlovable, if they were critical or negative or hurt you emotionally or physically, you may unconsciously choose what is familiar to you and what you have come to expect: the negative.

Now not *all* your friendships may be harmful or destructive. Indeed, many may be supportive, wonderful, and positive. There might be just one that is negative, one friend who has betrayed you. It could be a casual friend at work. It could be a close or best friend in your personal life. That one negative friendship could be the exception, not the rule. But even one destructive friend is too many in anyone's life.

However, first you have to recognize patterns from your childhood. This is not an easy task and may require the help of a professional. A therapist can often help identify the early-childhood traumas that get woven into our unconscious like roadmaps for future behavior. Breaking the negative relationship patterns is as difficult as breaking any lifelong habit. You really have to work at it.

Of course, there are different kinds and degrees of bad family relationships. Therapist Susan Forward, co-author with Craig Buck of *Toxic Parents*, points out that all parents do things wrong from time to time when it comes to raising their children, but the toxic parent has a pattern of verbal, sexual, or emotional abuse toward their child or children that leaves the child with "damaged self-esteem, leading to self-destructive behavior. In one way or another, they almost all feel worthless, unlovable, and inadequate."[1]

Untreated, these children grow up to have tremendous self-esteem problems. As we saw in the last chapter, low self-esteem will have a negative impact on friendships, causing a person to select friends who will perpetuate the destructive patterns from childhood. Low self-esteem could even cause someone to feel unworthy of having any friends. For example, 50-year-old Claudia, a married computer programmer with two grown children who, starting when she was 10 was sexually abused for four years by her older brother, describes how her family relationships and home life—which she described as "rigid, tense, competitive, intimidating, dismissive and denying of emotions, and much teasing"—have affected her friendships:

> Sexual abuse was just one contributor to my poor self-esteem, but sexual abuse consolidated my self-perception as "being worthy of poor treatment." I am cautious about entering into friendships. I "sexualize" any friendly gestures by men. I am quick to challenge disagreeable behavior or views rather than let them slide and enjoy what is there to enjoy. I don't believe I'm important to others [and] do not always keep in touch. I am distrustful. [I wonder:] Does someone like me because they like me, or are they just softening me up with listening and jokes and later will ask me to do something [abusive] to satisfy their needs at my expense?

Family issues could even stop someone from being able to have even one close friend. Someone might genuinely want friends, but her nonverbal cues may convey quite the opposite. Instead of smiling and conveying warmth, she frowns, complains, and subtly pushes people away. Until she makes the connection between her own behavior, her childhood, her fears, and the way it all influences why she lacks the friends so dearly craved, the pattern, however unpleasant, will keep repeating itself.

The harsh reality you need to face is that if you want to stop the pattern of picking friends who end up betraying you or treating you in a harmful or negative way, you will have to deal with the unresolved childhood issues that lead you to pick these kinds of friends. Until you deal with such issues, negative or destructive friends will be drawn to you like a magnet.

There is hope. Trained professionals and self-help books and courses can teach you to see and help you to feel that you are a lovable, caring, kind, considerate, worthwhile human being who deserves caring, devoted, positive friends. For example, 40-year-old Sally, a married sales clerk, has used her therapy to help her deal with her childhood and to see how her current feelings are tied to her earliest relationships, as well as the sexual abuse she suffered from her father and her brother. These insights have enabled her to make progress in having more positive relationships and a happier life, rather than just repeating the negative patterns and relationships from her formative years:

Depression is a constant. I never knew I was depressed until I went into therapy. When I was a child, I held everything in, never told anyone. I was afraid to.

Ambivalence is a constant now, as it was when I was a child. When I realized what my father was doing, I didn't want to be part of it, but at the same time, I felt I had to because he was my father. Today, many situations at work or home have a lot of ambivalence.

Anger. Something I don't express. I really don't know how to without hurting myself. Distrust is a biggie. [When I was a child] I put my trust in some people in my life [my father and brother] and I got a lot of pain because of it. I find it hard to really trust anyone.

Rage goes along with anger. I don't do it. When I do, I am hurtful to myself mostly. I have many intimacy problems. Just ask my husband. I have a rough time with being close to anyone. Touching, even if it is just a hug or handshake, I find it hard.

I don't feel worthy of good things in my life. When a friend does something good, I feel unworthy. I want to give but can't accept in return.

Fortunately, even though Sally wants to learn how to allow herself to accept intimacy, she has done enough work on herself that she and her husband are still together, despite her intimacy problems. She has two best friends; one helped her to get her current job "and that was almost 25 years ago." They still work together "and take our break together every day."

Change how you deal with the underlying issues from your childhood, change how you see yourself and how you react to people, and you will start making different friendship choices.

There's a wonderful book about fostering self-esteem in children; written by Dorothy Corkille Briggs, it's entitled *Your Child's Self-Esteem.* Briggs shows how a child learns her self-worth through messages with and without words, as she emphasizes that *"body language always speaks louder than words."*[2] (Which is why I feel so strongly that cyberspace friendships are not enough for adults, no matter how busy they are. They too need the physical and verbal language of their friends, face to face or at least a voice on the phone.)

You may be seeking out destructive friends because you lacked the early positive parenting that you needed. But the shoe could be on the other foot: You may be the one who is sought out. You may have had a marvelous childhood, you have high self-esteem, and because you have the self-confidence and happiness that others want, those who lack what you have seek you out. Out of guilt or a wish to give your friend what he lacked growing up, you think your friendship will help your enraged or unhappy friend to heal.

Sadly, too often it is the act of liking your unhappy, angry, melancholy friend that causes him to betray you; your friendship makes him uncomfortable because it brings up the feelings of loss for what he never had. Rather than deal with those painful and conflicting feelings, with the long-term positive outcome of working through and overcoming a disappointing childhood, your friend betrays you and forces you to reject him.

It is not your job to cure your friend of her low self-esteem issues. However, understanding the causes of this behavior may at least help you to avoid blaming yourself for the end of the friendship. Understanding the pattern, and, if it seems comfortable or a good idea to you, pointing it out to your friend or former friend, might help her to get professional help so she can break the cycle. But unless your friend gets help and can change her friendship-related problems caused by early parent-child bond issues, consider getting out of the friendship before your self-esteem is brought down to her low level.

It may seem like a stretch to have to work on your early family relationships as a way of improving your current friendships. But in the emotional and developmental progression we all typically go through, the first relationships are with our parents, followed by siblings, and then with other authority figures or peers, followed by romantic partners, and then to those we parent ourselves.

If we get "stuck" as we try to sort through those primary parental relationships we can't move forward. Social psychologist Dr. Duffy Spencer notes that the issue of friendship rarely comes up among her clients, not because friendship is unimportant, but because they are so consumed with sorting through parent-child or sibling relationships. Friendship is not yet even an issue or a source of strength. (Interestingly, the second relationship her clients are most likely to discuss is a work-related problem with a co-worker or boss.)

Even if you complain about destructive friendships, you may still be drawn to negative friendships. That is because perpetuating a pattern is less painful than confronting it and trying to change it. For example, by picking friends who have family or romantic relationships that are far worse than yours, you can avoid reexamining your own disappointing intimate relationships. That may sound simplistic, but in most cases friendship replicates early family patterns. As Dr. Spencer notes:

> We're always recreating family relationships around us. Because most people have unresolved issues from their family of origin, they might feel antagonistic toward someone who reminds them of a sibling or a parent and not even realize it. The majority of people don't realize it. A good warning is if you feel a conflict toward a person and that conflict seems out of proportion to what is really happening at the moment.

For 48-year-old Melissa, an unemployed, divorced artist, poor friendships are an outgrowth and repetition of her childhood:

> I came from a large family, and friendships were not encouraged. I tried to change that with my daughter, and she does have some long-lasting and close friendships. My [ex-] husband was anti-social, like my parents, and only once in my life did I feel like I was a good friend who had good friends. Now, with the upheaval of leaving my marriage and starting over, I am without friends, except one long-distance [friend]. I no longer know how to start again and am lonely. Painting is what brings me comfort and insight now, along with prayer and meditation.

The Sibling Bond

Even if you had a positive relationship with your parents, a negative relationship with one or more siblings could lead you into repeating this pattern in your friendships. Especially important is sibling sexuality: What is normal? When does it become abuse? Also important are teasing, fighting, and name-calling. What's normal? When is it pathological and probably related to your current destructive or negative friendships, either directly or indirectly, and your self-esteem issues?[3]

Vikki is the 29-year-old single working woman whose definition of best friendship (based on the TV show *Cybil*) was introduced in Chapter 1. Vikki's story includes her distress over her best friend of four years, Joachim, a platonic male friend with whom she works and who reports to her. Vikki explored her anger at Joachim for not being there for her on an emotional level. Only then was she able to see how her childhood—she had a hostile and distant relationship with her only sibling, a brother, as a child and into her adult years—was causing her to try to make her male platonic friend into the brother she never had. Understanding this enabled her to see that Joachim could offer her enough to make the friendship worth continuing; she was able to stop being upset about his limitations once she understood them in the context of her unresolved sibling issue.

Gretchen was the oldest of three. The younger two, a brother and a sister only a year apart, were much more bonded to each other. Her parents were constantly comparing the three, but of even greater significance is the life-long jealousy Gretchen has felt for her younger siblings' closer relationship. Gretchen confides that when she introduces two of her friends to each other, the jealousy she feels is overwhelming if those friends then become friends. It stirs up the old unresolved jealous feelings from childhood. Being aware of that, she tries very hard to avoid fostering such friendships between her friends, although it is clear that trying to work through those early conflicts so she could appreciate friendships among two or more of her friends offers a better long-term solution.

How you and your parents handled sibling rivalry when you were growing up will have an impact on your friendships today. The way your parents treated each child, and how you emotionally dealt with any disparity, may color your feelings toward your peers as acceptable or as overwhelmingly envious or jealous. Although it is impossible for parents to treat siblings exactly equally, especially if there are wide disparities in age and abilities, it is the *perception* of fairness and equal treatment that siblings need to feel if they are to avoid long-term negative sibling-related friendship problems. For example, if your parents made you feel as if you were as loved and as capable as your siblings, you are more likely to handle a friend's success and achievements well than if your parents always made you feel as if you were less successful, lovable, or worthy compared to your siblings.

But why would these unresolved sibling issues crop up in a friendship five, ten, or twenty years down the road when you seemed, until now, to be getting along just fine? You and your friend met at a point in time when you were equals. You attended the same school or were co-workers. Perhaps you were both single. But then you get engaged or your friend gets promoted, and unresolved sibling rivalry issues may be called into play. You or your friend feel, on an unconscious level, that a romantic partner is "favoring" a friend over a mate, or a promotion makes you or your friend feel less than the other person, who has become, for the moment, a sibling replacement.

If you or your friend was an only child, you may still have to deal with how lacking siblings has impacted on your current friendships. Even if rivalry between siblings is common, there is much love and friendship between siblings that offers a positive training ground for future friendships. Being an only child need not rule out someone's ability to find and maintain close and intimate friendships throughout life, as long as there is time and opportunity for fostering caring friendships outside of the family. In my friendship research, I observed that only children are often encouraged to develop good peer-relation skills, since their parents, aware that there are no peers at home to play with, are more likely to make sure that the child has opportunities for playing with friends (or cousins). Parents with two, three, or more children, especially if those children are close in age, sometimes feel that "they have each other," and consequently may be inclined to invest less time and energy in arranging for playdates outside the home.

Sibling physical, emotional, or sexual abuse presents a more extreme problem. I don't mean the sexual curiosity between siblings who are close in age that is mild and considered "non-abusive." Abusive sexual activity is more dramatic, including oral sexual contact, fondling, and touching. Fondling and touching are the most common types of sibling sexual abuse reported, especially between the ages of 10 and 12, the time victimization first is most likely to occur, and intercourse between siblings may be referred to as sibling incest rather than sibling sexual abuse.[4]

Even though abuse by an older opposite-sex sibling is five times more common than parent-child sexual abuse, it is hard to know precisely how often it occurs since it is rarely reported to the authorities. When parent-child sexual abuse comes to light, it almost automatically becomes a criminal matter. Sibling sexual abuse, even if it is by a much older sibling, is not viewed with the same seriousness since it is usually considered merely an aberrant behavior between two consenting children. But that consent is gained through psychological coercion, although sometimes physical threats or the use of weapons is involved.

Having spoken with adult survivors of childhood and adolescent sibling sexual abuse, and having attended the national annual meeting of an association of survivors of childhood sexual abuse as well as workshops for survivors including a day-long workshop for married couples where the wife had been an incest survivor, I have discovered that it dramatically affects the survivors as well as their mates. The most frequent victim is a young girl victimized by her older brother, although brother-brother or sister-sister sexual abuse, although less common, does occur as well. Many of these adult survivors did not even realize that sexual abuse by their older brothers might have had a negative impact on their childhood as well as their adult years until decades after it had ended. But the negative impact of the childhood sibling sexual abuse on peer and romantic relationships can linger for decades or even a lifetime. The typical immediate effects are to become depressed, guilty, self-hating, sad, isolated, a compulsive eater, anorexic or bulimic, or withdrawn from peers. Some of the long-term consequences are anger, shame, food-related problems such as overeating, anorexia, or bulimia, overspending, guilt, ambivalent feelings about sex, and conflicts over intimacy, including difficulty in achieving and sustaining positive friendships or romantic relationships.

If we are to detect childhood and adolescent sexual abuse, we have to become more aware of its subtle signs since the unexplained bruises of physical abuse are usually missing. If we are to detect and treat childhood and adolescent sibling sexual abuse, we have to become more sensitive to some of the warnings. First, there's the familial atmosphere that's conducive to sexual abuse: brothers and sisters who have distant parents (whether emotionally distant, or chronically busy or absent). Second, parents and educators have to examine whether their attitude ("boys will be boys, you know") is stopping them from seeing that exploration or curiosity has crossed the line and is now in the realm of sexual abuse. Third, if we are to encourage a child, adolescent, or even an adult to confess to one incident or to years of sexual abuse, we have to make the victim feel that she will be heard and believed.

Being sexually abused by a sibling will certainly influence later friendship patterns, but the cause-and-effect need not be the obvious one of finding and repeating abusive peer relationships. Someone who had such a horrific childhood experience could actually seek out positive friends to give her what was lacking in childhood. That is what Lillian, 50 and divorced, has done. She explains, "For most of my life, friends took the place of a family that didn't work. They became my family." When she was 12, Lillian, who "tends to have a few deep friendships," was raped by her 18-year-old brother. (She also had another brother, three years her senior, and a sister, four years younger, with whom she did not have an abusive relationship.) Lillian tries to explain what happened to her and why:

I was 12 and "starved" for love and attention in a family with an alcoholic and workaholic father who was seldom there and emotionally absent and a mother who was there but very frigid with any verbal or physical displays of love (such as hugs, etc.). Boundaries in my family were muted or nonexistent and very patriarchal. So I felt guilt and shame that it was my fault. [There was] no one I trusted [enough] to tell because I was afraid of blowing up family dynamics and because I had an underlying dread that my mother would not believe me. When I did tell my parents, individually, at age 41, my father unquestionably believed and supported me. My mother denied it, even after my brother's first wife corroborated that it did happen. So I guess my childhood fears were correct.

Being sexually abused by my brother made me feel powerless, dirty and ashamed. It robbed me of my childhood, my sexuality, myself. . . . To have friends, you have to be a friend. That's what I've tried to do—treat others as I've wanted to be treated in my family but never was. This translates [into] being thoughtful, perceptive, and kind. I'm known for giving thoughtful gifts and advice. I'm a good listener and available to help. I also make time to get together with my friends on a regular basis.

Of course, you can try to work out a better relationship with your parents or siblings when you are an adult, but you could also get from others, and give to yourself, what you may have missed in your childhood. You cannot change the past, but the real tragedy is those who perpetuate an unhappy childhood by unconsciously recreating it in unsatisfying friendships fraught with betrayal and negativity. Fifty-year-old Brenda, mentioned previously because her friend pulled away as soon as Brenda had shed a few pounds on a diet, is trying to overcome the long-term consequences to her friendships because of her father beating her with a belt buckle and her older brother and his friends gang-raping her. Brenda notes:

As a child, I never brought any friends home. I never knew what would happen, and I always wanted to keep the secret of abuse. I thought I could protect [my family] too. I felt I could be a better friend if I was no friend at all. . . . I still find it hard to form new relationships. I find it hard to reach out to people, even my closest friends. I still have to fight the old tapes of not being worthwhile or good enough to be a friend. I have to fight my fear of getting close to a friend because of trust issues.

By the same token, even if you had a memorable, cherished, loving childhood, unless everyone you befriend has positive family roots to draw upon, you may still have to deal with how your friends have been shaped by their parent-child and sibling relationships.

Working through friendship issues can be an excellent opportunity for you to deal with early family relationships. But until you have an understanding of why you or your friend chooses certain friends, you or your friend will probably repeat, rather than change, the basic pattern. It is also important not to oversimplify the way earliest parent-child and sibling relationships impact on friendship choices. Yes, there is definitely a correlation, but it may not be that obvious to the untrained eye. As psychoanalyst Melanie Klein notes in her classic essay, "Love, Hate and Reparation":

> Although love-relationships in adult life are founded upon early emotional situations in connection with parents, brothers and sisters, the new relationships are not necessarily mere repetitions of early family situations. Unconscious memories, feelings and fantasies [sic] enter into the new love-relationship or friendship in quite disguised ways. . . . Normal adult relationships always contain fresh elements which are derived from the new situation—from circumstances and the personalities of the people we come in contact with, and from their response to our emotional needs and practical interests as grown-up people.[5]

Part 3

Coping

Chapter 5

Can This Friendship Be Saved?

Your immediate reaction to a friend's betrayal will probably be shock, denial, and disbelief, followed by anger and finally a resolution regarding what occurred. These stages are actually a variation on the famous five stages of grief that psychiatrist Elisabeth Kubler-Ross found patients and their families go through when finding out that an illness is terminal.[1]

Reaction Stages to Unexpected Betrayal
(based on the stages of grief)

1. Shock, denial, and disbelief
2. Fright and fear that the trauma will occur again, including clinging behavior, such as uncontrolled talking about the event
3. Apathy alternating with anger
4. Resolution

Your first impulse following the betrayal may be to end the friendship. But once you've calmed down and absorbed what has happened, you may wish to try to understand why the betrayal occurred, or even see it as a sign that your friendship needs work and help, not an ending. The first step here is to seriously consider the answer to the following question: *Do I care enough about this friend to invest the time and energy that it might take to turn this situation around?*

If your answer is "yes," great! This chapter will help you to work through conflicts in friendships that you would like to save.

You may not want to invest the time or effort that could be required to try to salvage this positive friendship that has turned negative, yet you may have to. It may be in your best interest to work through this friendship if any of the following conditions or situations describe this positive-turned-negative friendship:

1. You work together.
2. The friend is also your boss.

3. The friend is or was also your employee.
4. The friend is or was also a client or customer.
5. The friend is or was a service provider and you cannot or do not wish to find an alternative one.
6. You fear the friend might become vindictive.
7. You live nearby or are neighbors.
8. You and your friend are connected through your spouses or children.
9. You and your friend will probably run into each other in your town or community.
10. You and your friend go to the same house of worship.
11. You are the kind of person who doesn't like to think anyone has bad feelings toward you or might bad-mouth you.
12. You're in a 12-step program, and it's important that you understand why this friendship turned sour or to right any wrongs you may have unwittingly done to another.

If you answered "yes" to one or more of the above situations, and even if you could go on with your life and career quite merrily without resolving this positive-turned-negative friendship, it is probably in your best interest to at least try to salvage the relationship.

What You Can Do on Your Own

Step 1: Recognize that this friendship requires attention. The first step is to realize that this friendship requires your consideration. Too often friendships, especially long-standing ones, are taken for granted until it is too late. You think your friendship is just fine; you do not put the time and energy into calling or getting together because you are busy, and, besides, you feel very secure about the relationship. When you finally do call, however, you find out that your dear friend is cooler toward you; you discover you have been replaced by another friend who is more responsive and available to your friend. "Nothing personal."

Step 2: Clarify the details. Reflect back on your friendship, from its beginning to where it is now, trying to figure out what, if anything, you did that might have caused it to go astray. What did you or your friend do that could have caused this rift? Before you even confront your friend, you want to analyze the situation on your own, getting the facts straight to the best of your knowledge and memory.

Step 3: Decide whether you will confront your friend or let things ride for a while. You may decide that taking a deep breath, backing off, and at least temporarily electing to "do nothing" is the better course of action. Sometimes, however, intervention is necessary, such as when letting things ride translates into a worsening situation. Not working things out may further fade your friendship. If there is an immediate conflict that needs to be addressed but you fail to "clear the air," conflicts may deepen, disagreements may fester, and rage may boil over so that salvaging the friendship becomes even harder.

Step 4: Assess whether both you and your friend believe your friendship could improve. It is pivotal that you and your friend believe that it is possible to change the way your friendship is now. Unless you and your friend believe you have choices, you will simply perpetuate the way the friendship has been going and, since you no longer find it satisfying, it will eventually fade or end.

Improving a friendship may be one of the most difficult intimate relationship shifts to measure. The changes could be very subtle; it could be a nuance or even a gesture. It could mean becoming a better listener or asking fewer favors of your friend. It might mean that your friend has to become less of a gossip or get a better grip on the jealousy she feels that causes her to unfairly put you down. It could mean you have to train yourself to share fewer secrets or accept that your friend cannot help himself about canceling your lunch get-togethers because of work-related crises that always seem to come up. It might just mean that when you get together, you need to find a way to have more fun than you have ever had before.

My research has found that friendships that last either have less conflict or, when conflict arises, the friends have better coping skills at handling the conflict. Fortunately, conflict resolution skills can be taught; you may be able to turn around friendships that you did not think you could salvage.

Handling Conflict with Friends

The first step toward working out a conflict with a friend is to understand the conflict or the betrayal. Why did it happen? You have already considered the possible conscious and unconscious reasons, as discussed in detail in Chapters 3 and 4, but here are additional factors to assess. What does each friend believe actually happened? Perhaps each one has her facts wrong. For example, two friends are angry because one kept the other waiting an hour at a restaurant. When they compared notes, they discovered that each one got the time wrong about when they were supposed to meet.

So clarifying the facts may actually allow some conflicts to be resolved immediately, and that's good news. But if the conflict cannot be resolved quickly and easily, you may still need more help. Remember that unresolved conflicts may lead to irreversible hostility.

Here are nine mediation techniques, typically used by experts as well as those who teach communication skills, for settling neighborhood disputes or disputes between companies or married couples, that are also useful for friendship disagreements:

1. *The IBB model (interest-based bargaining model).* This technique helps you to learn to look behind problems to the reasons they may have been created. For example, "I want to go out to a movie, but you want to work overtime," or "I want to borrow your computer, but you have a 'no loan' policy" could be reconsidered from an interest-based bargaining model that would focus on the positions raised: "I want to go out to a movie *because* we both work hard, you'll burn out if you keep working, and it's a fun way to spend time together as friends," and, "I want to borrow your computer *because* I can't buy one right now, I need it to create some flyers for my company, I've never broken anything else you've loaned me, and I promise to take really good care of it and return it quickly."

Interest-based bargaining or problem solving is really about asking the question, "Why?" and, alternatively, "Why not?" In that way, you get each friend to focus on the issues, rather than just the personalities involved. "Find out what each side's interests are by asking 'why?'" says Eileen B. Hoffman, a federal mediator and an expert in conflict resolution. Hoffman continues: "Once you figure out the *why* someone wants something, you can figure out the *how.* There may be more than one way to resolve it. People get locked into positions. [But] if you can satisfy somebody's interest, you can resolve things."

2. *Putting yourself in someone else's situation.* Try to understand your friend's motivations by comparing them to your own: When did I want something the way my friend wants this? How can I satisfy my friend's needs while still satisfying my own? When I got a new job and was ex-

tremely busy trying to adjust to the changes, was I able to return every personal phone call I received, or did it take me a while to get caught up on things? Just by putting yourself in your friend's situation, or asking your friend to put herself in yours, you might minimize the conflict.

3. *Listening carefully and thoughtfully.* One of the most important skills in conflict resolution is listening. By carefully listening, you validate someone's opinions as well as his own worthiness. You or your friend may not even realize that you have actually stopped listening to each other. If you are tuning each other out it will be difficult or impossible to resolve your conflicts.

4. *Step outside the situation and take a cinematic view.* When you are in the midst of a conflict, try for a moment to get yourself out of it. Pretend you are in the audience watching it on a screen, as if it were a movie. If you can give yourself some distance from the conflict, you will see it more objectively because you're seeing it played out by other people, not by you and your friend.

5. *Agree to disagree.* Do what the communication experts suggest you do, a technique I use when I work as a group facilitator and an approach parents often use when dealing with a conflict with a child: Validate your friend by acknowledging her point of view or position. "Agree to disagree," as they say.

6. *Validate the relationship.* Let your friend know you value your friendship. That will "up the stakes" in working things out, and motivate you both to move forward. An example of a statement that would validate your friendship is, "I want you to know that you and our friendship are very important to me and I really want to work things out between us."

7. *Allow for a cooling-off period.* Sometimes a friendship, especially a best or close one, can be saved simply by deciding to step back from the annoying situation and postpone dealing with any irreversible words or actions that might have occurred in the heat of the moment. A cooling-off period is an adult version of the "time out" parents impose on their kids. This cooling-off time—minutes, hours, days, or weeks, or longer, if needed— is a self-imposed period to step back, reassess, calm down, or chill out. It is amazing how much less important most issues, comments, or situations are when put in the perspective that sometimes only *time* provides.

Of course, you must reinitiate contact. Only then should you decide if it is even necessary to bring up whatever it was that enraged you. For example, your friend does not return your calls as quickly as you would like. Perhaps you can work out a system where you indicate you need to be called back right away, versus a "hello" call that could take longer to get to.

However, in some cases, failing to come to terms with the original conflict may result in a second, permanent rupture. If working out the difference is essential to the friendship, calmly bring up the conflict and deal with it with your friend so that your friend does not feel judged, criticized, or blamed. If you decide what happened was silly or irrelevant, let it ride. Not every problem or issue needs to be discussed continually. But if the initial conflict highlighted value differences, you probably need to iron those out.

8. *Ask for understanding.* If your friendship conflicts are based on your inattentiveness or not giving your friend what she needs, let your friend know if the causes are temporary. For example, perhaps you have been overwhelmed lately because of work, or perhaps you have been traveling and unavailable. Explain to your friend that you need time to get caught up and that he should not take your inattentiveness personally. If you are busy because of a new job, pressing deadlines, a family illness, or other pulls, let your friend know that as well and ask that she "cut you some slack."

9. *Saying "I'm sorry."* Whoever caused the conflict could just take responsibility and express remorse by saying, "I'm sorry." Admitting to words or deeds that upset or harmed a friend might be enough to salvage the friendship. Adding, "I'll try hard not to let it happen again" may help as well. If you share with your friend that you were disappointed that she wasn't there for you when your parent died, and your friend feels bad about her insensitivity and distance, and she says, "I'm sorry," that is a big step. Saying "I'm sorry" is not as easy as it sounds; uttering those two words may be a very big step for you or your friend, especially if childhood or current relationships or experiences do not applaud the admission of culpability. Still, it is a conflict-resolution technique to consider. (By the same token, it may be hard to hear or accept someone's "I'm sorry." But the first step is being able to feel it and to say it.)

It's tempting to avoid conflict, because it involves more stress in the short term, but dealing with difficult situations head-on makes for less stress in the long run. Furthermore, handled well, conflict may actually strengthen a relationship. The cost of avoiding conflict in a friendship may turn out to be the end of the friendship itself.

Offering Forgiveness

Even if you are the party who was "at fault," in certain instances a simple "I'm sorry" may not do the trick. That is because friendship is a relationship based on the needs and feelings of both parties. You may ask for forgiveness, but it is up to your friend to forgive you.

Even if your friend wronged you, begin by offering her your forgiveness. Why are you offering your forgiveness even if you are the one who was wronged and should be *offered* forgiveness? There are several reasons. The first is that you cannot control someone else's behavior, only your own. If you offer forgiveness, you may inspire your friend likewise to offer forgiveness, as she will learn from and maybe even be inspired by your example. The second reason is that being forgiven could be a humbling experience to your friend. Remember the old adage, "To err is human, to forgive, divine." Finally, it is much harder to stay angry with someone if she has ceased being angry with you.

Make no mistake, though: forgetting and forgiving can be hard to do. As columnist Harry Stein wrote in *Esquire* magazine:

> From strangers I anticipate nothing more than courtesy (and if I don't get it, my irritation generally passes quickly). From colleagues I insist upon respect and equitable treatment. And from friends I demand not blanket approval but patience, understanding, and loyalty—all of which I offer in return. And if I am crossed, I do not forget easily.[2]

Accepting Forgiveness

By the same token, you may need to brush up on how to graciously accept your friend's offer of forgiveness. Especially if this friendship is important to you, allowing your friend to ask for your forgiveness and to make amends may actually be harder than ending the friendship. But accepting your friend's forgiveness is a step toward salvaging this friendship and even strengthening it so it becomes more rewarding than ever.

How do you accept forgiveness graciously? It is so tempting to make your friend grovel or crawl, especially if he has been wrong.

If your friend asks for forgiveness and you wish to continue the friendship, offer forgiveness and accept her apology as quickly as possible. As noted before, "I'm sorry" can be the hardest two words someone needs to say. Knowing that, you can ease your friend's angst by granting your friend forgiveness and moving on. Avoid harking back to this conflict or harping on your friend's seeming mistake or slight that caused the strife. Be cautious about unwittingly developing a "one-upsmanship" attitude toward your friend or misusing her apology to inflate your own self-righteousness. Even if you have not yet done something that would require your friend to grant you forgiveness, you might need her compassion in the future. Your behavior will set the tone and provide the example for how similar situations will be handled in the future.

Facing Unrealistic Expectations

Facing unrealistic expectations has two parts. First, are your expectations about friendship realistic, based on what researchers tell us about friendship—namely, that friendship is an optional role and that its prominence in your current life is tied to where you are in your life cycle as well as the competing demands of obligatory family ties (spouse, children, parents, siblings, extended family) as well as any work, school, or community responsibilities? (You may also wish to refer back to Chapter 1, "What Is a Friend?" for a more detailed discussion of practical friendship considerations.)

If your friendship expectations are unrealistic, you may be constantly disappointed and consistently find that others don't live up to your standards. Your own exaggerated expectations about what your friend should be providing you may get in the way of having a satisfying relationship. In this case, it is *you* who has to change. Your neediness or unrealistic expectations about the role that any one friend can play in your life may be pushing this friend away. They may even be causing your friends to say or do hurtful things in a desperate attempt to stop their guilty feelings about not being able to give you what you need or want.

Failing to face impractical friendship expectations may cause a friendship to go by the wayside. That is what happened to Natalie's friendship with her best friend from fifth grade. Forty-year-old Natalie explains what happened to end their friendship, 20 years later, faulting her friend Claire for failing to come through for her, rather than her own excessive demands on Claire:

I had reached an all-time low. I was going through a terrible divorce, and I was forced into giving my ex the kids for about two years until I could get on my feet. I moved into this cheap six-unit apartment house, and my apartment desperately needed work. I was young and didn't know my rights as far as what was considered acceptable by the board of health. I would scrub walls and paint at night and work during the day at a company an hour away. For the first five days, I had no running water and had to get water out of the cellar sink to clean up the paint brushes. I had no fridge or stove, but I did have a cot and an electric coffee pot for soup, teas, and a poor substitute for a hot plate. I asked the "spoiled one" [my friend Claire] if she would mind if I came over to shower on a daily basis until my landlord could fix the problem the following weekend. She said no. Years later, I realized she [was] jealous of her husband [who might have been attracted to me]. I never forgot that. What a horrible way to treat a "friend."

If Natalie had realized that she had an unfair friendship expectation of Claire and had decided against making the request—if, say, she had gone to a community center or an inexpensive hotel to shower, or to a single girlfriend's apartment or home—it is possible her friendship with Claire might have been saved.

Another consideration is whether the person you have chosen, because of her personality or even the timing of your request, simply cannot fulfill your friendship expectations. This was what was going on with Doris, a 48-year-old entrepreneur who, upon reflection, realized that her friend wasn't getting from their friendship what she needed and deserved. "At that point in my life, I was very self-absorbed," Doris explains. "My son was a nightmare. I was taking care of my mom. My friend got pushed aside. There was not enough to maintain a friendship."

Doris's friend's needs were realistic, but at that time, because of what was going on in Doris's life and career, she was unable to give her friend what she needed. These insights did not occur to Doris for many years after the friendship abruptly ended when her friend failed to return her phone calls.

Dealing with Chemistry Issues

There may be clashes you have to face that may be a factor in why a friendship is no longer viable. Often this occurs because one or both friends "couple off" and the foursome that results is far from harmonious. Think of how challenging it is for two friends, who used to spend time together, to now include two others, who may be total strangers to the others and who may or may not have anything in common. Whether someone starts a romantic relationship or marries, how friends respond to the new romantic relationships in their life can spell bliss or trouble.

These chemistry issues, like the underlying reasons for some friendship issues that arise, may have as much to do with early family or sibling relationships as they do with how you really feel about your friend's new beau or how he feels about you. How easily did your friend or her boyfriend share a parent with the other parent or her siblings during the formative years? If sharing a loved one is a deep-seated issue, "sharing" a romantic partner with her friend, especially a close or best friend, may bring up as many feelings of jealousy and possessiveness as the sexual jealousy that occurs when someone tries to tell a romantic partner or spouse that she and her platonic friend are "just friends," not lovers.

First and foremost, when such changes occur and you and your friend now have to deal with one or more new relationships as well as your own friendship—whether it's a new romantic partner, another close or best friend, a sibling who moves back to town, or even a new baby—the chemistry issues have little to do with your original friendship. Of course, this won't help soothe your injured feelings if your best friend's newborn screams his head off every time you try to hold him or your girlfriend's husband doesn't say one word to you or your husband when you all go out for a celebratory dinner.

In these situations, you and your friend may decide there is a way for you to continue your friendship, but without the new relationships in tow. That might mean meeting for lunch during the workday, if you both work nearby, or hiring a babysitter for a "Girls' Night Out," or leaving the baby with your spouse while you keep the connection going with your friend.

To stubbornly try to throw people together who just do not want to be in the same room will result in a miserable time for everyone. The good news is that you don't have to abandon or be left behind by your friend just because your lives lead to other relationships and the chemistry, for whatever conscious or unconscious reasons, is not right from the get-go and never will be.

It may take some ingenuity on your part to keep your friendship going when chemistry issues emerge, but certainly being aware of what is going on and discussing it with your friend without rage, judgment, or ultima-tums will definitely help the situation.

If having a new relationship causes you to cut loose an old friend, or if your friend ends the relationship with you and a paramour or baby is of-fered as the reason, you have to decide if that's really what's at work or if it's an excuse. Those current ties may help your friend realize that the friend-ship has been strained all along; you may come to the same conclusion if you're the one with preferred new "pulls."

But if it's just the poor chemistry between others over whom you have no control, if you value your friendship enough and your friend cares about you, fight to avoid ending your friendship because of someone else. If you do someday end your friendship, it should be because you and your friend no longer care about each other or want to spend time together.

The Silent Treatment

Unfortunately, some people are so overcome with rage and conflicting emo-tions about a friendship or a particular incident that they give their friend or former friend the silent treatment. This is different from "cooling off," which is meant to allow one or both parties to "chill out." The assumption is that the cooling-off period is just that—a period of time, and not permanent.

By contrast, the silent treatment may be a way to permanently deal with (or, more likely, avoid) the conflicts that have occurred in the friendship. The silent treatment is all about power. It is the nonverbal way that some-one tries to demonstrate that she is above discussing the issues at hand. Out of an unconscious or even a conscious fear of the angry words or accu-sations that might flow from the mouth of the angry one, the silent alterna-tive emerges.

On a certain level, the silent one may rationalize that she is actually avoiding conflict since, unlike angry words, the treatment is indeed silent. No words that could be misinterpreted or repeated to others are shared. No nasty e-mails or letters are exchanged. No, there is silence. Nothing.

But within that silence there is an action, even though the action, on the surface, seems to be inaction. The silence is as strong an act as any letter, e-mail, or phone call for the one on the receiving end of the silent treatment.

The one who is initiating the silent treatment probably does not see it that way. He probably figures it's better to avoid saying things that might be regretted just in case, at some point, there is a wish to start the friendship up again or, as is likely, there may be a necessity to deal with each other. You might work in the same business or run into each other at the supermarket or at open school night or even on the street, if you live nearby.

Those who use the silent treatment are probably just overwhelmed by the need to cope with an ambivalent situation involving conflict. Twenty-seven-year-old Max, a mailroom clerk living in New Mexico, has a hard time trusting anyone because of early abuse by his older brother. The silent treatment he received from a platonic female friend was especially cruel:

> She had promised to buy tickets for an upcoming concert I really wanted to see. We were not dating. I was going to go with her and her boyfriend. We were just friends. So I waited all night for them, and nobody showed.

Perhaps the friend realized that she had created a potentially awkward situation—having Max along on a date, a third wheel—but rather than discuss the situation honestly with him, she stood him up (a form of the silent treatment), disappointing him and embarrassing him. Furthermore, those who were sexually abused as children or teens are especially sensitive to being kept waiting: They had to wait for the dominating, abusing older sibling, parent, or authority figure to come and go, often without warning, so they need clarity and predictability from those they become emotionally attached to.

Unfortunately, rather than discussing these issues with his friend, Max cut off the friendship.

If you are using the silent treatment, be aware of how it could be affecting your casual, close, or best friends. It may, in some instances, be better than a confrontation, but you still need to be aware that there are consequences to it. It could bring out rage, anger, and despair in the one on whom you use the silent treatment, rather than the smooth end to the friendship that you hoped it would achieve.

If you are on the receiving end of the silent treatment, you need to see it as a very strong hint that the friendship is fading or ended. You may have to deal with others besides your friend, such as other friends you trust, a spouse or romantic partner, a family member, or a therapist, if the feelings of abandonment and betrayal brought up by the silent treatment prove overwhelming and debilitating. If an angry parent practiced the silent treatment as a means of punishing you when you were a child, you may be particularly sensitive to the silent treatment, even if it lasts for only a brief period.

Getting Help

If you feel you've done everything you can do on your own, as well as asking your friend to try to make changes, and you feel you're not getting anywhere, it may be time to bring in outside help. A good hint that it's time to call in a third party is if you or your friend find yourself saying to the other or even thinking, "You're not listening to me!"

A third party can indeed be helpful if you and your friend are at a point that you are unable to hear each other. Rage, anger, misunderstandings, feelings of betrayal, grievances, and a whole host of other emotions also could be getting in the way of an amicable solution to your friendship problems. Another friend, a family member, and a religious leader are all possible mediators.

If you want to go to a professional mediator, there are national mediation associations that might be able to make referrals on the local level. These include the Association for Conflict Resolution (ACR), which was formed in 2001 by the merger of three associations—the Society of Professionals in Dispute Resolution (SPIDR), the Academy of Family Mediators (AFM), and the Conflict Resolution Education Network (CREnet)—as well as the American Arbitration Association. (For the web site and mailing addresses of these associations, consult the Resources section in the back of this book.)

In a new approach called "transformational mediation," a third party works with the two disputing friends to have them acknowledge each other and empower each other. Transformational mediation is a powerful tool. One of its components is that when those who are disputing speak to each other, they need to use "I" words, indicating how the speaker feels, rather than judging the other person. In other words, each disputing friend would say something like, "When so-and-so does something, I feel like _____."

A third party will help reinforce the most pivotal conflict resolution skill noted before, namely listening. Experts in conflict resolution are trained to know when people are actually listening and when they are tuning out. If someone cannot or will not hear what is being said, it is impossible to resolve the issues. A third party could help if the friendship problems get to the point that neither friend is able to communicate or listen, by providing a sounding board, acting as a facilitator or mediator, or even deciding the issue as an arbitrator. (The arbitrator is given the right to make a binding decision that both parties agree, in advance, they will abide by.)

For more suggestions specifically about how to cope with work-related friendship disputes, see the suggestions in Chapter 7 on work and friendship.

A therapist is another source of help for handling conflict with a friend, but traditionally the therapist will be treating just one of the disputing friends. Unlike couples or family therapy, which has a tradition within the therapeutic community as well as a treatment option, friendship therapy in which the friends are in treatment together is uncommon. More commonly, one or both friends would discuss the friendship-related conflicts within the context of their separate individual or group counseling.

Conflict patterns that reoccur with friend after friend will certainly be red flags to you, your friend, and your therapist that there are probably unresolved issues from the past impacting on current relationships. The advantage of consulting a therapist to sort through these friendship conflicts, in contrast to a third-party mediator or even another friend, is that hopefully a competent therapist will facilitate the self-awareness that can help you make permanent changes rather than dealing with only one problematical friendship situation.

Doing this work in therapy is crucial, however, if you find yourself either picking the wrong friends most of the time or consistently losing good friends or pushing them away through your own behavior or your inability to effectively handle conflict in a friendship, when it arises.

Chapter 6

When and How to End It

Okay, so you've tried all the conflict resolution techniques suggested in the previous chapter. Or maybe your friend simply refuses to try to work things out. You may be the one to decide that this friendship simply has to end.

When a best or close friendship does end it is usually because of a trigger incident, the feeling that someone has "crossed the line," often through an act of betrayal. Here are examples of betrayal or disagreements that were offered as reasons for ending a close or best friendship:

- "I had a girlfriend who was good at scoring the boys I was interested in. We had been best friends for about 10 years. A boyfriend I had then for a couple of months was killed in a car accident and after that, she told everyone that he was more interested in her than [in] me."
- "She wasn't there for me when my mom passed away."
- "Their beliefs and mine contrasted to the point of argument."
- "My best girlfriend was so jealous of me and my talents that she sabotaged me every chance she could."
- "She stole from me after I took her in and gave her a place to live."
- "I had a close friend in high school betray me in many ways, just [by] being mean and spiteful."
- "I shared some private secrets with a best friend and she told others."
- "A friend 'borrowed' some of my video games, then ended up selling them to a store that buys and sells used games."
- "Used me for money, verbally abused me, and physically abused me."
- "My best friend misunderstood a conversation I had with her boyfriend. I told him I'd like to hang out with him after my best friend moved away. I wanted someone to talk with about losing my best friend, and they both misunderstood [that I was making a play for him] and wouldn't talk to me ever again."

Deciding to End a Negative Friendship

You need to gain strength to end a friendship. Ending a friendship is not something to consider or do lightly. Friendships, especially close or best ones, stir up very strong emotions. Your friend may know secrets about you that might be shared with the public at large if you are no longer friends and that could hurt you or embarrass you. You are rejecting someone and that isn't something to do without good reason.

But if you have good reason to believe it is best to end your friendship, you now need strength to do the unconventional: Decide that you do not want to continue this particular friendship. Here are some affirmations to help you stay strong in your decision:

Affirmations to Reinforce Your Decision to End a Friendship

1. I have tried my best, but I cannot change this negative friendship.
2. I am ending this friendship because it is in my best interest, and I have to put myself first, before all others, including this friend.
3. I am a nice person, and I do not come to this decision lightly.
4. I will end this friendship in as kind and compassionate a way as I can, but I will stick to my decision to end it.
5. I am not a vindictive or cruel person. I am doing this because I think it is best for me.
6. I know my friend may not agree with my decision and may try to convince me to continue our friendship. But I have to do what my considered judgment tells me is preferred.
7. I will not gossip about my friend or about our failed friendship.
8. I will respect my friend's secrets and privacy after the friendship ends, just as I expect my friend to respect mine.
9. When the friendship is ended, I will avoid obsessing over my decision.
10. I will give myself time to grieve and mourn this failed friendship, just as I would grieve or mourn the ending of any intimate relationship that I once treasured and valued.
11. Ending one destructive friendship does not mean that I have a pattern of harmful friendships in my life.
12. I am entitled to have upbeat, positive, and trustworthy friendships.

13. I have learned a lot from this failed friendship and will use that knowledge to benefit the other friendships in my life even if I could not salvage this friendship.

Guidelines for Ending a Friendship

How you end a destructive friendship, especially a close or best one in which feelings are intense and intimate information has been exchanged, is very important since you do not want to enrage your former friend. In most instances, you will want this friendship to fade, rather than dramatically end; you will want to wind down your relationship rather than have a direct confrontation, to minimize the possibility of someone launching a vendetta against you. You may also want to avoid a dramatic ending because it will require you to invest so much emotion and energy in a relationship that you probably feel has already taken too much of your valuable resources. If "living well is the best revenge," then "the best revenge is having a positive friendship."

You may simply want to "be busy" when this friend asks to get together; after a while, she will get the hint.

If your friend does not "get the hint" and her attention seems pathological or extreme, consider getting help from appropriate sources, such as the police or other local authorities including crime victim advocates, especially if you feel you are being stalked. It will probably be helpful to those who will try to help you with the situation if you have a detailed written journal of dates, times, and incidents, documenting any phone calls or encounters that substantiate your feeling that you, or someone you love, is being stalked.

You've decided that ending this friendship is the only solution that will work right now or in the long run. But you've heard stories about ended friends sabotaging each other or you're afraid that that might happen to you.

What is the optimum way to dissolve a friendship to avoid the chance of imminent or long-term retaliation especially by a friend who may be in the position to adversely affect you and your reputation?

Here are seven guidelines for ending a friendship:

Keep your lips sealed about the ending. Gossiping about ending friendships—even if it feels good to "get it off your chest," and unless it is to a trusted spouse or romantic partner unrelated to the friendship situation, or a therapist or clergy member—may backfire. It is extremely difficult to control secrets, especially juicy ones. You want to handle the ending so discreetly that no one else knows you are doing it.

Avoid bad-mouthing your former friend. As before, you don't want your failed friendship to become grist for the gossip mill, nor do you want to get a reputation for telling tales out of school. Plus, your friend may then feel she has the "right" to start telling tales about you.

Try to wind down the friendship by "being busy" rather than having a confrontation. Defuse the situation by pulling away from your friend rather than doing something dramatic, like writing a letter, confronting her in a direct and public way, "having it out" over the phone or in person. For example, 52-year-old Teresa, who has 60 people reporting to her at work, had a very negative close friendship that she decided to end. "She and I worked for the same company, in different branch offices. I was leery about honestly expressing myself to her. She always asked my opinion about actions that her boss and fellow employees made. Her negative attitude was depressing, so I just stopped returning her calls."

Keep the emotions calm and in check. The calmer you are, the less you will be giving your former friend emotional fuel to fire up a possible vendetta.

If you do have to discuss your decision to end the friendship, make it clear you are not rejecting your friend but the way that you interact. This will allow your former friend to save "face," minimizing the rage that often is associated with rejection.

Be careful what you say or do that could come back to haunt you. Some friendships are relationships fraught with as much emotion and pathos as that of a romantic or familial one. Don't minimize how upset your former friend might be by the ending of your friendship either because you were "just friends" or even by citing the degree of intimacy of your friendship—say, casual, as opposed to close or best. Some casual friendships that have lasted for decades become a familiar, positive force in someone's life. Ending one, especially abruptly because of a dispute, could cause a great deal of stress. So "cool off" and "chill out" as you avoid saying or doing anything that could be held against you, particularly if you someday want to try to repair this damaged and ended friendship.

Remember that every friendship has two points of view that may be distinctly contradictory. You may not get the sympathy you want by sharing what happened in the friendship since others may wonder, "What really happened?" so be cautious about looking to others to validate what you did or did not do. Only you and your former friend know what really went on between you. You need to deal with the ending of this friendship in as dignified and private a way as possible.

Remember, to end destructive friendships in a way that minimizes the creation of rage and anger, which could bring on a vendetta, follow these suggestions:

- Minimize contact. Be "busy" if your friend tries to initiate contact, and hope that he or she finally gets the "hint."
- Avoid an abrupt ending by suggesting a "cooling off" period that may lead gently to a permanent ending.
- If you and your friend decide to have a dialogue about why you are ending your friendship, emphasize that you are not rejecting your friend but how the two of you relate. You could even put the onus on yourself, "It's not you, it's me," reducing the potential of despair related to the end of an intimate relationship.
- Replace the friendship with a positive one.

Coping After the Friendship Ends

If you are obsessing or having trouble getting over a failed friendship, even if your reasons for ending it were valid, and especially if you were not the one who ended it, refer back to the discussion of getting over addiction to a person, introduced in Chapter 3.

I am not using the term "obsessing" in a clinical way. These obsessions are not the same as someone who has an obsessive-compulsive disorder, as manifested by constant hand-washing, cleaning, checking, and ordering rituals. Obsessing in this context refers to dwelling on the failed or harmful friendship to the point that you are paralyzed. Just saying that you need to stop obsessing about this failed or negative friendship is probably not going to help you to do it. What may help is to rethink the friendship.

First, try to figure out what it is about this failed friendship that is causing you so much distress. I've found that the strongest trigger in these situations is a cut-off: The other friend just stops calling, and, unlike letting the friendship fade, the other friend's calls and requests for contact are turned down or ignored, or the other friend does something negative and then ends the friendship without further discussion or contact, or simply "disappears"—relocates, changes a phone number, or even changes a name without leaving any clues as to how she can be found again. The theme that runs throughout these situations is lack of closure.

You could try to find closure by seeking out your former friend and, if your friend will answer the phone or agree to meet with you, trying to sort through what happened. But in some instances, that is absolutely the wrong way to go about dealing with this situation, and it could actually put you in jeopardy—if your friend is homicidal, suicidal, a sociopath, a chronic liar, psychotic, or just so negative that any contact whatsoever could derail you from the positive path you are now on.

So if you decide that actually confronting your former friend is not the way to deal with your obsession, you now have to work on the only person you can truly control: yourself. It might help if you ask yourself the following questions:

1. Why am I obsessing about this failed friendship?
2. What is obsessing about this failed friendship stopping me from doing? Seeking out new friends? Forgiving myself for the end of the friendship? Taking responsibility for the part I played in the end of the friendship?
3. Can I channel my energy in a different way by trying to find a new positive friendship, or putting more time and energy into the valuable friendships or romantic relationships I do have?
4. Is there a program I can attend or professional help I can seek out if this obsession continues to get in the way of my enjoyment of my life?
5. Is this obsession the reflection of a valid concern for my physical safety? If it is, have I taken precautions to protect myself as much as possible from this perceived danger?
6. Have I ever had a similar situation before that I can look to, and learn from, to help me to know how to get over this obsession now?
7. Is there another friend or family member I can share my concerns with who might have another point of view that could help me deal with my obsession?
8. Have I tried writing down my thoughts about this former friend and our friendship as a way of working through my unresolved feelings about what happened?

Negative Friendships among Children and Teens

The tragic school violence in the last five years has forced parents, educators, government officials, and social-service organizations to place a greater emphasis on the friendships of elementary, middle, and high school youths. The bullying that has always plagued the school years can no longer be dismissed by saying, "Kids will be kids." Not when disgruntled youths, overcome with rage because of being bullied, as well as deep-seated emotional problems, pick up shotguns and rifles and injure or kill their classmates and teachers.

Students are learning that they cannot be silent about any knowledge they obtain about the threat of violent acts. Parents are also learning that they have to be more aware and involved in their children's friendship choices and behaviors. If violent or illegal behavior is suspected, a parent or educator has the duty to find out more information and take the necessary action if intervention can prevent tragedies.

Also, research has shown that kids with positive friendships do better at school, have lower absenteeism, and have higher self-esteem.

Dealing with Bullies, Violence, Drugs, Criminal Activity, Dysfunction, and Gangs

Bullying is certainly not a new phenomenon. For as long as there have been children or teens interacting, there has been bullying. But that was all before Columbine and the tragedy of two students, allegedly believing themselves to be bullied and not part of the clique at school, went on a shooting rampage, killing 12 classmates and a teacher before killing themselves. Columbine and other school shootings that have resulted in critical injuries or deaths have put a whole new spin on the issue of bullying.

Now bullying is seen as the reason behind many instances of school violence because it can produce a completely inappropriate, unacceptable overreaction from the alleged victim of the bullying.

Kate Cohen-Posey, a social worker and counselor and author of *How to Handle Bullies, Teasers, and Other Meanies,* has advice for parents and kids who need to deal with bullies. She suggests three main strategies for dealing with bullies:

1. Turning Insults into Compliments. Ignore the bully's words and pretend he has said something nice. If you can't think of anything else to say, you can always say, "Thank you."[1]

2. Asking Questions. Bullies and pests don't really think. They ask out of habit. Questions make people think.[2]
3. Agreeing. Bullies expect people to disagree with them. When someone agrees, they are surprised.[3]

Staying involved and aware of what is going on with your children and teens, without being so over-involved that you prohibit your children from developing their own secure sense of self, is a key step in reducing the tragedies that have occurred throughout the United States in recent years, as well as in other parts of the world. A 46-year-old married mother from India, with two adult children, recalls what she did during her children's formative years to address friendship issues, noting that children may themselves figure out if a new friend is a relationship that they should really pursue:

> It is a good idea for parents to be watchful of their children's friends without obvious meddling. If your normally well-adjusted child suddenly becomes closed and secretive, resentful, unreasonably rebellious, off his/her studies or commitments, and most important of all, does not want to bring his new friend/friends home, be on the alert. My husband and I have always kept an open house for the friends of our children and insisted that within a reasonable span of time, they introduce their new friends to us. If they are still reluctant to do so, we have asked them to reason out for themselves why. It generally works.

Even if you find yourself displeased with the friends your child or teen is bringing home, you will probably want to stay out of your child's choices unless you suspect the presence of weapons, drugs, illegal behavior, or violence. You could, of course, still use these friendship choices as information that lets you assess how your child or teen sees himself or herself. Those insights could help you to work with your child or teen to help him change his self-image and behavior; his friendship choices will probably shift as his self-image changes.

Forty-four-year-old Lidia reflects back on why, for a year, she hung out with a friend who was a very bad influence:

> We became friends during a rebellious time. She introduced me to drugs. It only lasted about a year. My mom didn't like her and forbade me to see

her. I would see her anyway, but then we grew apart after a while. She was depressed, would sleep with lots of different guys, and steal money from her parents. *I could be rebellious through her* [emphasis added].

If your child or teen's friends are involved in dangerous or criminal behavior, a decided proactive role may also be required. As a first step, try to get your child or teen to see the possible consequences to him or her of spending time with these friends. Share predictable scenarios, using newspaper or magazine clippings, television or feature film documentation, to concretize the very real risks to their safety, welfare, health, and even their life. That includes any youths who drink and drive, putting themselves, their passengers, pedestrians, and other drivers at risk as well.

If your child or teen is unable or unwilling to cut off the negative friendship on his or her own, it is your responsibility to stay involved and firm in your conviction that this crowd could do your child or teen (and others) real harm. Impose restrictions on your child or teen, if necessary; whenever possible, facilitate your child or teen making different or new friendship choices that will lead to more positive relationships.

In fact, being liked and being part of a group are so pivotal to so many children and teens that you want to avoid taking away your child or teen's negative friends until positive friendship replacements are already in place. The situation is much the same as when marriages become strained—one or both spouses may start to invest heavily in alternative relationships, minimizing the overwhelming loss they feel when a marital tie comes apart. In the same way, when a child or teen needs to divorce from a peer group that is not in his or her best interest, other ties will smooth the transition period from group A to group B (even if eventually your child or teen ends up in group C or D).

The experiences of the last few years with school violence in middle-class suburban communities has emphasized that all children, their parents, and educators have to be concerned with deviance and violence—not just in inner-city neighborhoods, where gang violence had been perceived as more likely and prevalent.

Gang membership has a common denominator: disgruntled youth. This is true whether a gang draws its membership from the ghetto, where members may deal drugs, mug people, and use weapons; or from middle- or upper-class communities, where the gang may have only two members, as happened at Columbine. The disgruntled youths see themselves as outcasts, unable to achieve status and notoriety by being part of the mainstream. They create what sociologist Albert K. Cohen and others have called a "delinquent subculture." In the classic *Delinquent Boys,* Cohen cautions that it is the group (or gang) and the nature of the group itself that could account for the dramatic (and negative) changes that can occur once a youth becomes part of that gang:

> Countless mothers have protested that their "Johnny" was a good boy until he fell in with a certain bunch. But the mothers of each of Johnny's companions hold the same view with respect to their own offspring. It is conceivable and even probable that some of these mothers are naïve, that one or more of these youngsters are "rotten apples" who infected the others. We suggest, however, that all of the mothers may be right, that there is a certain chemistry in the group situation itself which engenders that which was not there before, that group interaction is a sort of catalyst which releases potentialities not otherwise visible.[4]

There has always been a debate over whether the clothes make the man or the man makes the clothes; similarly, you could ask whether the gang makes the youth or the youth makes the gang. But as Cohen points out, the nature of the gang is so powerful as an entity all its own that you cannot separate the gang from the youth.

If your child has become part of a gang that is deviant, especially if the gang is involved in illegal activity and there are weapons present, direct and swift intervention may be necessary and recommended. If you need help on how to do this, you might contact a trusted local authority on juvenile delinquency or juvenile issues. This may not be the time to wait until your child "finds" himself and decides, on his own, to get out of the gang.

Here, in summary, are warning signs that your child or teen may be in a destructive or negative friendship; the severity of the behavior, or situation, will help you decide whether your intervention is necessary or your child or teen can work it through on his own:

- You find yourself trying to explain away or justify too many actions that your child's friend is engaged in that just "don't feel right" because those actions are cruel, illegal, bizarre, or just plain offensive.

- Your child's friend is a pathological liar.
- Your child's friend is a thief.
- Your child's friend engages in violent behavior.
- On more than one occasion, someone else has said to you, "I need to talk to you about your child's friend."
- Your child's friend uses illegal drugs.
- Your child's friend is a known gang member.
- Your child's friend seems to be "taking over" your child's life, far too quickly and too completely, spending an inordinate amount of time at each other's apartments or homes, "hanging out" all the time.
- The quality of your child's schoolwork has dramatically worsened since this friendship began.
- Your child's friend is disrespectful toward you to a degree that is intolerable, including using foul language or making inappropriate comments.
- When your child is invited to a party, he is told, "Please don't bring your friend so-and-so along."
- Your child's friend has bragged about violent or illegal acts that he is planning to commit.

Unless the situation is serious enough that your child's safety, life, liberty, or health, or that of the school or community is at risk, you may want to let your child work through a friendship choice that fosters your disapproval. First of all, if it's just a question of you or your spouse, or even your other children, not liking a friend because of a completely subjective reason, it is unfair to impose that opinion on your child or teen. Friendship enables your child or teen to explore a far wider range of personalities and sensibilities than in her family of origin. Furthermore, by imposing your friendship choices on your child without a good enough reason, you are preventing your offspring from acquiring the first-hand experience of working through a relationship from its beginning and, if she decides to end it, to its ending, including how she handles the ending and how it makes her feel. Of course, you certainly have a right to point out anything about your child's friend that annoys you, but without going the next step: demanding that your child cut off the friendship. You will, however, want to try to express yourself with an "I" statement, qualifying your observation, if you wish to share it, as just your opinion and not a judgment. The hope is that by verbalizing and denoting a specific behavior or characteristic, your child or teen will now become aware of it herself and make any adjustments about the friend or friendship on her own. For example, if it annoys you that your teen's friend spends hours at your home, eating with your family, but has never said "thank you," you might say to your teen, "I hope when you are a guest at your friend's house, you always thank his parents for whatever food they give you." That way you are not directly criticizing your child's friend but instead are reinforcing the behavior you expect your child to exhibit, letting your child draw his own conclusions about his friend's conduct. It is even possible, when you are not around and it could be done with tact and subtlety, that your teen will actually say something to his friend so he could correct his behavior and regain your approval, which children do seek.

If you feel your child or teen is consistently choosing friends who are not at his level and who seem to be a bad influence, without it being so pathological that intervention is recommended, use this as information about where your child or teen is at and what this friend says about him. If you find ways to help your child improve his self-image, whether on his own or through outside counseling, that, combined with exposure to new friendship possibilities, may help your child to eventually choose friends who are also more to your liking.

But if drastic measures are essential because your child or teen has befriended someone who puts him in immediate danger, you may have to take a more active role in resolving the situation. Although an extreme solution, if it is necessary you may have to remove your child from a violent or criminal gang, or a negative friendship that is causing social, legal, or academic problems, by sending him to a different school. You may even have to consider moving to another community where he could have a fresh start. It may be the only way to get your kid away from a "bad" crowd. One mother even moved her 14-year-old son to another country after he became involved with a middle-class gang that was arrested for beating up several other youths, many of whom had to be hospitalized for their injuries. While some of the gang spent time in a juvenile detention center, and everyone involved had to work hard to remove the stigma of being arrested from their community and school profile, he finished his high school education at a private school in Europe, graduating and going on to college without incident.

Part 4

Business, Work, and Friends

Chapter 7

Friendship at Work: Are the Rules Different?

Betrayals in personal friendships can be painful and emotionally debilitating, and they can even destroy an intimate relationship or break up a family. Work-related friendships come with such a particular set of ups and downs that they've evolved into their own category, especially as we spend more and more time at work. Betrayals in work-related friendships also have particular consequences: They can damage a reputation, derail a rise up the ladder, get someone fired, even obliterate a career.

When Friendship Works in the Workplace

If work-related friendships that go sour are so horrific, why not just avoid them altogether?

Because that is a poor alternative. It's no surprise that a positive, healthy friendship at work and in business not only makes the day more pleasant but actually increases productivity. And it is definitely a contributing factor in career advancement and success.

Supervisors approve because having friends at work also means lower employee turnover; you are more likely to stay at a job if you like the people you work with and they like you. The three factors that are key considerations about work friendships are: Are the friends at the same level? What is the level of intimacy? Can you trust your friend?

Workplace or business friends who are at the same level are more likely to have fewer conflicts and problems than friendships between boss and employee or when friends are at an unequal status, even if they do not work in the same department. Furthermore, although a tried-and-true, well-managed close or best friendship can be an asset in work or in business, it needs to be a friendship that was tested out before the two people worked together, or it needs to evolve slowly and cautiously so that the friendship is strong and safe. Aware that a workplace friendship between those unequal in status can strain the friendship, Beverly, a 40-year-old executive at an information management corporation, wondered whether asking her friend to work for her was a good idea. "When I moved to another division, there was an opportunity for my friend, who had been my peer in another division, to work for me. We discussed the pros and cons and said that we're basically putting our friendship on the line. If things don't work out in the workplace, we could risk our friendship. But we felt it was okay to go ahead, and it worked out fine. I actually left the company [and started my own company], but my friend is still there."

As a 35-year-old screenwriter says:

> I helped someone get in a door, and I went out of my way to work with someone and it just didn't work out, and we had to work very hard to separate the work experiences from the friendship. Ideally the friendship should triumph, but I can't say that always is the case. But we're not an industry where you could rely on some clear little moral like "don't work with friends" because that's what we do. It's a risk that you take constantly.

If you have a track record with your friend, and reason to trust her, your friendship will have a better chance of enduring the additional work challenges, as well as benefiting from the rewards. As 29-year-old Barbara, a researcher for a health-care facility, notes:

> When you're spending eight hours a day somewhere, it's real easy to develop a real close friendship. I think it's a good thing. We're spending so much time at work as a society we do consider our work another family. It's important that we feel good about the relationships at work. To the extent that friendships help establish trust or, on the downside, when lost friendships destroy trust, friendships can greatly enhance or hurt the work relationship.

But if you have a friend at work who betrays you, it may be a lesson that forever turns you away from work-related intimate friendships. That's what happened with a 27-year-old administrative assistant:

When I was going through my divorce, I worked in a very small office. I had a friend I worked with who called me every night after work. She stated how concerned she was and I told her many personal things. She went to my boss a few months later and told her my personal life was affecting my work. My boss told me later about it. My boss stated she did not feel that way, nor did my co-workers.

I vowed I would never get close to a co-worker again. I now work somewhere else, and they know very little about my life outside of work.

Therefore, in general, it is casual friendship—not close or best—that is the safest and preferred relationship at work and in business. Although there are certainly numerous exceptions—such as when a close or best friendship has been successfully tested and is so long-standing, strong, and low-maintenance that it could endure the additional challenges of working together—it is still true that the information shared between close or best friends is so intimate that in some instances it may create conflicts of interest among employees. For instance, if you and your close or best friend are co-workers and one of you is promoted over the other, how will you handle having to now report to your friend?

Still, in the best of situations, workplace friends aren't just a team; they are a kind of family, especially if they are equals, working together on the same task in the same space, whether the company is small, medium, or giant.

Although I am now a self-employed entrepreneur, conducting seminars or interviews, working with freelancers or teaching, I can't help being nostalgic for my very first job after graduate school. At Macmillan Publishing Company, where I began as an editorial assistant, we had such a workplace family for about a year. Not only did we work day after day on the same projects, but we often went out to lunch together; our boss, who was also a friend, invited us to her home for after-work get-togethers. While I worked there, I felt a bond of friendship with several co-workers and my two bosses that enriched my workday. The workplace environment closely replicated the daily camaraderie of the school years, especially from kindergarten through high school, when you see the same classmates, some of whom become friends, and share with them homeroom, classes, and participation in extracurricular activities. Decades later, I am still friends with Gail, a co-worker whom I met at that time.

Writer and teacher Karen Lindsey shares the value of her workplace friendships with Ed, Dale, and Jane, whom she befriended when she got a job as a part-time proofreader at *Newsweek* magazine. In her book, *Friends as Family,* which was way ahead of its time with its pro-friendship message when it was published in 1981, Lindsey writes:

> Though we rarely discussed one another's personal problems, we were acutely aware of them. . . .
>
> Sometimes, of course, we got on each other's nerves; sometimes we hurt each other's feelings. These times, too, we never talked about. But for the most part, we simply hung out together, chatted, and enjoyed each other's company with an easy and casual acceptance.
>
> When I left New York and moved to Boston ten years ago, the hardest part was leaving Newsweek. . . .
>
> Ed, Jane, Dale, and I were a fine example of the workplace family. We spent long hours together every day for a period of years. We spent more time with each other than any of us—even Dale with his wife and son—spent with anyone else.[1]

Lillian Vernon, founder and CEO of Lillian Vernon Corporation, a mail-order and on-line retailer based in Rye, New York, believes that it is good to have strong workplace relationships that are familiar but not best friends. She notes:

> I believe it is possible to be close to the people you work with but not best friends. My business requires that I travel several weeks a year throughout the world in search of new products for my catalogs. During these trips, my chief merchant and two other merchants accompany me. We grow close on these trips because we spend so much time together. We normally work seven days a week and eat all our meals together, so naturally our conversations become more personal. When we travel, we rely on each other because we're away from our family and friends. However, once back in the office, I make it a practice rarely to discuss personal matters with my staff, and our meetings together are always very businesslike. I also don't socialize with my staff out of the office unless we're attending a business engagement together. This has made our working relationships more objective and professional.

For close or best friends it can be especially tricky to keep personal details separate from professional situations. For example, your boss is considering you for a new project. You're ready, willing, and able to take it on. But you shared with your dear friend at work just the other day how exhausted you are trying to juggle all the projects you already have on your plate with your spouse and parental responsibilities. When your boss mentions she is planning to give you this new project, your friend, without even thinking, blurts out how overwhelmed you already feel. Your friend quickly apologizes for that comment, instantly realizing he had no right to share with your boss what was said "between friends." The boss, of course, says that she forgot anything was said, but the damage was done. What was said cannot be unsaid; perceptions are reality. The new project, which could have advanced your career, and even brought in a big bonus, is given to someone else. You probably never even find out why unless your guilty friend decides to get it off his chest.

That scenario is based on many situations I have heard about or observed over the years. In fact, it is actually a pretty mild version. Another typical scenario involves someone playing up to a new employee, trying quickly to become a friend. The object is to gain a competitive edge over the fresh hire by finding out what he knows, as well as what he doesn't.

Still, friendship at work is sometimes recommended, even friendships between managers and employees, as William D. Marelich does in his article "Can We Be Friends?" published in *HR Focus.* Marelich sites numerous benefits of manager and employee friendships, including, "Managers and employees who are friends enjoy working together. The friendships lead to positive work environments, with less anxiety and stress. A positive work environment leads to increased productivity."[2]

For all types of workplace friends who start off at the same place on the corporate ladder, one of the most difficult and challenging work situations that will "test" their friendship is if one is promoted. In highly competitive businesses or workplace environments, where employees may be competing for the same customers or clients (as in real estate) or where just one can make it to the next level (as in the granting of tenure in a college department), it may be very hard to balance the pulls of workplace competition and the developing friendship.

CEO Lillian Vernon points out that it is because of the potential pitfalls for best friends working together, as well as the importance of safeguarding close friendship, that she is strongly against best friends working together. Vernon explains:

> My company doesn't encourage best friends working together and nei-
> ther do I. I'm aware of best friends who start businesses together, only to
> see the friendship fail when problems occur and they can't agree. Often,
> when something goes wrong between two friends who work together, they
> blame each other and their productivity declines because they are filled
> with resentment and anger. The situation can become very destructive for
> the business. In life, it is much more difficult to find a close personal friend
> than a good employee.

The results of my friendship survey of 180 men and women bear out Vernon's pronouncement: Of the 139 who answered the question about workplace friendships, so few had a best friend at work that the average number of workplace best friends was 0 (only 24 out of 139 had 1 or more best friends at work, school, or in business, for an average of less than 1 for the sample, or 0.25). The average number of workplace close friends was only 1; on average, there were also 6 casual friends. (This compares to the higher averages in the sample of 180 men and women for close, best, and casual friends outside of work, as noted in Chapter 1: 26 casual, 6 close, and 2 best friends.)

To avoid conflict of interest, the appearance of trading favors, or the consequences of revealing personal information, highly placed executives that I have interviewed expressed the necessity of forming friendships outside their industry or, in one market research consultant's case, across the river in another city and state. Some have even confided that they do not have close friends at work; another explained that he and his boss were best friends, but they had to carefully manage their friendship, which pre-dated their working relationship.

But you don't have to be a highly placed executive to want to keep work and friendship separate. As a 47-year-old married computer consultant with two schoolage children, who works at a company with several hundred employees, explains: "I don't interact with many at my workplace, and I am the only one in my particular position. At times, I feel a bit isolated in a place with many employees. At other times, this makes keeping work and home separate easier."

Rosalie, the 34-year-old married Massachusetts-based public relations manager with three-way friendships mentioned in Chapter 1, explains why she has revised her views on friendship at work. When Rosalie notes that she now recommends "work friendships" instead of "friendships" she is referring specifically to a change in the level of intimacy (and confidentiality) that is shared:

> Right now I am working in an office with 110 people, but I am also working toward having my own public relations firm. I used to have a team of 11 people reporting to me . . . but I've stepped down in order to have time to pursue my own business. I have been very close with people that I work with, and this has been very difficult at times. I will not do this in the future, but rather will keep my friendships at work as work friendships because it just becomes too difficult and there are too many conflicts of interests.

Rosalie goes on to share how one of her close friends, who was a former boss, betrayed her:

> In a business dealing . . . one of my very close friends (who happened to be my ex-boss) left my company to go work for a competitor. She was ruthless in trying to take an account with her, looking to "stick it" to the company she was leaving. What she didn't realize was that in the course of doing it, she was also "sticking it" to me . . . her friend.

It is in work-related friendship that the gender differences that have long been documented in friendship are most dramatic. Boys and men tend to have friendships that are based on doing things together with a minimum of sharing confidential information and emotional support, while girls and women tend to have friendships that are based on conversation, emotional support, and confessions. The male president of a small company completed my questionnaire about workplace friendships; to the question about how many friends he had at work, he answered "100." To the question about how many employees there were at the company, he answered "100." Certainly those friends were casual friends, but it is by considering all 100 employees to be friends that he probably gained the positive work environment and boss-employee relations to have a company with higher worker satisfaction than if he answered "2" or "0" to the number of friends he had at work.

By contrast, a female human resource manager at a construction company of 4,500 noted that she did not have any friends at her current job. "There is a very low trust level in this organization because most people are motivated by fear," she added.

Women, especially as they get higher up the ladder, are finding out that it can be "lonely at the top." They are discovering that befriending another woman at their level at another company or in another industry or someone with a completely different job at a less prestigious level is better than being isolated and lonely. Fifty-eight-year-old Annie, after she retired from her high-powered corporate job and relocated back to her Midwestern hometown to start her own company, befriended Margaret, who worked at the manicure salon Annie frequented. "Margaret started doing my nails, and we quickly became fast friends."

Francine, who has 60 men and women reporting to her at the training company that she runs, would like to find out "how to have friends on the job when you are the boss." For now, Francine is pursuing friendships outside of her company. That decision follows her ending a close friendship at her current job with someone who "did not support me when I needed her moral support. She acted as if she did not know about my situation." But friendship is a priority for Francine, even though it is hard to find time for friends because of her job as well as taking care of her home, her spouse, and her 10-year-old daughter. "I barely have enough time for my family, job, and church," Francine explains. Her closest friend is someone she met at work although they are no longer co-workers. "We talk once or twice a week by phone," Francine explains.

I also discovered that for many, working together is where a casual friendship forms, planting the seeds for a close or best friendship that blossoms after the friends no longer work together. Gloria met her friend Suzie when Suzie interviewed for Gloria's job (Gloria had been promoted). Although they bonded instantly, Suzie left the company after two years, at which point their relationship flourished into a friendship that has lasted more than two decades. Initially working together helped the friendship by providing Gloria a close look at her friend; it was having that positive snapshot of Suzie that formed the basis of the friendship that has persisted to this day. As Gloria notes:

I also enjoyed the way she [Suzie] could and would interact with people and her ability to make them feel important and loved—it again made a difference in my life. These are the things she provided me with. It was a joy to be around her and feel so accepted.

Lies, Deceit, and Revenge: Misusing Friendship at Work and in Business

Of course the horror stories also abound. Here is a representative sample:

- "[A friend who was] on a hiring review committee told the others that I was 'still too wounded' from my divorce to handle the position I was applying for." (48-year-old divorced unemployed artist)
- "Basically [he] kept up our friendship to use my expertise in investment strategy." (51-year-old male financial adviser)
- "Told the boss my secret." (50-year-old female occupational therapist)
- "Fired me." (43-year-old single female entrepreneur)
- "Lied to get me fired." (24-year-old single female teaching assistant)
- "Sometimes knows too much about situations, and that causes problems." (36-year-old male director of personnel at a health-care corporation)
- "Told my personal business." (45-year-old divorced female sales representative)
- "Tried to take a customer from me." (20-year-old self-employed female)

Each of these examples has to be handled according to the personalities involved. Do the friends wish to preserve the friendship? Do they want to continue working together? Have they gone past the "point of no return" so that the friendship, or working together, is no longer an option?

Fifty-year-old Roger reflects back on the betrayal at work by his friend, who was also his boss, and how it changed their relationship. There was a power struggle at work between two departments, and Roger's boss allowed the other department to decide what job Roger should be allowed to perform:

He gave me up, basically. He asked me to stop doing what I was doing, so I felt betrayed by him. I called him a coward. I was really disappointed.

He felt so bad that he cried. [But] he felt there was nothing he could do about it.

I thought there was. He could have fought for me. He could have stood up for me. Instead of supporting my side of the situation or my integrity, though, he just buckled under.

This scenario was definitely not a positive step for Roger's career, since they continued to work together and his ex-friend continued to be his boss:

I hated him. I didn't want anything to do with him, which wasn't a good thing because he had to evaluate me. I've never been very trusting so [what happened] might have reinforced earlier feelings of untrustworthiness, [about] never letting myself get too close to somebody because of being burned, that kind of thing.

Roger feels that his former friend betrayed him because "He was afraid. He was saving his own ass." Whatever the reason for the betrayal, within a few months the negative situation proved too much for Roger, who not only quit his job but decided to switch careers as well.

Rules for Work and Business Friendships

Here are ten simple tips for conducting friendships at work.

- *Avoid creating, or becoming part of, a friendship clique at work.* Cliques are counterproductive at work. By creating a feeling of favoritism, they create morale problems outside the clique. Excessive socializing may occur with workplace cliques; there may be the real or perceived idea that clique members get preferential treatment. New hires may feel particularly isolated and left out, making their acclimation more difficult and longer than it needs to be. If managers and subordinates are in the same clique, it could make it hard to supervise; objectivity and productivity could suffer.
- *Be cautious about friendships at work.* Camaraderie or a casual friendship is fine, and an enhancement to productivity; close or best friendships, unless carefully managed, can interfere with the work-

place, especially if confidential information, such as what salaries or bonuses someone is receiving, are shared and become the source of jealousy and envy. Keep such intimate relationships separate from your work as much as possible, but if you take your time to make sure you and your close or best friend are tried and true, and you have enough information or evidence that you can handle any work-related issues that arise, a close or best work friendship could be blissful.[3]

- *Be discreet about your friend's confidences.* Whether the workplace or business friendship is a casual, close, or best friendship, keep your friend's confidences to yourself.

- *Shun gossip.* Gossip is especially harmful if you overhear or are tempted to share information about a co-worker, subordinate, boss, client, customer, or supplier that you received because of your friendship. That includes any personal information as well as any "hush-hush" career plans, new product releases not yet shared with the public, etc.

- *Never misuse a work or business friendship for opportunistic reasons.* There is a fine line between asking a favor of a friend that is appropriate and acceptable and crossing the line into opportunism. Some guidelines: Is the request a reasonable one to be asking of your friend? How would you feel if the positions were reversed and a friend asked the same of you? Is the favor within the expertise and knowledge of your friend, so he or she would not feel compromised by complying with your request? When in doubt, put the friendship before the request, or you could damage your relationship.

- *Avoid bragging or name-dropping about your friendships.* Instead of looking well connected and popular, you will probably look like you're trying to parlay your friendships to your own advantage. The friendship should be its own reward, not what mileage you might get out of the association. (This is different from putting your friend forward in an appropriate way, like recommending that the friend attend or chair an activity you're organizing.)

- *Use your instinct and your judgment to withdraw yourself from (or avoid) any situations that might put you or your friend in a potential conflict of interest.* For example, if your friend's company prohibits accepting gifts from clients, and you are a client as well as a friend, don't send your friend's birthday present to her office; you might both agree that exchanging cards is better. If your friend has a job opening but hiring a friend is frowned upon, do not press your friend to get you an interview.

- *Watch your body language, gestures, and nonverbal cues.* At the office, or if you attend a trade show and you run into a very close or best friend, remember how your behavior will be viewed by those surrounding you. Do you really want to be hugging, kissing, and jumping up and down from the sheer joy of reconnecting with your friend if you're in a workplace or business setting? Avoid language or even a tone of voice that is too familiar when talking to a friend.

- *If your opposite-sex friendship becomes a romance, a whole new set of concerns needs to be addressed.* Don't kid yourself, your co-workers, employees, or boss that "nothing's changed" now that a workplace friendship has turned into a romance. There are guidelines to consider once a workplace friendship becomes a romance, to minimize the possibility of jealousy or resentment at the office, or even allegations of sexual harassment or inappropriate conduct. Keep in mind that your friendship-turned-romance might not last; just as working with, or for, a former friend may prove uncomfortable or intolerable, working for or with a former romantic partner (who used to be a friend) may be even more challenging.[4]

- *If your workplace opposite-sex friendship is truly just a friendship, watch your behavior so you do not unwittingly give credence to any rumors.* Opposite-sex friendships are more prevalent than ever before, especially in the workplace. Just be aware that you will probably have to be more cautious about what you say and do with an opposite-sex friend than with a same-sex one, if you are to avoid any rumors that your friendship is more than just platonic.

Dealing with Friendship-related Workplace Conflicts

The conflict-resolution techniques described in Chapter 5, "Can This Friendship Be Saved?" in the section "Handling Conflicts with Friends" all apply here. In summary, here are the basic options available to you and your workplace or business friend with whom you are having a conflict:

- You could change.
- Your friend could change.
- You could both change.

- You could try to step outside of the conflict and view it as if you are an objective observer.
- You could work out the conflict through discussion.
- You could allow for a cooling-off period.
- You could call in a third party to help mediate your friendship dispute (a professional mediator, arbitrator, human resource department professional).
- You could decide to stop having contact with your friend by ending the friendship, getting transferred to another department, or leaving the company.

If you are having conflicts with a workplace friend, the first thing you need to figure out is if the problems are arising from the friendship or from the work. If you and this person were not friends, would you handle the situation differently? If the answer is "yes," consider what you would do. Just figuring out the answer to that question may help you immediately resolve the problem by focusing on the work or business issues.

If the conflict is caused by friendship, you may need to handle this situation differently from one involving a personal friend. Let's say you and your friend know how to "push each other's buttons," get on each other's nerves, competing with each other in everything and anything. That may be fine outside of your shared business situation. But if the way you interact with each other as friends is a problem at work, you can train yourself to separate how you respond to your friend in work versus non-work situations. You need not always automatically respond to your friend the same old way.

For example, you and your friend may have a history outside of work or business; for instance, your friend always has trouble making a decision about what movie to see or what restaurant to go to. At work or in business, that hesitancy can have drastic consequences. So if you find your friend equally slow to make business decisions, don't let him get away with it. Ask him directly for his opinion. Explain that you need his feedback as you try to bolster his confidence and offset his tendency to waffle or procrastinate.

If you find that your friend, who you know in her personal life often never gets around to washing the dishes or sending out holiday greeting cards, is missing deadlines at work as well, talk about it. You know from your friendship that this is a pattern that your friend has in her entire life, and maybe you could help your friend with it by discreetly pointing out the similarities. "Say, let's talk about deadlines and priorities," you might say, adding, "Let's see if we could delegate some of these tasks so you can focus on what's really important."

What are the policies at your company for friends at work? Some companies discourage it; others encourage it so much that they even offer a financial reward to those employees who are instrumental in getting their friends to join the firm.

Part 5

Breaking the Pattern

Chapter 8

Finding Good Friends

Now that you know how to deal with bad friendships, you're probably wondering how to avoid them in the first place. How do you know if someone you meet will turn into a positive or a negative friend? There are no clear answers. Befriending someone new, whether it is in business or in your personal life, always involves risks. There are no guarantees except that, if you do not take chances and develop new friendships, your life will narrow. You may become lonely if all of your friends move away, are too busy to get together, or, as you age, they pass away.

In my first book, *Friendshifts®*, I developed a quiz that I called the Friendship Compatibility Quiz. Those 15 questions were a convenient way to do some reflecting about yourself as well as about a new acquaintance, to consider if you even want to cultivate a friendship with this man or woman.[1] Here, I have modified and expanded it. This new Friendship Attunement Quiz includes five additional questions that might help you to detect if this potential friend might betray you, or if your association could turn into a destructive or harmful friendship. Once again, there are no guarantees or sure predictors. These questions are simply designed to help you think about some issues and concerns that could be red flags. Circumstances and personalities can change for a host of reasons, ranging from career or financial setbacks or advancements to personal relationship upheavals, relocations, and so forth. You may want to take this quiz again from time to time to see if your answers have changed.

Friendship Attunement Quiz

1. Does your acquaintance always tell the truth?
2. Does your acquaintance treat co-workers, subordinates, or superiors (if a work-based acquaintanceship) or family members or romantic partners (if it is an acquaintance that started outside of work) in a respectful, reliable, and polite way?
3. If this acquaintance reminds you of someone from your present or past, is it someone you liked, admired, and respected?

4. Are you impressed by the loyalty and quality of the other friends of this new acquaintance?
5. Do you find yourself looking forward to seeing your acquaintance again, or to receiving the next e-mail, or the next phone call?
6. Have you have gotten verbal or nonverbal signs from your acquaintance that she wants to become your friend?
7. Do you have the time and the energy to add this friend to the friendships you already have?
8. Are you taking enough time to get to know this acquaintance?
9. Do you and your acquaintance have fun together?
10. Do you and this potential friend have any similar interests?
11. Do you feel comfortable when you and this acquaintance talk on the phone?
12. Are you aware of any value disparities between you and your acquaintance but believe those value differences will not pose a problem?
13. If your religion, ethnic group, racial background, or age is not the same, is this acceptable to both of you?
14. If your socioeconomic class is different, is the contrast unimportant to both of you?
15. Are you in agreement about how often you want to call or see each other?
16. Do you reside or work near each other, or, if you live far away, will you get around any obstacles physical distance might present to a friendship evolving?
17. Whenever possible, will you return phone calls from your friend within 24 hours?
18. Would you keep a prior date with your acquaintance even if your romantic partner, date, or spouse suddenly asked you for the same time, or at least reschedule your appointment with your new friend?
19. Do you have the gut feeling of liking this person?
20. Do you think your acquaintance would answer "yes" to questions 18 and 19?

If you answered "yes" to all of the above questions, the character of your new acquaintance seems to be excellent and positive; you seem committed to this acquaintance and compatible with her; there is a good likelihood she could become your friend and a trustworthy one.

If you answered "no" to just a few questions, think about what those "no" answers reveal. Are these situations, feelings, or value conflicts you could overlook or work through within yourself or with your acquaintance, or are these obstacles that may prove insurmountable? Now that you have considered your answers to these questions, you have to consider what your acquaintance might answer to these questions as well.

Reconnecting with Old Friends

Today more than ever before, because of the Internet, there are numerous ways to try to relocate a former friend. (See the list of web sites for tracking down lost friends listed in the Resource section of this book.) But should you? Here are questions to ask yourself to help you decide if a friendship is one you should try to rekindle.

Quiz: Do I Want to Reconnect?

Answer always, often, sometimes, or never to the questions that follow.

1. My friend and I had fun together.
2. My friend brought out the best in me.
3. I find that I miss my friend.
4. I find myself wondering what my friend is up to.
5. I've tried to find this friend before but didn't know where or how to start looking.

If you answered "always" or "often" to four or all the above questions, you seem ready and interested in finding this old friend. If you answered "always" or "often" as well as "sometimes" to at least three of the above questions, you may still benefit from tracking down this particular old friend, but you may also want to reevaluate your past together first. You might also want to ask yourself if you want to find a specific friend or if you are just reaching backward because all your friends are out of town this weekend or you just moved to a new town and are afraid of meeting new people. (Be clear about your motives for reconnecting; if you misuse your old friend because of a temporary lull in your life and your friendship was never all that great anyway, you might push your friend aside again once things are back on track for you.)

But if you answered "never" to two or more of the above questions, this specific friend is probably not a good candidate for reconnecting right now.

That does not mean you could not reconsider this friend at another time if you or your friend have changed or if circumstances have changed for you or your friend.

What I Learned at My High School Reunion

What I learned by attending my thirty-fourth high school reunion relates directly to the possibility of reconnecting with old friends. After months of anticipation, I returned to my mother's house in the borough of Queens in New York City, not far from the hotel where the reunion was to be held.

As I looked at myself in my mother's mirror, the same mirror I had peered into as I stared at myself in my high school prom dress, I wondered who would be at the reunion. I was eager to reconnect with so many of the friends I had lost contact with, the boys and girls who had mattered to me and been such a big part of my life.

I arrived at the airport hotel ballroom excited to be reconnecting with my classmates. It seemed like maybe 10 or 20 years had gone by at the most, not 34.

My older sister had traveled from Washington, D.C., to attend this reunion with me since we had gone through high school in the same grade. Her husband was away on a business trip, but my husband was in attendance, too.

For almost half an hour after I arrived, I read name tags and tried to connect them with faces but did not recognize one. No familiar faces from the class of '65 greeted me at the door. Instead an employee of the reunion company officially greeted me, someone whose job it was to move the evening along as efficiently as possible.

I realized it was going to be hard to find anyone that I knew. Not only because our graduating class had more than 1,500 (the school had around 4,700 students and was on triple session) but also because they had included three graduating classes in the reunion: '63, '64, and '65. As my husband later pointed out, if you add in the spouses or guests also in attendance, you had only a one in six chance that someone was actually in my class.

Finally I recognized a name. It was someone that had been in an after-school activity with me. I shouted out her name.

She seemed to recognize me instantly. We jumped up and down gleefully.

I reminisced with her about her outstanding talents.

"You have a good memory," she said.

She told me about what she was doing now, about her husband, the ages of her children, and then she brought out the pictures.

I made "ooh" and "ah" sounds as I looked at the pictures of her children and husband.

Then I pulled out my wallet and showed her the only picture I carry around of my two sons, taken of them six years ago, before I went back to being so involved in my career, in the days when I was more focused on putting pictures in family albums instead of getting articles and books published again.

She then started talking to my sister, who was standing next to me.

Their conversation was short and to the point.

And then my friend with whom I had spent so many days after school for two years of my life those 34 years ago, said to my sister, "And where's your sister? Is she here?"

My heart sank! She had been talking to me all that time and did not know who I was.

Later I went over to someone else that I thought I recognized.

When I said my name she replied, "You're the writer."

Someone else read my name tag and said, "I remember you. You ran for office."

I spotted someone who had been in "the clique." I said hello. She said hello back, but our eyes did not meet. She was looking over my head to the sea of faces around me.

She and I had not connected 34 years ago, and it was clear we were not going to connect tonight, either.

Then I remembered why those high school years had been so hard on me and why I think they are for so many of us. Yes, I had been in chorus, a cheerleader, a leader, in the future teachers club, and feature editor of the high school newspaper. Yes, I had good grades and a really close friend who was in the class after mine. But by and large, I felt like to everyone else I was a symbol rather than a person. "A writer." "Someone who ran for office." "A cheerleader." "A leader." "An alto in the chorus."

And that was why this reunion did not work for me—although others report more positive reunion experiences.

As we left the parking lot I thought out loud: "Am I glad I'm not in high school anymore."

And then I took out my traveling, all-purpose "Personal Journal" and wrote:

"There can be no present when all you have in common is your past."

But the $62 I had paid the reunion company was actually money well spent. Why did I care if those I met recognized me as an older version of the girl who had an outrageous hairdo in her high school yearbook photo, a severe bun pulled high on my head, a hairdo that I was not about to recreate for this reunion? Whatever I looked like on the inside is what really mattered, something so few know during those vulnerable high school years, and, from the reunion, I'd say too few had come to understand it.

I also thought about those high school friends who were not at the reunion; why was I waiting for someone else to give us a reason to reconnect? If those friends were so important to me then, could I seek them out and rekindle the friendship or at least have enough contact so if we all showed up at the fortieth or fiftieth, there would be some more recent history to build upon? Upon reflection, I realized that I was still friends with Judy, my one very close friend from high school; the other friends with whom I had considered reconnecting would take a lot of time and effort to see if those friendships could be rekindled.

Going Forward by Going Backward

But sometimes there are gains to going backward to an old friend. There may be unresolved issues that you still need to work out with this old friend. There may be situations you need to explore to see if your understanding, then and now, matches your friend's. You might want to revisit a specific friendship for self-development or just for curiosity's sake.

Lauren, a 38-year-old married nurse's assistant with two teenagers, had a positive experience after reconnecting with an old friend from her school years. Describing herself as "shy," Lauren, who grew up in Asia and attended boarding school in India, far from California, where she now resides, explains why and how she reconnected with a casual friend from high school, who has become her closest friend:

> I was trying to make some attachments, any attachments at all, and thought that of all the people I went to school with, she was the one I would most likely want to get in touch with again. I didn't know her very well in school—a casual friend—so I don't really know why I chose her. I had her parent's e-mail address. They live in England. And I tried to reach her

that way but never got a response. Not more than a month later, she e-mailed me, having seen my e-mail address in an alumni directory.

We have been writing almost daily for over two years now, picking up where we left off. We accomplished what takes most people three years to accomplish: we have bared our souls, we poured out our sorrows, shared our joys. We haven't seen each other face to face in about 22 years, but she is [now] my closest friend.

Reconnecting worked for Lauren and her old friend. But each situation is unique, so you obviously want to be careful about reconnecting, even if there could be some educational benefits to doing so, if you fear that your friend was or is engaged in any activities that are illegal or dangerous or in any way sociopathic, homicidal, or suicidal. Friendship provokes powerful feelings—and failed friendships, especially if you were the one to end it, can bring out the same feelings of rejection and despair as a failed romance. The emotion and pathos that was dealt with and put on a shelf could come back to haunt you, or could be revived, if you do reconnect.

By contrast, if a friendship ended because of a structural change, such as moving away or changing jobs, rather than a conflict or betrayal, reconnecting may be great for you both. You could also test the waters and see what response you get, whether that means sending an e-mail, making a phone call, or sending a letter. Based on that exchange, you may decide if you want to go the next step, setting up a get-together. Sometimes the way we feel emotionally when we physically see a friend or hear her voice on the other end of the phone says it all. Do you feel excited, happy, and joyful? Or do you feel angry, annoyed, or even bored? Recognize and heed those feelings.

Where Do I Start?

Every friendship begins with two strangers meeting, whether over the Internet, by phone, or in person. Those strangers then become acquaintances and, in time and because of a testing out of that relationship, it will either become a friendship, dissolve into no contact, or, even worse, degenerate into hostility.

Obviously, in order to begin the process, interaction has to occur. To people who are loners, to those who work at home, or to retirees who may have reduced opportunities for new relationships, that may not be as easy or as available as it seems.

But by just getting out there, someone sets the stage for positive friendships that could fight the depression that often results from being alone or isolated. Certainly if you are new in town, or just starting a job, being accessible for new acquaintanceships is the first step.

After meeting a potential friend, the next step is to extend your contact. Friendship, like romance, is a relationship that is built on details, so you need to lay a solid foundation. There has to be something about the acquaintanceship that causes you both to feel something valuable will be gained by going further with the relationship.

No matter how busy you are or your friend is, you have to make the time for your relationship to grow and blossom. I've found it takes, on average, three years from the time two people meet and become acquaintances until a genuine tried-and-true friendship develops.[2] The time frame makes sense; by that time, most acquaintances are no longer convenient. They have been tested. Someone has graduated, switched schools, gotten a promotion, changed jobs, moved away, gotten married or divorced, or had a child. All those changes are "tests" of your relationship. Interestingly, psychologist Dorothy Tennov, in her study of love entitled *Love and Limerence,* likewise found it took an average of three years for a romantic relationship to be proven a true love or just an infatuation.[3]

Structural changes, such as getting a new job or relocating to a new community, are real challenges. If you replace your acquaintance with someone more convenient, or if you have reduced or no contact with each other, you probably didn't care enough about the relationship to make the extra effort. If your relationship lasts and you still find time for each other, if you and your chum still care about each other, it's a real friendship.

Although the wish to become friends must be shared by both acquaintances, *what* you share need not be equal. That is a pivotal concept that will help you avoid many friendship conflicts related to unmet expectations. There are simply some people who like to receive phone calls, but they do not like to place calls, whether because of their personality, finances, or lack of time. There are friends who may think nothing of recommending a place to get together and others, fearful that their decisions will backfire, who refuse to make suggestions of any kind. That does not make them bad friends. They simply bring different preferences and personalities to the friendship, and friends need to respect those variations. Of course, the overall balance sheet of give and take has to even out, but not on each and every item, as if there is a friend "to do" list that needs to be checked off.

A key ingredient in the progress of a friendship is whether you think your future friend will offer companionship—someone to do things with or talk to, share interests with, and offer emotional support. As noted before, friends tend to be similar—like attracts like—so most of the time acquaintances that are most like you are most likely to become your friends.

Besides "the test of time," there are specific ways to help move an acquaintanceship along to a friendship:

- Emphasize shared values and interests.
- Take your acquaintance's temperature about what frequency of contact and intensity of feeling will be most comfortable for her.
- Don't gossip about your relationship.
- Don't ask favors that might make your acquaintance feel compromised, used, or confused about whether your wish to become a friend is based on feelings or opportunism.
- Communicate regularly.
- Remember your acquaintance's birthday or any other significant occasions in his life. That includes new jobs, anniversaries, awards, achievements, or activities of her close family members.
- Show a concern for your acquaintance's life—family, work, hobbies, and personal matters—but without getting so overinvolved that you're accused of being nosy.
- If an acquaintance asks you to come through, do it. Show that you care.
- Get together with your acquaintance in as many varied situations as possible, beyond the narrow context in which you originally became acquainted.
- Avoid taking your evolving friendship for granted or leaning on it too heavily.
- Emphasize the fun or play factor. Since your acquaintance, like you, has so many other competing relationships and responsibilities to deal with, try to keep emphasizing the joy and merriment in this evolving relationship.

As the old saying goes: "To have a friend, be a friend." But what does that mean?

For starters, friends who listen (as well as speak) are more valued than friends who just want to share and unload. Listen empathetically and sympathetically, not critically or judgmentally.

Listening will go a long way toward adding the other necessary ingredients, as noted in Chapter 1 of this book, "What Is a Friend?"—such as building trust, discreetly handling self-disclosures, and respecting privacy.

In most relationships, people slowly but surely develop trust by sharing confidences while sharing activities, not the other way around. The friendship develops and intensifies through doing and participating in experiences, in addition to talking.

Regular contact is the premium way to keep your friendships in good shape, as well as dealing with conflicts as they arise. Decide what way of keeping in touch with friends works best for *you*. For you, are parties the most desirable way to keep connected with your friends, or do you prefer "one-to-one" interactions if at all possible?

If a friend invites you to a key event in her life, try to get there. Make it a priority, even if you have to go without a spouse who is unable to get away. (Of course if you can not attend, find other ways to celebrate from afar.)

Use the holidays to catch up with your friends and to show them they matter to you, whether that means a holiday phone call, a personalized card or letter, or an appropriate gift. But the holidays should not be the *only* time you remember your friends, or they will begin to wonder just how much of a friend they really are.

If you are really pressed for time but still want to maintain contact with your friends, try to combine what you have to do with getting together with a friend. For example, meet over lunch during the workday if you just do not have a minute to spare at night or on the weekends. If you are planning to take in a movie with your spouse, invite another couple along, and talk over a cup of coffee before or after the picture. Ask a friend to join you for a necessary holiday shopping. It will keep your friendship going and might even make the chore more fun.

Make a master list of birthdays and anniversaries, and note those dates on a wall calendar or in your weekly planner, so you will find it easier each year to remember those special dates for your friends.

If you find yourself wondering when you last saw or spoke to some of your best, close, or casual friends, consider keeping a log that records your contact beyond just holiday cards. If you find too many months—even years—

going by without getting together, it might help you to get an overview of your friendship contact. Decide how often you would like to talk to or see your friends, especially those who live out of town. Try to commit to definite get-togethers.

Fear of Friendship

I hope enough positive statements about healthy friendships have emerged in this book to show you the benefits of having even one close or best friend.

But what if you or someone you care about is afraid of friendship? The fear could be based on a specific incident or relationship: As the victim of betrayal in friendship, you may be afraid to try again, fearful the same thing will happen.

Hopefully, what you have learned in this book will help you make better choices so betrayal is less likely to happen again and, if it does, you will have the tools to deal well with the situation.

But what if this is a long-standing, deep-seated fear, a dread so strong that you have never had a friend? Yes, over the years I have received letters from teens as well as men and women who confide in me that they have never had even one friend. I have also interviewed adults who, because of one terrible experience with a friend, have been afraid to try again, and have remained friendless for years or even decades.

Sometimes this friendlessness is part of a larger rejection of all intimate relationships; the friendless may be single, depressed, isolated, shy, and frightened. In that case, learning to open up and risk rejection, and acceptance, by becoming someone's friend probably has to be part of an overall program to improve social relationships. Short- or long-term therapy with a counselor or therapist may be helpful. Personal referrals are always an excellent way to find a potential therapist in your community. If you are too shy to ask someone to recommend his or her therapist, there are associations that will make referrals to local affiliated therapists. A list of several well-regarded professional associations are listed in the Resources section at the end of this book.

What if you or someone you care about has excellent social relations in all areas *but* friendship? Then you will want to ask yourself what it is about friendship that frightens you so much more than romantic or family or even business relationships. If you can understand what it is about friendship, or a particular friend, that brings up a fear so strong that it stops you from having friendships at all, you may be on the road that will help you change your behavior.

Sometimes it is not until a change occurs in your life and shifts around your intimate relationships that you realize you do indeed want a friend. That is what happened to 30-year-old Marilyn, the married nurse's assistant mentioned previously in connection with the theft of money by her maid of honor at her bachelorette party. Fearful that a friend would betray her, she was willing to depend on just her parents, her husband, and the relationships (but not friendships) at her demanding job. But then her parents moved "pretty far away," and she suddenly wanted and needed a friend. Marilyn, who does not have any children, explains:

> I haven't cared too much about having close friends until recently. My parents moved pretty far away, so I really don't have a social network anymore, except my husband, his friends, and some people I socialize with at work. For a while it didn't bother me, I was so busy at work (purposefully, I think, so I didn't have to deal with reality) that I didn't have time to think about it. But today I went to lunch with my husband and his boss, and I saw these friends (about seven of them) having lunch together, and I realized I was lonely. I miss just gabbing with people. I'm not a telephone talker, but I like getting together in person. I'm just wary of putting a lot of time in with friendships and getting burned in the end.

Or someone may not consciously fear friendship, but their behavior may nonetheless push away potential friends. Social psychologist Dr. Duffy Spencer describes a patient who is reluctant to reach out to develop friends because she does not think she is "good enough": "She just cannot understand why she doesn't have any [friends]. What she doesn't see is the way she nonverbally communicates that she feels very shut down and hurt. She is always frowning and unhappy. She doesn't understand that she's not reaching out in a receptive way. She wants friends but is not seeing what she's doing not to have them. She's a perfectionist about herself."

The kind of pushing away, frowning, and deep-seated fear of intimacy reflected in the previous example is a far cry from feeling the apprehension around strangers and acquaintances that we would label shyness. Unlike the debilitating shyness just described, some degree of shyness is quite common. Psychologist and shyness expert Dr. Philip G. Zimbardo found that 80 percent of the nearly 5,000 people who completed the Stanford Shyness Survey reported feeling shy at some point in their lives; more than 40 percent described themselves as being "presently shy."[4]

Fortunately there has been a lot of research into the causes of shyness as well as how to overcome it. Overcoming shyness is often the first step in conquering a fear of friendship. Very shy people are so cautious of interacting with others that they avoid any contact, sometimes even eye contact, with a potential friend. Shy people need to learn how to build their self-esteem and self-confidence and to be able to set in motion the mutual connection that might become a friendship.

Anxiety about Opposite-sex Friendship

The fear of having an opposite-sex friendship is distinct from the fear of friendship, usually same-sex friendship, discussed above. A woman shares her concern about having an opposite-sex friendship. Describing herself as "a normal female," she sent me this question: "I've had a very long-standing, deep, and personal relationship with a male that is totally non-sexual. I am teased about this by many people. They don't believe the non-sexual aspect. Is this type of friendship so *very* unusual and/or inappropriate?"

Her question is a very common one, and more than ever before, the answer to that question would be no, an opposite-sex friendship that is purely platonic is more acceptable and prevalent today than ever before. Still, you know yourself and—if you are involved in a romantic relationship or married—your partner's ability to handle your opposite-sex friendship, better than anyone else. Just because, in theory, an opposite-sex friendship need not involve any romantic feelings does not discount that your romantic partner or spouse might be jealous of your opposite-sex friendship because of the sexual jealousy your friendship evokes in him, even if he is completely comfortable about the time you spend with your same-sex friends.

Psychologist Linda A. Sapadin did a very interesting study of the same- and opposite-sex friendships of 156 professional men and women. She discovered that the women gave high marks to their same-sex friendships for overall quality, intimacy, enjoyment, and nurturance, whereas the men rated their opposite-sex friendships higher in those areas, except for intimacy.

Essentially, for women, opposite-sex friendships were just another positive friendship; for the men, their opposite-sex friendships were favored over their same-sex friends.[5]

Another key question that researchers R. Lance Shotland and Jane M. Craig addressed was whether men and women interpreted the same behavior as "friendly" or "sexually interested." They concluded that although both men and women were able to distinguish the difference in the two types of behavior, men were more likely to label behavior as reflecting sexual interest than were women.[6] What that suggests is that because of that predisposition, a man might be more likely to misinterpret a wish to be friends as the desire for a romantic relationship.

If you and your opposite-sex friend are careful to be clear about what your motives are, and if you are both confident that your romantic partner or spouse can handle this friendship, an opposite-sex friendship is not only possible but, for some, the preferred kind of friendship.

Knowing that opposite-sex friendships can truly be platonic and normal, however, does not mean you have to pursue them. As 28-year-old Mary points out, she has only one close or best "friend" of the opposite sex: "I consider my husband my best friend as we have been through hell together, emotionally and financially."

Do Men Want Friends As Much As Women Do?

In ancient days men were said to have valued friendship even more than marriage, which until recently, often was prearranged and based on practical concerns rather than romance. Until the twentieth century, women were not even considered "capable" of friendship, which was seen by some as an ever "higher" relationship than marriage.

Furthermore, the social-science literature on gender differences in friendship has always emphasized that men and women may define that friendship quite differently. Traditionally these differences go back to elementary school and persist through the teen, college, and adult years. Men's and boys' friendships tend to involve sharing of activities more than the sharing of feelings. Men tend to be in friendship groups, rather than in one-on-one relationships. By contrast, women and girls tend to share on a more personal level, and they are more likely to be friends in twosomes, or dyads.

Over the last decade, I have observed that the more pronounced gender differences in friendship are diminishing for a number of reasons. The proliferation of male support groups during the 1980s and 1990s, and the articles and books reinforcing that "it's okay for men to feel and share their feelings" is transforming male friendships into something closer to the friendships typically associated with women.

The increase over the last few decades of opposite-sex friendships that are strictly platonic has helped men to have a "safe" friend outside of marriage, someone to turn to for reinforcement about emotionally charged relationships or situations. If a man opens up to a female friend, he may be more willing to also share some intimacies with a male friend. No longer is there an automatic assumption that if a man and a woman are "just friends," that it has to be something more. The proliferation of opposite-sex dorm rooms, more women at higher levels in the workplace, and a wider acceptance of opposite-sex friendship groups throughout elementary, middle school, and high school years are all fostering the notion that opposite-sex friendships can and do occur that are just that and nothing more.

We have also come a very long way, in the last few decades, from the time when platonic feelings for a woman were assumed to be a camouflage for the "real" romantic ones.

We have also made strides so that being part of a female friendship network or a male friendship group after a certain age no longer automatically leads to rumors or allegations of lesbianism or homosexuality.

Getting Help

As you now know, friendship is important enough to your personal happiness, as well as your career success, and even your physical and emotional health, that you may want to consider getting help with your friendship-related challenges and concerns, whether they are a fear of friendship, a pattern of picking friends who end up betraying you, or getting involved with friends who disappoint you.

Professional help is one option. There are numerous qualified therapists available. Whether they are psychologists, psychiatrists, clinical sociologists, social workers, or psychotherapists, all could work with you on your friendship-related concerns. How to find the right therapist could be the topic of an entire book. At this point, let me just emphasize that you and your new therapist have to be a good "fit." In addition to considering the credentials and training of a new therapist, as well as the referrals and evaluations you have received from current or previous patients or clients, you need to look for a mutual rapport that gives you confidence that real change is possible. (For a listing of professional associations that provide referrals to local member therapists, see the Resources section at the end of this book.)

But are there other options for working on your friendship-related issues, in addition to professional counseling? What if, at this time, you do not or cannot go into one-on-one therapy? Dr. Duffy Spencer suggests that although a friend is definitely not a therapist, there is a way that with some guidance a friend could help you with your self-growth. Dr. Spencer points out that you may have to help your friend to learn one skill of an effective therapist—namely, being an empathetic listener. If your friends have a tendency always to jump in and offer solutions to whatever concerns you share, you may need to suggest an alternative way that you want them to respond to you. Says Dr. Spencer:

> The first thing I recommend is that you contract with a friend to basically just listen and give empathy, to be a sounding board. I ask that my clients and students have someone listen to them for five or ten minutes, and then return the favor at some point.
>
> You can actually contract with a friend. Say, "I don't want you to take my side. I don't want you to get mad *with* me. That's not going to help. That's just co-opting the situation. Just listen to my feelings without judgment. That's all."

No, friends certainly cannot be therapists, nor should therapists be friends. But when some reconditioning to be a better listener is required, friends can at least learn to provide one of the many benefits of sharing about one's life, concerns, or fears—the sense of relief that occurs just through the act of sharing. The bonding occurs when you feel someone listens with empathy. And you will benefit: You get a chance to see the situation differently just through the act of reporting it to a second party. It is amazing what you can learn this way.

Dr. Spencer suggests other ways that you could work on your friendship issues:

- Go to seminars. Take adult education classes.
- You can join support groups, professionally led, 12-Step, or self-help groups.

- Bibliotherapy [books that help healing] is very useful. You can also get inspirational tapes and CDs.
- You can even go to inspirational movies [cinematherapy] like Sandra Bullock's *28 Days, Groundhog Day, Regarding Henry*. If you allow yourself to cry, that can be very helpful.
- Try ventilation writing. You just write any which way. You don't worry about penmanship or grammar, and you must destroy it afterward.
- But if you do have the time, there is journaling. In *The Artist's Way*, Julia Cameron advocates something called "the morning pages." Your assignment every morning is to fill up four pages. . . . and don't stop writing until you do.[7]
- The final thing to do is some of your own physicalizing. This is more than simply physical activity. It has another edge to it, like penciling in somebody's name on the bottom of your sneakers and pounding them on the floor. Or twisting a towel or hitting a pillow. Or just let yourself shake. Close the windows and scream. There's a lot of good information on this approach in *Growing Yourself Back Up*, by John Lee, and Peter Levine's book *Waking the Tiger*.[8] It's really all about completing the impulse to fight or to take flight. We're taught not to express our feelings, to close down. So you allow yourself to complete the process.

In addition to joining a support group, reading books, attending classes, or watching movies, here are several additional ways for you or your friend to work on your friendship skills:

- Surround yourself with positive friendships, and observe what it is about those friendships that you admire. Just as it is often recommended to couples that they associate with other happy couples, being in the presence of empathetic and nurturing friendships can educate you by example.
- Keep a friendship journal to share your thoughts about friendship and specific friends, especially if you are too quick to say things to friends in anger that you later regret uttering, after the damage has been done to your friendships.[9]
- Pick one friendship-related issue that you wish to work on and focus on that one concern for a couple of weeks. Whether it's trust, empathy, your listening skills, finding one new friend, or putting more time into the friendships you already have, taking the time to work on your

friendship skills or on a specific friendship will benefit you and your friends.

- Another example of "physicalizing" I once heard about is a store that allowed you, for a fee, to throw crockery at the wall.
- Write a letter to your friend but put it aside and only mail it after a time if you are absolutely sure that is what you want to do. But just the act of writing out your feelings and thoughts, and spelling out any grievances, could help you to understand and even work through the issues this friendship needs to address to go forward.
- If you have fears related to friendship, consider the worst thing that could happen related to your fear, such as imagining that you call someone you've met and ask her to go out for a cup of coffee and she tells you she has all the friends she needs and does not want to spend time with you. Now picture yourself surviving that rejection: Rather than let it destroy your self-esteem, commend yourself for having the courage to reach out to someone new.
- Attend a lecture or workshop on friendship or related issues such as anger, intimacy, dealing with conflict, or communication skills.

Time for Friends

I have written about finding time for friends, and it is a friendship topic I am often asked about.[10] But in my new survey, when the question was "What is the one thing you would like to learn about friendship?" "finding time for friends" was the second most popular concern of those who answered the question. (The Number One concern was "how to handle conflict with a friend.") It's worth summarizing the 10 best ways to make time for your new and old friends:

1. Make it a *priority* to schedule time to get together with your friends.
2. Take a class together or create a club, like a cooking, book, or bowling club, that meets regularly.
3. Volunteer together.
4. Plan a "friends' night out."
5. Spend birthday or holiday time together—just you and your friend or with your families as well.

6. If you live far away, schedule reunions or vacations together, even a day trip.
7. If you work nearby, meet for lunch.
8. If you're both too busy to visit or call, send an e-mail or a letter.
9. When you do get together, schedule your next get-together.
10. Remember that *friendshifts* happen. Allow for those changes so your friendships can continue even if the level of intimacy or frequency of contact is different than before.

Chapter 9

Where to Go from Here

If you are better able to deal with friendship problems as a result of reading this book, then I've done my job! But you've only done part of yours. The rest of it is to take the energy that you may have been pouring into ruminating over a betrayal or coping with negative friends into creating or emphasizing pre-existing positive friendships. Focus on celebrating the joy those positive, self-affirming, and trustworthy friendships bring as those beneficial relationships reshape your life. Furthermore, if you're happier with your friends, you will be more content with yourself and your life. That sense of well-being will spill over into other areas and relationships in your life, including your romantic, family, and business relationships.

- "I've had to phase out a few close friends who became too annoying. They thought we were best friends and acted that way. So they became more work than they were worth." (26-year-old freelance artist)
- "Most friendships I have had in the last few years have been very one-sided, it seems. Most people want lots more than they are willing to give in return and want to tell troubles but not listen. Friendship is a two-way street and most people are not into that." (55-year-old married man, retired, one of eight siblings, who does not have friends right now)
- "A friend at work did not support me when I needed it. . . . I felt that she did not want to be associated with me because I was not in with 'the power group.' I was just another lowly employee." (51-year-old married female executive)
- "I was close friends with an ex-boyfriend and had to end it because he was getting married and his girlfriend was jealous of me." (35-year-old married copy editor)
- "I had a good friend all through high school who became just wicked after we graduated. About two years ago, I just stopped returning her calls. She talked about everyone to me, she was mean to my children, and I felt we had just grown apart. The relationship was very unhealthy for my family." (27-year-old divorced administrative assistant)

All of these friendships ended, whether or not a dramatic betrayal was involved, and freed these men and women up to get greater enjoyment out of the other friendships or intimate relationships in their lives.

In your own life, you will go farther faster and enjoy the journey more if you have valued, caring, loyal, and trustworthy friends to help you along. Have you really thought about who your casual, close, or best friends are? In your personal life? In your work? What are you doing to keep those friendships current?

You may need only one or two close or best friends in your personal life, and as many casual friends and neighbors as you can handle. But at work or in your field of business, especially if you are a freelancer, self-employed, or an entrepreneur, you will probably need one to two dozen casual friends who will help keep you current in your field and provide feedback. One or two carefully managed close or best low-maintenance, tried-and-true friends are ideal.

Make a list of your personal friends and then your business friends.

How often do you see each other? Call? Meet? Communicate?

Do you remember their special days?

If you lack the friends in your personal or business life that you need and want, what are you going to do about your situation? Wishing will not make the necessary changes that you need to create the genuine friendship network that is proven to enhance your personal happiness and career success.

Create an action plan for finding and cultivating positive friends in your personal life and business. First, commit to friendship as a priority goal. Second, make sure you are visible and accessible enough for meeting new people who might become friends. Are you too busy working or taking care of children or an elderly parent to cultivate an acquaintanceship that might become a friendship if you do meet someone new? If there are activities that you have to do, such as exercising, do it at a gym, if you have been working out alone at home, since you might meet people at the gym or health club. If you have a personal concern that you want to explore, such as overeating or dealing with grief, consider joining a self-help group where you may meet others who share your problem. Take a class, being careful not to always arrive late and leave early so you avoid the possibility of interacting with potential friends. If your shyness or other personality or work problems are hampering you from forming new friendships, seek out the professional help that you need. Build your self-esteem and self-confidence so you will be more daring about starting conversations and cultivating new friendships.

Take a course in non-verbal communication if you need help reading the subtle cues that others are communicating to you as well as the positive or negative messages you are transmitting by your frown, smile, stance, clothing, and body language. If you are so busy that it is hard to reach you by phone, let potential friends have multiple ways to contact you including e-mail, cell or mobile phone, or beeper.

The rewards, personally and professionally, will certainly justify the time, energy, and self-searching that may be necessary. Despite the pitfalls of friendship gone awry, friendship has a strong power to heal. An article in *Psychology Today* by Natasha Raymond cited research that came out so strongly in favor of friendship that the title of her article was "Friendship: The Hug Drug." Raymond notes that in a study of women who became friends with the volunteers they saw throughout the year, 72 percent reported a remission in their depression, as compared to only 45 percent in the control group who did not receive the same regular visits. That is a comparable success rate to antidepressants or cognitive therapy, according to the study.[1]

Epidemiologist Dr. Lisa F. Berkman earlier did research into the way that friendship improved the survival rate following a heart attack in 194 men and women over the age of 65. More recent research found that "for women diagnosed with moderately serious breast cancer, a large network of supportive friends and relatives cuts the risk of recurrence and death by 60 percent over seven years."[2]

Getting Over a Harmful Friendship: What If You Never Know Why It Happened?

I hear it over and over again, in similar words, "I don't know what happened. We were always so close. Then, for no apparent reason, she stopped returning my phone calls. It's as if we were never the close friends we had become for the last fifteen years."

We live in an information age where most everyone wants to know the "why" behind something. So, if you have been betrayed by a former friend, no matter how close the relationship or whether the context was business or personal, it may be important to you to find out *why* your former friend treated you that way.

You already know some of the reasons that seeking out a former friend to get the all-important "closure" about the relationship may be a bad idea.

Your former friend may be completely unaware of what she "did" to you. She may be unaware because she is in denial—the unconscious defense mechanism that lets someone deal with something unpleasant by refusing to acknowledge it. Or she might know perfectly well what she did, but the costs to her self-esteem would be too great to admit it outright.

You may also just decide that you do not want your former friend to know what the rift meant to you. Doing so could give your former friend even more power over you or the ability to harm you more than he already has. So turning the other cheek, moving on, and getting over it may be in your own best short- and long-term interests.

Doris, a 48-year-old entrepreneur, had two different friendships that were both close and long-term. One lasted more than 10 years and the other lasted more than 25. In both cases, the close friend ended the friendship by not calling or returning calls. To this day, Doris has never seen or heard from these friends again. It was up to Doris if she was going to continue to be plagued by wondering what happened, consumed with rage and anger, or instead was going to try to make sense out of what happened and turn it into a learning experience. As Doris explains:

> The same thing happened with both of them. They both cut me off, just like that, just stopped calling, wouldn't take my phone calls, sent back letters, wouldn't communicate with me in any way, shape, or form. With no explanation as to why.
>
> When this happened I felt like somebody had taken a sword and shoved it into my heart and twisted it. I felt bodily pain. It felt like my heart hurt. I felt very raw and very scared. Now and then I got angry.
>
> First it was guilt and shame.
>
> Then I went to being really pissed off.
>
> It would sort of fluctuate, and then I went through incredible mourning. These friends were a really big loss.
>
> I had repeatedly tried to get through, and at some point I just said, "I need to stop. They know where I am."
>
> One of the women and I shared a therapist together so I even used the therapist as an intermediary. "Look, she's not calling me back. Would you ask her if she's willing to sit down and discuss this?"
>
> And she said, "She said she's not willing to sit down. She wants nothing to do with you," and that was all I got.

Doris came to realize that the answer would not be a simple one. It was a combination of where Doris was in her life at the time (she had a demanding husband, a young child with learning issues, and an intense full-time job), where her friends were (both were single women without children), and Doris's definition of friendship as a relationship that has more to do with getting than giving. That changed in time, partly because of these two dramatic failed friendships. Doris explains:

It was very disheartening, and I look back and I understand, taking my part of it, understanding it's what I thought friendship was at that point, and I realized that I didn't give my share to it.

At those points in my life [when these friendships ended], I was very self-absorbed. I was very involved with a dysfunctional husband, a child with special needs, and work so I could barely keep my head above water. The women were single with no kids and so had more free time, and I realize I wasn't available in a lot of ways to these two women.

It used to be the sort of friendship you'd just pick up where you left off kind of thing and suddenly it was all kind of gone. I was really shocked.

Doris's family background made the end of these two friendships all the more traumatic. The victim of sexual abuse by her father, Doris had a hard time trusting people, especially women. Although her father was the one to abuse her, Doris faulted her mother for failing to intervene and stop it.

I asked Doris how she dealt with the stonewalling from these two former close friends:

It took me a good year or longer, almost daily [of thinking about the ended friendship]. Everything made me look at myself. It crept around every corner. [But] it made me look at myself. And I have to say that in many ways it showed me and made me really look at myself and what I wanted from relationships, and it helped me to get out of myself. Where are my priorities in life? I always say family and friends come first, but that's not what I'm living.

It was a gift in so many ways, rising out of the ashes of the mourning and looking at my part. I have truly come to the other side where I have developed healthier, more reciprocal, and caring, real friendships.

Roger, whose friend and boss betrayed him when he failed to go to bat for Roger (see Chapter 7, on work and friendship), also looked upon that horrific betrayal as a catalyst to finding a new job. Unable to work for his former friend, Roger eventually left the company and followed his dream to pursue a freelance career.

In addition to trying to learn about yourself from the ending of a friendship, you can also think about the benefits to you if you find a way to forgive. Just consider the energy drain that revenge can be for most people who ruminate about how they might get back at a friend who betrayed them.

You do not have to confront those whose friendship you no longer wish to maintain, nor do you have to respond to any confrontations that others try to engage you in. The choice is yours. But, as Doris's example demonstrated, you can always examine the friendship, the betrayal, and the possible causes. It may help you in your present and future relationships and choices.

Knowledge fosters power and self-confidence. Hopefully the knowledge you have gained by reading this book will give you confidence to try to figure out what, if anything, was behind the falling out that you had with your friend. Perhaps you can now fill in the blanks yourself, based on your own instincts and interpretations of the possible motives or reasons. True, you may never definitively know, much less understand, the reasons behind a betrayal, or why you chose a destructive friend. But even if you never find out for certain, through your own self-awareness, you can give yourself the closure that you are seeking. That is what Doris did, and you can certainly, too.

I hope you have learned enough about friendship and betrayal, as well as the difference between positive and negative friendships, that you will be less afraid of friendship. You have learned how to recognize 21 distinctive types of friends who are more likely to make your relationship a less than wonderful one. But you have seen plenty of examples in this book and you probably can point to numerous instances in your own life of wonderful friendships that exist and thrive, based on truth, honesty, and loyalty. There are also friendships that end, or should end, because of betrayal, lies, deceit, jealousy, and downright vindictiveness. I hope that now you are better equipped to recognize and deal with those friends as well.

But the evidence is undeniable: Friends extend life and improve the quality of life. Sometimes you can salvage a friendship, if you are secure enough within yourself, by diffusing a potential rift that might permanently separate you and your friend. For example, Alma, who is gay, explains:

> I told [my friend] Barbara I was in love with her, and she said that as much as she loved me, she wasn't in love with me. But if she were a lesbian, I'd be the person she'd want to be with. And we continued to be good friends. Just the way she handled the whole situation—it was such a gift.

The catch-22 is that sometimes you have to be the one to change so you can become a better friend, accept friendship, or even appreciate the friends you already have. As a married middle-aged woman who has struggled to overcome early child abuse shared with me: "I don't feel worthy of good things in my life. When a friend does something good, I feel unworthy. I want to give, but can't accept in return. [I want to learn] how to allow myself to accept."

I've tried to show that a positive change in attitudes toward friendship and friendship patterns is possible without changing friends. Bonnie, the 49-year-old woman whom I first interviewed in 1996 for my book *Friendshifts*®, said that she considered her dog Buster "the best friend I've ever had" as she went on to espouse her belief that a dog makes a better friend than people. She concluded her comparison of people and dogs with the words "I vote for dogs."[3]

Fast-forward five years. After working on herself, getting some counseling, learning more about friendship, and going through a life-altering personal experience, Bonnie's life and friendship patterns have changed.

> [Today] I wouldn't say that dogs are better than people are. I don't feel that way today. I don't think that today. I still love my dog, but I'm really grateful for the people in my life. I was very angry [five years ago]. I was very unhappy. Now I wouldn't say that I'm happy, but I wouldn't say I'm unhappy.
>
> What happened was that my [only] sister died. If you wrote a play and said, 'What would be the incident that made the change happen?' that would be it.
>
> [My very close friend] Regina was there for me when my sister died. But in terms of becoming someone, growing in life, and this sort of thing, [the change in my attitude toward friendship] was happening over time. I went from being very unhappy and having no self-esteem to being someone who just has a better outlook on life.

Our friends are usually a mirror of ourselves. Sometimes in order to change who our friends are *we* have to change, just like Bonnie. By changing how we view ourselves, even the same friend may be seen in a different light. But Bonnie's friend Regina also, over the years, became less of a Controller than she used to be and a more accessible, accepting close friend.

As 55-year-old Michael, who left his corporate job and his best friend at work to become an independent consultant, says, "The better I feel about myself, the better I feel about everybody else." He's not as hard on his friend and others, since he is kinder to himself.

I want to end this book by returning to the question that I posed in the introduction: If friendships do not always last a lifetime anymore than marriages do (because of divorce, widowhood, or singleness by choice), what's left to believe in as a lifetime relationship that's forever?

As Bonnie has learned, the strongest friendship needs to be with oneself (and, some will say, also with God). And Brenda, whose recovery from childhood physical and sexual abuse, as well as obesity, was discussed earlier in this book, shared with me how crucial it is to learn forgiveness and self-love as a help to her in finding the close and best friends she wants:

> In years past, I was too frightened of people to let anyone get close. Now I am more self-confident and sure about who and what I am as a person in all areas of my life. I still get frightened sometimes. But I no longer push people away. I have nothing to hide or be ashamed of in my life. I also feel I have something worthwhile to give a friend.
>
> The other thing is that we have to learn to forgive. We have to forgive those who hurt us and harmed us, who stole our childhoods from us. In doing that, we learn to forgive ourselves. Without self-forgiveness we cannot learn to love. Without love, life is empty. If we love ourselves as we would have others love us, think of all the good people—friends, special people— we can have in our lives.

Friends are not a quick fix for loneliness, career problems, romantic disappointments, mental illness, or failure. Yes, friends, especially positive close or best ones, will help enrich your life and enhance your happiness. But befriending yourself makes it less likely that a friend will betray you or that you will allow a toxic friendship to continue.

Finally, it was not my intention in this book to encourage you to dwell on negative friendships. There are so many positive friendships available to you that you are worthy of experiencing. Perhaps by freeing up some of the energy that may have been drained out of you because of a betrayal, or perhaps by feeling more confident that if you did detect a negative friendship you could deal with it, your friendship fears have been replaced with optimism and hope for one of the most glorious intimate relationships readily available to all of us. None of us can change the past, whether that past included a joyful childhood or a bleak one, whether you had a 54-year marriage that ended because your spouse died or you have been single your entire adult life. Nor does friendship take the place of romance (or children, siblings, parents, or an extended family). It is a relationship of choice with its own complexities and rewards.

If your friends have been glorious, that is wonderful; build on those exemplary relationships. But if your friends have betrayed, disappointed, or hurt you, you have a fresh start. Right now. You are deserving of at least one caring, nurturing friend in your life. Whether you have been a devoted friend to others or have been befriended by a caring person, there is hope for you, this moment, that you will find such a friend.

Notes

Introduction

1. For substantiation that friendship helps extend your life as well as increasing the chances of surviving breast cancer or a heart attack and contributing to mental health, see Lisa F. Berkman and Leonard Syme, "Social Networks, Host Resistance, and Mortality: A Nine-Year Follow-up Study of Alameda County Residents," *American Journal of Epidemiology*, Vol. 109 (1979): 186-204; L. F. Berkman, "Social Support Predicts Survival in Myocardial Infarction Patients," paper presented at American Heart Association, Science Writers Seminar, Santa Barbara, California, January 18, 1995, 5 pages; Derek L. Phillips, "Mental Health Status, Social Participation, and Happiness," *Journal of Health & Social Behavior*, Vol. 8 (December 1967): 285-291; James S. House, Karl R. Landis, and Debra Umberson, "Social Relationships and Health," *Science*, Vol. 214 (July 1988): 540-545; Rebecca G. Adams, "Which Comes First: Poor Psychological Well-Being or Decreased Friendship Activity?" *Activities, Adaptation & Aging*, Vol. 12 (1988): 27-41; Natasha Raymond, "Friendship: The Hug Drug," *Psychology Today*, December 1999, page 17; Marilyn Elias, "Friends May Make Breast Cancer More Survivable," *USA Today*, March 8, 2001, page 01D; "Emotional Support Predicts Survival After Heart Attacks," Yale School of Medicine, Office of Public Information, December 14, 1992 (research of Dr. Lisa Berkman); Karen Thomas, "Cyber-friends Finally Embrace: Breast Cancer Survivors Meet Their Sources of Online Support," *USA Today*, May 30, 2000, page 05D; R. Daniel Foster, "Friends as Healers," *Modern Maturity*, September-October 1997, pages 44-45; and Jacqueline Olds, "The Healing Power of Friendship," *Bottom Line/Health*, August 1997, pages 1-2.

2. See Kevin Vaughan and Jeff Kass, "Columbine Had 'Red Flags': Officials Had Many Chances to Prevent Shooting, Panel Says," *Denver Rocky Mountain News*, May 18, 2001, page 4A; Lisa Belkin, "Parents Blaming Parents," in *The New York Times Magazine*, October 31, 1999, pages 61-67, 78, 94, 100; and Nancy Gibbs and Timothy Roche, with reporting by Andrew Goldstein, Maureen Harrington, and Richard Woodbury, "Special Report/ The Columbine Tapes: In Five Secret Videos They Recorded Before the Mas-

sacre, The Killers Reveal Their Hatred—and Their Lust for Fame," *Time,* December 20, 1999, beginning on page 40.

3. On the shootings in Santee, California, see Terry McCarthy, with reporting by Polly Forster, Jeffrey Ressner, and Margot Roosevelt, "Andy Williams Here. Unhappy Kid. Tired of Being Picked on. Ready to Blow. Want to Kill Some People. Can Anybody Hear Me? How Did Things Get so Bad?" *Time,* March 19, 2001, page 24+; and Betsy Streisand, Angie Cannon, Anna Mulrine, and Randy Dotinga, "Betrayed by Their Silence?" *U.S. News & World Report,* March 19, 2001, page 22.

Chapter 1: What Is a Friend?

1. On number of friends, see J. L. Barkas (a.k.a. Jan Yager), "Friendship Patterns Among Young Urban Single Women" (Dissertation, City University of New York, Sociology, 1983), and Jan Yager, *Friendshifts®: The Power of Friendship and How It Shapes Our Lives,* Stamford, CT: Hannacroix Creek Books, 2nd edition, 1999, page 178.

2. Michael Levin, *A Woman's Guide to Being a Man's Best Friend,* Kansas City, KS: Andrews and McMeel, 1996. Robert D. Putnam makes a similar point in "The Story Behind This Book," when he concludes his list of thank-you's in this way: "Everyone needs a best friend; I am blessed to be married to mine." Robert D. Putnam, *Bowling Alone: The Collapse and Revival of American Community,* New York: Simon & Schuster, 2000, page 513.

3. Montaigne, "Of Friendship," translated by Donald M. Frame, in *The Complete Essays of Montaigne,* Stanford, CA: Stanford University Press, 1958, pages 141–142.

4. Streisand, Cannon, Mulrine, Dotinga, "Betrayed by their silence?" *U.S. News & World Report,* March 19, 2001, page 22.

5. Mary Alice Kellogg, "When True-Blue Turns Green," *Savvy,* May 1986, page 28.

6. Mary Kay Shanley, *She Taught Me to Eat Artichokes,* Marshalltown, IA: Sta-Kris, Inc., 1993.

7. Yager, *Friendshifts®*, page 38.

8. *Ibid.*, pages 12, 20-21, 30, 76, 129, 177.

9. On cliques, see "Anatomy of a Clique," by Noelle Howey, *Seventeen*, November 1998, pages 158-161; Karen S. Peterson, "The Years of Living Dangerously: Need for Kids to Fit in among Peers Arriving Earlier, Stronger," *USA Today*, January 23, 2001, page 08D; and Terri Apter et al., *Best Friends*, New York: Three Rivers Press, pages 62-65.

10. Suzanne Vaughan, *Potholes and Parachutes: Stories of Hope and Healing for Getting Up, Getting Out, and Landing Safely*, Aurora, CO: Valbeck Press, 2001.

11. Jan Yager, *Business Protocol*, Stamford, CT: Hannacroix Creek Books, 2nd edition, 2001, pages xvi and 208.

Chapter 2: Detecting Harmful People *Before* They're Friends
1. Yager, *Friendshifts®*, page 60.

2. Florence Rush, *The Best-Kept Secret: Sexual Abuse of Children*, Blue Ridge Summit, PA: TAB Books, a division of McGraw-Hill, 1981, pages 177-178. Rush quotes a victim who was molested as a child and who "identified so positively with his molester that he, in turn, grew up to molest other children."

3. John Lutz, *Single White Female*, New York: Ballantine Books, 1992.

Chapter 3: What's *Really* Going On?
1. Linda Tripp, interviewed by Nancy Collins, in *George*, January 2001, page 94.

2. Linda Tripp, interviewed by Nancy Collins, in *George*, January 2001, page 96.

3. John Amodeo, *Love and Betrayal*, New York: Ballantine Books, 1994, page 64.

4. Lois Duncan, "How Not to Lose Friends Over Money," *Woman's Day*, March 25, 1986, page 20.

5. Liz Smith, "Bravo! Lipton Gets What He Deserves," *The [Stamford] Advocate*, March 6, 2001, page A2.

6. J. L. Barkas (a.k.a. Jan Yager), *Single in America*, New York: Atheneum, 1980.

7. Ian Robertson, *Sociology*, 2nd edition, New York: Worth Publishers, 1981, page 163.

8. Theodore Isaac Rubin, *The Angry Book*, New York: Collier Books, 1969, page 205.

9. Howard M. Halpern, *How to Break Your Addiction to a Person*, New York: Bantam Books, 1982, pages 188-238.

10. "Like attracts like" was espoused by the ancient philosopher Aristotle in *The Nicomachean Ethics* (translated by H. Rackham, Harvard University Press, 1968) and has been proven by social-scientific empirical evidence by social scientists, including psychologist Theodore Newcomb in his experiments in the 1950s with University of Michigan transfer students: Theodore Newcomb, "The Prediction of Interpersonal Attraction," *The American Psychologist* 11, November 1956, pages 575-586.

Chapter 4: It's All in the Family

1. Susan Forward, co-author, with Craig Buck, of *Toxic Parents: Overcoming Their Hurtful Legacy and Reclaiming Your Life*, New York: Bantam Books, 1989, page 6.

2. Dorothy Corkille Briggs, *Your Child's Self-Esteem*, Garden City, NY: Doubleday, 1970, page 19.

3. See Stephen P. Bank and Michael D. Kahn, *The Sibling Bond*, New York: Basic Books, 1982, and Adele Faber and Elaine Mazlish, *Siblings Without Rivalry*, New York: Avon Books, 1987.

4. See David Finkelhor with Sharon Araji, Larry Brown, Angela Browne, Stefanie Doyle Peters, and Fail Elizabeth Wyatt, *A Sourcebook on Child Sexual Abuse,* Beverly Hills, CA: Sage Publications, 1986, and D. Finkelhor, "Sex among Siblings: A Survey on Prevalence, Variety, and Effects," *Archives of Sexual Behavior,* Vol. 9, (1980) pages 171-193.

5. Melanie Klein, "Love, Guilt, and Reparation," in Melanie Klein and Joan Riviere, eds., *Love, Hate and Reparation,* New York: Norton, 1936, 1964, page 89.

Chapter 5: Can This Friendship Be Saved?
1. Elisabeth Kubler-Ross, *On Death and Dying,* New York: Macmillan, 1976, 1969. Psychiatrist Martin Symonds described similar stages experienced by crime victims; see M. Symonds, "Victims of Violence: Psychological Effects and Aftereffects," *American Journal of Psychoanalysis,* Vol. 35 (Spring 1975): 19-26. See also: J. L. Barkas (a.k.a. Jan Yager), *Victims,* New York: Scribner's, 1978, page 10.

2. Harry Stein, "On Not Turning the Other Cheek," *Esquire,* March 1980, page 13.

Chapter 6: When and How to End It
1. Kate Cohen-Posey, *How to Handle Bullies, Teasers and Other Meanies,* Highland City, FL: Rainbow Books, 1995, page 14.

2. *Ibid.,* page 18.

3. *Ibid.,* pages 22-23. Cohen-Posey cautions that these are three tactics intended for the annoying, obnoxious name-calling of bullies. "For more dangerous situations, other strategies may be needed."

4. Albert K. Cohen, *Delinquent Boys: The Culture of the Gang,* New York: Free Press, 1955, pages 135-136.

Chapter 7: Friendship at Work
1. Karen Lindsey, *Friends as Family,* Boston: Beacon Press, 1981, pages 79-84.

2. William D. Marelich, "Can We Be Friends?" *HR Focus*, Vol. 73 (August 1996): 17.

3. See Barbara A. Winstead, Valerian J. Verlega, Melinda J. Montgomery, and Constance Pilkington, "The Quality of Friendships at Work and Job Satisfaction," *Journal of Social and Personal Relationships*, Vol. 12 (2): 199–215. These researchers, studying 722 faculty and staff at two universities, found that those with a best friendship at work that was problem-free had higher job satisfaction; conversely, a best friendship at work that had "maintenance difficulty" (problems) had more of a negative impact on job satisfaction.

4. As long as both friends are single and the romance is appropriate and acceptable to management, workplace friendships that evolve into romance need not be a problem. But anyone having a romance needs to consider how the friendship-turned-romance might be seen as a betrayal by co-workers.

What if a co-worker has a crush on your beloved? What about co-workers who may be lonely at home and long for romance? A workplace romance, flaunted in their faces daily, may make them feel all the lonelier, causing feelings to be aroused at work that employees would prefer to keep in check.

If the romance is inappropriate—if one or both parties is involved with or married to someone else—it could further put co-workers in the uncomfortable position of having to keep a secret or being privy to a clandestine affair that disturbs them.

Workplace friendships that become a romance need to be handled with caution to prevent feelings of betrayal that such relationships may bring out in other employees. Furthermore, if there is a policy against such relationships, that has to be addressed. If the friendship-turned-romance is between those of disparate status, there may be reason to show caution: If the romance cools, allegations of sexual harassment could compromise each party or the company.

For further comments on office romance protocol, see "When Work Friendship Becomes Romance," in Yager, *Friendshifts*®, pages 182–183, and "Company Romance" in Jan Yager, *Business Protocol*, Stamford, CT: Hannacroix Creek Books, 2nd edition, 2001, pages 56–59. See also: "Office Romance," transcript of National Public Radio interview with Ray Suarez, host, and Jan Yager, as well as Gary Neuman and Gary Matyhiason, October 7, 1998; Dennis M. Power, *The Office Romance: Playing with Fire without Getting Burned*, New York: AMACOM, 1998; and Carol Hymowitz and Ellen

Joan Pollock, "The One Clear Line in Interoffice Romance Has Become Blurred," *The Wall Street Journal,* February 4, 1998, pages 1, A8.

Chapter 8: Finding Good Friends

1. Yager, *Friendshifts*®, pages 42-43.

2. *Ibid.,* p. 36.

3. Dorothy Tennov, *Love and Limerence,* New York: Stein and Day, 1979.

4. Philip G. Zimbardo, *Shyness,* Reading, MA: Addison-Wesley, 1977, pages 13-14.

5. Linda A. Sapadin, "Friendship and Gender: Perspectives of Professional Men and Women," *Journal of Social and Personal Relationships,* Vol. 5 (1988): 387-403.

6. R. Lance Shotland and Jane M. Craig, "Can Men and Women Differentiate Between Friendly and Sexually Interested Behavior?" *Social Psychology Quarterly,* Vol. 51 (1988): 66-73.

7. Julia Cameron, *The Artist's Way,* New York: Jeremy P. Tarcher/Perigree, 1992.

8. John H. Lee, *Growing Yourself Back Up,* New York: Three Rivers Press, 2001; and Peter A. Levine, with Ann Frederick, *Waking the Tiger: Healing Trauma,* Berkeley, CA: North Atlantic Books, 1997.

9. Jan Yager, *Friendship Journal: Selected Quotes from Friendshifts*® *and a Journal,* Stamford, CT: Hannacroix Creek Books, 2001.

10. Yager, *Friendshifts,* pages 214-220; Jan Yager, *Creative Time Management for the New Millennium,* Stamford, CT: Hannacroix Creek Books, 1999, pages 149-150; "Why Even Busy Working Moms Need Friends," posted at workingmom.com, May 18, 2000; "Wise College Students Find Friends for Life," *Wall Street Journal'*s www.collegejournal.com, released February 14, 2001 (Part 1), and "How to Stay Connected with Your College Crowd," *Wall Street Journal'*s www.collegejournal.com, released February 14, 2001 (Part 2).

Chapter 9: Where to Go From Here

1. Natasha Raymond, "Friendship: The Hug Drug," *Psychology Today,* December 1999, page 17.

2. "Emotional Support Predicts Survival After Heart Attacks," Yale School of Medicine, Office of Public Information, December 14, 1992. See also: "Social Support Predicts Survival in Myocardial Infarction Patients," paper presented by Lisa F. Berkman, Ph.D., at the American Heart Association Science Writers Seminar, Santa Barbara, California, January 18, 1995; Dr. Karen Weihs of George Washington University Medical Center in Washington, D.C., according to the report on her research in *USA Today,* found that "for women diagnosed with moderately serious breast cancer, a large network of supportive friends and relatives cuts the risk of recurrence and death by 60% over seven years. . . ." (Marilyn Elias, "Friends May Make Breast Cancer More Survivable," *USA Today,* March 8, 2001, page 01D.)

3. *Friendshifts®*, p. 205.

Selected Bibliography

The literature relevant to the topic of negative friendships is voluminous, covering everything from scholarly sociology and psychology articles and treatises on friendship formation to popular books on coping with anger, conflict, and self-esteem. This bibliography is not intended to be definitive; it is just a selection of some of the excellent seminal and contemporary research and writing that is available. References are grouped by topic; inclusion in this list does not imply an endorsement, nor should exclusion from this list because of space or other considerations be construed as criticism of those works. Please note that there are additional references in the chapter-by-chapter Notes that precede this selected bibliography. In the Resources section that follows, you will find names, addresses, and web sites, if available, for related associations and information sources.

Anger

Lerner, Harriet. *The Dance of Anger: A Woman's Guide to Changing the Patterns of Intimate Relationships.* New York: HarperCollins, 1997.

Rubin, Theodore Isaac. *The Angry Book.* New York: Collier, 1969.

Betrayal and Trust

Amodeo, John, and Charles L. Whitfield. *Love and Betrayal.* New York: Ballantine, 1994.

Bode, Janet. *Trust and Betrayal.* New York: Delacorte Press, 1995.

Greer, Jane, and Margery D. Rosen. *How Could You Do This to Me?: Learning to Trust After Betrayal.* Garden City, NY: Doubleday, 1998.

Communication Skills

Lerner, Harriet. *The Dance of Connection: How to Talk to Someone When You're Mad, Hurt, Scared, Frustrated, Insulted, Betrayed, or Desperate.* New York: HarperCollins, 2001.

Nierenberg, Gerard I., and Henry H. Calero. *How to Read a Person Like a Book.* New York: Simon and Schuster (Fireside), 1986 (1971).

Rawlins, William K. *Friendship Matters: Communication, Dialectics, and the Life Course.* Hawthorne, NY: Aldine de Gruyter, 1992.

Tannen, Deborah. *You Just Don't Understand: Women and Men in Conversation.* New York: Ballantine Books, 1990.

Jealousy

Chambers, Veronica. "Taming Envy." *O* magazine, November 2000, pages 103-104.

Curtis, Jean. "When Sisterhood Turns Sour." *The New York Times Magazine,* May 30, 1976, pages 15-16.

Friday, Nancy. *Jealousy.* New York: Bantam Books, 1985.

Gaylin, Willard. "Feeling Envious," in *Feelings: Our Vital Signs.* New York: Harper and Row, 1979, pages 130-147.

Stern, Barbara Lang. "Is Jealousy Healthy?" *Vogue,* October 1988, pages 350, 352.

Loneliness

Lynch, James J. *The Broken Heart: The Medical Consequences of Loneliness.* New York: Basic Books, 1979.

Perlman, Dan, and Letitia Anne Peplau, eds. *Loneliness.* New York: Wiley-Interscience, 1982.

Putnam, Robert D. *Bowling Alone: The Collapse and Revival of American Community.* New York: Simon and Schuster, 2000.

Weiss, Robert S., ed. *Loneliness: The Experience of Emotional and Social Isolation.* Foreword by David Riesman. Cambridge, MA: MIT Press, 1973.

Girlfriends

Apter, Terri, et al. *Best Friends: The Pleasures and Perils of Girls' and Women's Friendships.* New York: Crown Publishers, 1998.

Beanland, Ame Mahler, ed.; Emily Miles Terry, ed., and Jill Conner Browne. *It's a Chick Thing: Celebrating the Wild Side of Women's Friendship.* Berkeley, CA: Conari Press, 2000.

Bernikow, Louise. *Among Women.* New York: Harper and Row, 1980.

Berrey, Carmen Renee, and Tamara Traeder. *Girlfriends: Invisible Bonds, Enduring Ties.* Berkeley, CA: Wildcat Canyon Press, 1995.

Coleman, Chisena. *Just Between Girlfriends: African American Women Celebrate Friendship.* New York: Simon and Schuster, 1998.

Cott, Nancy. *The Bonds of Womanhood: "Woman's Sphere" in New England, 1780-1835.* New Haven, CT: Yale University Press, 1977.

Degler, Carl N. *At Odds: Women and the Family in America from the Revolution to the Present.* New York: Oxford University Press, 1980.

Eichenbaum, Luise, and Susie Orbach. *Between Women: Love, Envy and Competition in Women's Friendships.* New York: Viking, 1987.

Goodman, Ellen, and Patricia O'Brien. *I Know Just What You Mean: The Power of Friendship in Women's Lives.* New York: Simon and Schuster, 2000.

Pogrebin, Letty Cottin. *Among Friends.* New York: McGraw Hill, 1985.

Shanley, Mary Kay. *She Taught Me to Eat Artichokes.* Marshalltown, IA: Sta-Kris, Inc., 1993.

Shapiro, Patricia Gottlieb. *Heart to Heart: Deepening Women's Friendships at Midlife.* New York: Berkley Books, 2001.

Sheehy, Sandy. *Connecting: The Enduring Power of Female Friendship.* New York: Morrow, 2000.

Male Friends

Bahr, Robert. "Passionate Friendships Between Men." *MGF (Men's Guide to Fashion),* Dec. 1987, pp. 18-20.

Lewis, Robert A. "Emotional Intimacy Among Men." *Journal of Social Issues* 34 (1978): 108-121.

Miller, Stuart. *Men and Friendship.* Boston: Houghton Mifflin, 1983.

Nardi, Peter M., ed. *Men's Friendships.* Newbury Park, CA: Sage, 1992.

Pleck, Joseph H. "Man to Man: Is Brotherhood Possible?" in Nona Glazer-Malbin, ed., *Old Family, New Family: Interpersonal Relationships.* New York: D. Van Nostrand, 1975, pp. 229-244.

Sharpe, Anita. "How to Find Guys to Hang Around and Do Stuff With." *Wall Street Journal,* May 9, 1994, pp. 1, A6.

Shotland, R. Lance, and Jane M. Craig. "Can Men and Women Differentiate Between Friendly and Sexually Interested Behavior?" *Social Psychology Quarterly* 51 (1988): 66-73.

Opposite-sex Friends

Booth, Alan, and Elaine Hess. "Cross-Sex Friendship." *Journal of Marriage and the Family,* Feb. 1974, pp. 38-47.

Hacker, Helen Mayer. "Blabbermouths and Clams: Sex Differences in Self-Disclosure in Same-Sex and Cross-Sex Friendship Dyads." *Psychology of Women Quarterly* 5 (April 1981): 385-401.

Sapadin, Linda. "Friendship and Gender: Perspectives of Professional Men and Women." *Journal of Social and Personal Relationships* 5 (1988): 387-403.

Werking, Kathy. *We're Just Good Friends: Women and Men in Nonromantic Relationships.* New York: Guilford Press, 1997.

Friendship over the Life Cycle

Dickens, Wenda J., and Daniel Perlman. "Friendship Over the Life-Cycle," in *Developing Personal Relationships,* S. Duck and R. Gilmour, eds. New York: Academic Press, 1981.

Fischer, Claude S., and Stacey J. Oliker. "Friendship, Sex, and the Life Cycle." Berkeley: Institute of Urban and Regional Development, University of California, March 1980.

Hess, Beth B. "Friendship and Gender Roles over the Life Course," in *Single Life,* Peter J. Stein, ed. New York: St. Martin's Press, 1981, pp. 104-115.

Hughes, Michael, and Walter R. Gove. "Living Alone, Social Integration, and Mental Health." *American Journal of Sociology* 87 (July 1981): 48-74.

E-mail and Friendship

Adams, Rebecca G. "The Demise of Territorial Determinism: Online Friendships," in *Placing Friendship in Context,* Rebecca A. Adams and Graham Allan, eds. London: Cambridge University Press, 1998, pp. 153-182.

Collins, Clare. "Friendships Built on Bytes and Fibers." *New York Times,* Jan. 5, 1992, p. 32.

Sklaraoff, Sara. "E-mail Nation." *U.S. News & World Report,* March 22, 1999, p. 54.

Classic Friendship Writings

Aristotle. *Aristotle in Twenty-Three Volumes/Vol. 1, The Nicomachean Ethics.* Translated by H. Rackham. Books 8 & 9. Cambridge, MA: Harvard University Press, 1968.

Bacon, Sir Francis. "Of Friendship" (1625), in *Classic Essays in English,* Josephine Miles, ed. Boston: Little, Brown, 1965.

Cicero. *On Old Age and on Friendship.* Translated by Frank O. Copley. Ann Arbor: University of Michigan Press, 1967.

Emerson, Ralph Waldo. "Friendship," in *Essays by Ralph Waldo Emerson,* New York: Harper and Row, 1951, pp. 121-156.

Enright, D.J., and David Rawlinson, eds. *The Oxford Book of Friendship.* New York: Oxford University Press, 1992.

Lazarsfeld, Paul F., and Robert K. Merton. "Friendship as Social Process: A Substantive and Methodological Analysis," in *Freedom and Control in Modern Society,* M. Berger, T. Abel, and C. Page, eds. New York: Van Nostrand, 1954, pp. 18-66.

Montaigne. "Of Friendship," in *The Complete Essays of Montaigne*, edited and translated by Donald M. Frame. Stanford, CA: Stanford University Press, 1958, pp. 135-144.

Plato. *Lysis, or Friendship,* in *The Works of Plato,* Irwin Edman, ed. New York: Modern Library, 1928.

Thoreau, Henry David. *The Portable Thoreau.* New York: Viking, 1964.

Welty, Eudora, and Ronald A. Sharp, eds. *The Norton Book of Friendship.* New York: Norton, 1991.

Yager, Jan. "Perspectives on Friendship." Special issue on Sociological Practice, edited by Ray Kirshak. *International Journal of Sociology and Social Policy.* Vol. 18, No. 1, 1998, pp. 27-40.

Friendship Studies

Barkas, J. L. *Friendship: A Selected, Annotated Bibliography.* New York: Garland, 1985.

Barkas, J. L. (Janet Lee). See also Yager, Jan.

Bell, Robert R. *Worlds of Friendship.* Beverly Hills, CA: Sage, 1981.

Blieszner, Rosemary, and Rebecca G. Adams. *Adult Friendship.* Thousand Oaks, CA: Sage Publications, 1992.

Block, Joel D. *Friendship.* New York: Macmillan, 1980.

Bloom, Allan David. *Love and Friendship.* New York: Simon and Schuster, 1993.

Brain, Robert. *Friends and Lovers.* New York: Basic Books, 1976.

Brenton, Myron. *Friendship.* New York: Stein and Day, 1975.

Davis, Murray S. *Intimate Relations.* New York: Free Press, 1973.

Derrida, Jacques. *Politics of Friendship.* Translated by George Collins. London: Verso Books, 1997.

Duck, Steve. *Friends, for Life: The Psychology of Close Relationships.* Brighton, England: The Harvester Press, 1983.

Fehr, Beverley. *Friendship Processes.* Thousand Oaks, CA: Sage Publications, 1996.

Greeley, Andrew M. *The Friendship Game.* Garden City, NY: Doubleday, 1971.

Rubin, Lillian Breslow. *Just Friends.* New York: Harper and Row, 1985.

Yager, Jan. *Friendshifts®: The Power of Friendship and How It Shapes Our Lives.* Stamford, CT: Hannacroix Creek Books, 1997, 2nd edition, 1999.

Friendship Formation

Naegele, Kaspar D. "Friendship and Acquaintances: An Exploration of Some Social Distinctions." *Harvard Educational Review* 28 (1958): 232-252.

Newcomb, Theodore M. "The Prediction of Interpersonal Attraction." *The American Psychologist* 11 (Nov. 1956): 575-586.

Parlee, Mary Brown, and *Psychology Today* editors. "The Friendship Bond: PT's Survey Report." *Psychology Today,* Oct. 1979, pp. 43-54, 113.

Yager, Jan. "Why New Mothers Need New Friends." *McCall's,* Jan. 1988, p. 41.

Benefits of Friendship

Berkman, Lisa F., and Leonard Syme. "Social Networks, Host Resistance, and Mortality: A Nine-Year Follow-Up Study of Alameda County Residents." *American Journal of Epidemiology* 109 (1979): 186-204.

Brody, Jane E. "Personal Health: To Avoid Loneliness, Both Emotional and Social Attachments Are Necessary." *New York Times,* April 6, 1983, p. C10.

——. "Personal Health: Maintaining Friendships for the Sake of Your Health." *New York Times,* Feb. 5, 1992, p. C12.

California Department of Mental Health. *Friends Can Be Good Medicine.* San Francisco: Pacificon Productions, 1981.

Goleman, Daniel. "Stress and Isolation Tied to a Reduced Life Span." *New York Times,* Dec. 7, 1993, p. C5.

——. "Therapy Groups Yield Surprising Benefits for Cancer Patients." *New York Times,* Nov. 23, 1989, p. B15.

Gove, Walter R. "Sex, Marital Status, and Mortality." *American Journal of Sociology* 79 (July 1973): 45-67.

Raymond, Natasha. "Friendship: The Hug Drug." *Psychology Today,* December 1999, page 17.

Lying

Bok, Sissela. *Lying: Moral Choice in Public and Private Life.* New York: Pantheon, 1978.

Peck, M. Scott. *People of the Lie: The Hope for Healing Human Evil.* New York: Simon and Schuster, 1983.

Pets as Friends

Burke, Sarah. "In the Presence of Animals: Health Professionals No Longer Scoff at the Therapeutic Effects of Pets." *U.S. News & World Report,* Feb. 24, 1992, pp. 64-65.

Secrets

Bok, Sissela. *Secrets: On the Ethics of Concealment and Revelation.* New York: Vintage, 1984.

"Secrets." *New York Times Magazine,* December 3, 2000. Articles by Luc Sante, Thomas Powers, Howard French, Daphne Merkin, Jane Smiley, and others.

Simmel, Georg. "Friendship, Love and Secrecy." Translated by Albion Small. *American Journal of Sociology* 11 (1906): 457–466.

Self-esteem and Self-acceptance

Hillman, Carolynn. *Recovery of Your Self-Esteem: A Guide for Women.* New York: Simon and Schuster (Fireside), 1992.

McKay, Matthew, and Patrick Fanning. *Self-Esteem: A Proven Program of Cognitive Techniques for Assessing, Improving, and Maintaining Your Self-Esteem.* 3rd edition. Oakland, CA: New Harbinger Publications, 2000.

Newman, Mildred, and Bernard Berkowitz, with Jean Owen. *How to Be Your Own Best Friend.* New York: Ballantine Books, 1971.

Vienne, Veronique, with photographs by Erica Lennard. *The Art of Imperfection: Simple Ways to Make Peace With Yourself.* New York: Clarkson Potter, 1999.

Stages of Reaction to Unexpected Trauma

Callanan, Maggie, and Patricia Kelley. *Final Gifts: Understanding the Special Awareness, Needs, and Communications of the Dying.* New York: Bantam Books, 1992.

Kubler-Ross, Elisabeth. *On Death and Dying.* New York: Macmillan, 1976.

Dealing with Problematical Relationships and Friendships

Foa, Edna B., and Reid Wilson. *Stop Obsessing! How to Overcome Your Obsessions and Compulsions.* New York: Bantam, 1991.

Forward, Susan, with Donna Frazier. *Emotional Blackmail: When the People in Your Life Use Fear, Obligation and Guilt to Manipulate You.* New York: HarperPerennial, 1997.

Glass, Lillian. *Toxic People: 10 Ways of Dealing with People Who Make Your Life Miserable.* New York: St. Martin's, 1997.

Halpern, Howard M. *How to Break Your Addiction to a Person.* New York: Bantam Books, 1982.

Isaacs, Florence. *Toxic Friends/True Friends: How Your Friends Can Make or Break Your Health, Happiness, Family, and Career.* New York: Morrow, 1997.

King, Florence. "The Misanthrope's Corner: Linda Tripp, Friendship and Morality." *National Review,* September 1, 1998.

Lutz, John. *Single White Female* (originally titled *SWF Seeks Same*). New York: Pocket Books, 1990.

Wheelis, Allen. *How People Change.* New York: Harper, 1975.

Yager, Fred, and Jan Yager. *Just Your Everyday People.* Stamford, CT: Hannacroix Creek Books, 2001.

Developing Friendship Skills

Black, Hugh. *The Art of Being a Good Friend.* Manchester, NH: Sophia Institute Press, 1999 (1898).

Carnegie, Dale. *How to Win Friends and Influence People.* New York: Pocket Books, 1940 (1936).

Gabor, Don. *How to Start a Conversation and Make Friends.* New York: Simon and Schuster (Fireside), 1983.

Griffin, Em. *Making Friends (and Making Them Count).* Downers Grove, IL: InterVarsity Press, 1987.

Hibbard, Ann. *Treasured Friends: Finding and Keeping True Friendships.* Grand Rapids, MI: Baker Book House, 1999.

Kephart, Beth. *Into the Tangle of Friendship: A Memoir of the Things That Matter.* Boston: Houghton Mifflin, 2000.

Leefeldt, Christine, and Ernest Callenbach. *The Art of Friendship.* New York: Berkley Books, 1980.

McGinnis, Alan Loy. *The Friendship Factor: How to Get Closer to the People You Care For.* Minneapolis, MN: Augsburg Publishing House, 1979.

Robinson, Rita. *The Friendship Book: The Art of Making and Keeping Friends.* North Hollywood, CA: Newcastle, 1992.

Conflict

Coser, Lewis A. *The Functions of Social Conflict.* New York: Free Press, 1956.

Himes, Joseph S. *Conflict and Conflict Management.* Athens, GA: University of Georgia Press, 1980.

Simmel, Georg. *Conflict and The Web of Group-Affiliations.* Translated by Kurt H. Wolff and Reinhard Bendix. New York: Free Press, 1955.

Money and Friendship

Duncan, Lois. "How Not to Lose Friends over Money." *Woman's Day,* March 25, 1986, pp. 20, 22, 25.

Overcoming Shyness

Zimbardo, Philip G. *Shyness: What It Is, What to Do About It.* Reading, MA: Addison-Wesley, 1977.

Siblings

Bank, Stephen P., and Michael D. Kahn. *The Sibling Bond.* New York: Basic Books, 1982.

Faber, Adele, and Elaine Mazlish. *Siblings Without Rivalry: How to Help Your Children Live Together So You Can Live Too.* New York: Avon, 1987.

Irish, Donald P. "Sibling Interaction: A Neglected Aspect in Family Life Research." *Social Forces* 42 (March 1964): 279–288.

McDermott, Patti. *Sisters and Brothers: Resolving Your Adult Sibling Relationships.* Los Angeles: Lowell House, 1992.

Samalin, Nancy. *Loving Each One Best: A Caring and Practical Approach to Raising Siblings.* New York: Bantam Books, 1996.

Sibling Abuse

Caffaro, John V., and Allison Conn-Caffaro. *Sibling Abuse Trauma: Assessment and Intervention Strategies for Children, Families, and Adults.* Binghamton, NY: Haworth Press, 1998.

Wiehe, Vernon R. *Sibling Abuse: Hidden Physical, Emotional, and Sexual Trauma.* New York: Lexington Books, 1990.

Family

Erikson, Erik H. *Childhood and Society.* New York: Norton, 1950, 1963.

Forward, Susan, with Craig Buck. *Toxic Parents: Overcoming Their Hurtful Legacy and Reclaiming Your Life.* New York: Bantam Books, 1989.

Secunda, Victoria. *When You and Your Mother Can't Be Friends: Resolving the Most Complicated Relationship of Your Life.* New York: Delacorte, 1990.

——. *Women and Their Fathers: The Sexual and Romantic Impact of the First Man in Your Life.* New York: Dell, 1992.

Work and Friendship

Baron, Gerald R. *Friendship Marketing: Growing Your Business by Cultivating Strategic Relationships.* Grants Pass, OR: The Oasis Press/PSI Research, 1997.

Bird, Laura. "Lazarus' IBM Coup Was All About Relationships." *Wall Street Journal,* May 26, 1994, pp. B1, B10.

Hoffer, William. "Friends in High Places." *Writer's Digest,* October 1986, pp. 42–44.

Lindsey, Karen. *Friends as Family.* Boston: Beacon Press, 1981.

Love

Fromm, Erich. *The Art of Loving.* New York: Harper and Row, 1956, 1974.

Halberstam, Yitta, and Judith Leventhal. *Small Miracles of Love & Friendship: Remarkable Coincidences of Warmth and Devotion.* Holbrook, MA: Adams, 1999.

Levin, Michael. *A Woman's Guide to Being a Man's Best Friend.* Kansas City, KS: Andrews and McMeel, 1996.

Shain, Merle. *Some Men Are More Perfect Than Others.* New York: Charterhouse, 1973.

———. *When Lovers Are Friends.* Philadelphia: Lippincott, 1978.

Tennov, Dorothy. *Love and Limerence: The Experience of Being in Love.* New York: Stein and Day, 1979.

Self-esteem

Hillman, Carolynn. *Recovery of Your Self-Esteem: A Guide for Women.* New York: Simon and Schuster (Fireside), 1992.

Children and Teens

Aries, Philippe. *Centuries of Childhood: A Social History of Family Life.* Translated by Robert Baldick. New York: Vintage, 1962.

Asher, Steve, and John Gottman, eds. *The Development of Children's Friendships.* Cambridge, MA: Cambridge University Press, 1981.

Bigelow, Brian J. "Children's Friendship Expectations." *Child Development* 48 (March 1977): 246–253.

Boys Town Center. "Helping Friendless Children." Boys Town, NE: The Boys Town Center, booklet, n.d. (received Feb. 1983).

Briggs, Dorothy Corkille. *Your Child's Self-Esteem.* Garden City, NY: Doubleday, 1975.

Douvan, Elizabeth, and Joseph Adelson. *The Adolescent Experience.* New York: Wiley, 1966.

Frankel, Fred. *Good Friends Are Hard to Find: Help Your Child Find, Make and Keep Friends.* Los Angeles, CA: Perspective Publishing, 1996.

Hartup, Willard W. "Children and Their Friends," in *Issues in Childhood Social Development,* pages 130–170. H. McGurk, ed. London: Methuen, 1978.

Haskins, James. *Street Gangs: Yesterday and Today.* New York: Hastings House, 1974.

Meyer, Stephanie H., and John Meyer, eds. *Teen Ink: Friends and Family* (written by teens). Deerfield Beach, FL: Health Communications, Inc., 2001.

Michelle, Lonnie. *How Kids Make Friends: Secrets for Making Lots of Friends, No Matter How Shy You Are.* Evanston, IL: Freedom Publishing Company, 1995.

Rubin, Zick, et al. *Children's Friendships.* Cambridge, MA: Harvard University Press, 1980.

Selman, Robert L., and Anne P. Selman. "Children's Ideas About Friendship: A New Theory." *Psychology Today,* Oct. 1979, pp. 71–72, 74, 79–80, 114.

Stocking, S. Holly, Diana Arezzo, and Shelley Leavitt, in cooperation with the Boys Town Center. *Helping Kids Makes Friends.* Allen, TX: Argus Communications, n.d.

Thompson, Michael, and Catherine O'Neill Grace, with Lawrence J. Cohen. *Best Friends, Worst Enemies: Understanding the Social Lives of Children.* New York: Ballantine Books, 2001.

Weinraub, Bernard. "Bush Urges Youngsters to Help Friends on Drugs." *New York Times,* Sept. 13, 1989, p. A24.

Weston, Carol. *Girltalk: All the Stuff Your Sister Never Told You.* 3rd edition. New York: HarperPerennial, 1997.

Physical, Emotional, or Sexual Abuse

Bass, Ellen, and Laura Davis. *The Courage to Heal: A Guide for Women Survivors of Child Sexual Abuse.* New York: HarperPerennial, 1994, 3rd edition.

Farmer, Steven. *Adult Children of Abusive Parents: A Healing Program for Those Who Have Been Physically, Sexually, or Emotionally Abused.* New York: Random House, 1990.

Finkelhor, David. *Sexually Victimized Children.* New York: Free Press, 1979.

Helfner, Mary Edna, Ruth S. Kempe, ed., and Richard D. Krugman, ed. *The Battered Child.* Chicago: University of Chicago Press, 1999, 5th edition.

Pelzer, David J. *A Child Called "It": One Child's Courage to Survive.* Deerfield Park, FL: Health Communications, 1995.

Rush, Florence. *The Best-kept Secret: Sexual Abuse of Children.* New York: McGraw-Hill, 1981.

Depression

Golant, Mitch, and Susan K. Golant. *What to Do When Someone You Love Is Depressed.* New York: Henry Holt, 1998.

Papolos, Demitri, and Janice Papolos. *Overcoming Depression,* 3rd edition. New York: HarperCollins, 1997.

——. *The Bipolar Child: The Definitive and Reassuring Guide to Childhood's Most Misunderstood Disorder.* New York: Broadway Books, 1999.

Finding Time for Friends

Mosle, Sara. "The Importance of Being Busy." *The New York Times Magazine,* November 15, 1998, Section 6, p. 132.

Yager, Jan. See listing for *Friendshifts*® under Friendship Studies, above.

——. "How to Stay Connected With Your College Crowd." *Wall Street Journal's* www.collegejournal.com, released February 14, 2001 (Part 2).

——. "Wise College Students Find Friends for Life." *Wall Street Journal's* www.collegejournal.com, released February 14, 2001 (Part 1).

Resources

In the pages that follow, you will find associations, organizations, and self-help groups that offer information or help on friendship-related issues, including web site addresses. Inclusion in the list that follows does not imply an endorsement of any association, agency, or company by the author. Nor does omission of that association, agency, or company imply criticism. For space and other considerations, the listings that follow are representative, not comprehensive. Furthermore, since addresses may change, agencies can change their names, associations can merge, cease operating, and relocate, and web sites can be discontinued, the accuracy of any listing cannot be assured. The author and publisher specifically disclaim any responsibility for any liability, loss or risk, personal or otherwise, which is incurred as a consequence, directly or indirectly, of the use and application of any listings in this resource section.

Where to Find Professional Help

Help is available if unresolved childhood issues or current concerns stand in the way of you developing the positive friendships you want or ending a negative friendship that is harming you. (Friendship is just one of the many interpersonal relationships counselors are trained to deal with, in addition to marital and parenting issues.) The choices of trained counselors include psychotherapists, psychiatric social workers, psychologists, clinical sociological practitioners, family therapists, and psychiatrists. In addition to asking a family physician or friend for a referral, you might approach the local chapter of these national professional associations for recommendations to member professionals:

American Academy of Child and Adolescent Psychiatry
3615 Wisconsin Avenue, NW
Washington, DC 20016
www.aacap.org

American Association for Marriage and Family Therapy
1133 15th Street, NW, Suite 300
Washington, DC 20005-2710
www.aamft.org

American Psychiatric Association
1400 K Street, NW
Washington, D.C. 20005
www.psych.org

American Psychological Association
750 First Street, NE
Washington, D.C. 20002-4242
www.apa.org

National Alliance for the Mentally Ill
2107 Wilson Boulevard, Suite 300
Arlington, VA 22201
www.nami.org

National Association of Social Workers
750 First Street, NE, Suite 700
Washington, DC 20002-4241
www.naswdc.org

RELATED ASSOCIATIONS

National Association for Self-Esteem
Box 674
Normal, IL 61761
www.self-esteem-nase.org
This membership association publishes a related newsletter to help with building self-esteem.

The Shyness Institute
2000 Williams Street
Palo Alto, CA 94306
www.shyness.com
Lynne Henderson, Ph.D., is the director, and Philip Zimbardo, Ph.D., author of *Shyness,* is the co-director of this institute focused on understanding and treating shyness.

For Conflict Resolution Assistance

In 2001, the Association for Conflict Resolution was formed by the combining of three associations—SPIDR (Society of Professionals in Dispute Resolution), AFM (Academy of Family Mediators), and CREnet (Conflict Resolution Education Network). ACR's mission statement, as provided on its web site, is "enhancing the practice and public understanding of conflict resolution." The ACR sponsors conferences; maintains a mediator referral list and a directory of associations and organizations compiled by AFM (Academy of Family Mediators); conducts research; sponsors training and annual conferences; makes references; and produces videos and written materials that deal with conflict resolution.

Association for Conflict Resolution
1527 New Hampshire Avenue, NW, 3rd floor
Washington, DC 20036
www.acresolution.org

This association has referrals to arbitrators:

American Arbitration Association
Corporate Headquarters
335 Madison Avenue, Floor 10
New York, NY 10017-4605
www.adr.org

For Help in Finding Friends

Here are some ways to search for old or lost friends via the Internet:

www.gradfinder.com
www.alumni.net
www.asd.com
www.highschoolalumni.com
www.curiouscat.com/alumni
www.coolbuddy.com
www.classmates.com
www.switchboard.com

You could also try the free major Internet search engines:

www.google.com
www.altavista.com
www.hotbot.com
www.yahoo.com

Here is a sample of membership associations and organizations that address specialized concerns or volunteerism. These associations or organizations may provide a way for you to meet new friends if a formal group is a way for you to try to meet others who may share your interests or if you wish to contribute to your community through cultural, volunteer, or professional or work-related groups. Some have state affiliates or local chapters. You may also want to check your local paper or your community's web site for listings similar to the ones that follow.

National and international programs have local chapters to help children and teens develop new friendships. Here are two:

Big Brothers Big Sisters of America
230 North 13th Street
Philadelphia, PA 19107
www.bbbsa.org

Boys & Girls Clubs of America
1230 West Peachtree Street, NW
Atlanta, GA 30309
www.bgca.org

For those who are grieving, this is a helpful group:

The Compassionate Friends
P.O. Box 3696
Oak Brook, IL 60522-3696
www.compassionatefriends.org

Seniors who wish to go on educational programs and trips can contact:

Elderhostel, Inc.
11 Avenue de Lafayette
Boston, MA 02111-1746
www.elderhostel.org

An adult exchange program offers international opportunities for friendship:

Friendship Force International
34 Peachtree Street, Suite 900
Atlanta, GA 30303
www.friendship-force.org
Friendship Force was established in 1977 and now has chapters throughout the United States and in 45 countries. Its "citizen ambassadors" travel abroad to live with host families.

Here are web sites dedicated to friendship:

www.janyager.com/friendship
I created this web site to share information about friendship, the friendship seminars I offer, and samples of my friendship writings, including excerpts from my book *Friendshifts*® and information related to this book, *When Friendship Hurts.* (Selected friendship writings and information are also posted at my main site: www.janyager.com.) There are also additional free, related friendship articles and updated information about National New Friends, Old Friends Week, which has been held annually since I founded it in 1997 to celebrate new and long-standing friendships. You will find examples of how the week has been celebrated over the years by various individuals, associations, and institutions. For more information, go to www.janyager.com/friendship/nationalnew-oldfriendsweek.htm.

www.friendship.com.au
Australian Bronwyn Polson created her Friendship Page in 1996 and continues to add contemporary and classic quotes and poetry about friendship.

INDEX

Resources section, 7, 125, 167, 205-9
retirement, 46, 163-64
revenge, 7-8, 62-63, 88, 181
    in workplace friendships, 149-150
Risk-taker, the, 30, 35-36
Rival, the, 30, 41-42
romantic relationships, 56, 63-65, 170, 183
    cheating in, 4, 38, 63-64, 92
    chemistry issues and, 122-23
    disclosure of information about, 14
    friendship vs., 11, 13
    resentment related to, 70-73
    sibling issues and, 106-7, 108
    at work, 152
Rubin, Theodore Isaac, 75-76
rumors, 3, 4, 5, 33, 152

sadness, 6, 43, 108
Santee, California, murders in, 3
Sapadin, Linda A., 169-70
school violence, 2-3, 23, 133, 135
secrets, 14, 58
    confidentiality and, 16-17, 38-39, 149
    dangerous, 16
Self-absorbed, the, 30, 36
self-assessment
    of One-upper, 40
    of Taker, 33
self-confidence, 177, 181
self-development, foul-weather friends and, 20
self-disclosure, confidentiality and, 16-17

self-esteem, 177
    of children and teens, 133
    low, 4, 20, 32, 36, 40, 89, 101-4
self-image, of Competitor, 40
sexual abuse, 35, 45-48, 92, 102-3, 107-10, 180
sexual harassment, 2, 152
Shanley, Mary Kay, 21
She Taught Me to Eat Artichokes (Shanley), 21
shoplifting, 35
Shotland, R. Lance, 170
shyness, 168-69, 177
Shyness Institute, 206
sibling relationships, 95, 105-10, 122
    negative friendships and, 34-35, 42, 46-48
silence, 36, 123-25, 133
Single in America (Yager), 70, 82
Single White Female (Lutz), 50
Smith, Liz, 67
Society of Professionals in Dispute Resolution (SPIDR), 125, 207
Spencer, Duffy, 104, 105, 168, 172-73
spouses, 145
    as best friend, 12-13
    cheating of, 4, 38, 92
    chemistry issues and, 122-23
    death of, 46, 82, 91
    "no secrets" from, 17
starting friendships, 163-67
Stein, Harry, 119
stepping outside the situation, 117, 153
suicide, 2-3, 92-93, 133

Reading Group Guide for *When Friendship Hurts*

Discussion Points:

1. In *When Friendship Hurts,* Dr. Yager lists many possible reasons one friend might hurt another. Think of a friendship you care about that either has ended or needs to improve if it is to last. What concepts from *When Friendship Hurts* might explain the conflicts in this friendship and help you to mend it?

2. What is the definition of a positive friendship? What does Dr. Yager say are the key components of friendships that reaffirm us?

3. Dr. Yager writes that there are really three kinds of friendship: casual, close, and best. What is similar and what is contrasting in these three categories?

4. In addition to the level of intimacy involved, friendships are distinguished by the number of people in the friendship group. How do friendships between two vary from friendship groups including three, four, or more?

5. Dr. Yager suggests 21 different types of negative friends. Do you recognize any of those traits in your current or former friends? In yourself? Pick a type that describes one of your friends. Why do you think your friend is like that? What can you do, if anything, to help yourself and your friend so the friendship stays positive?

6. How can Dr. Yager's description of the Ideal Friend serve as a prototype? Do you have at least one friend who is ideal? Are you? In all your friendships or only in certain ones? If you are not the Ideal Friend, what could you change about yourself so you are a better friend?

7. How can the techniques of conflict resolution discussed in Chapter 5 apply to the conflict you may be having with a friend? Is there at least one technique you could try next time a conflict arises with a friend?

8. When, if ever, is it time to end a friendship? Why is it sometimes better to let a friendship fade than to have a dramatic confrontation?

9. What might you do if you don't like your child's friend? When might you want to intervene? What are other options to explore?

10. What is the answer to the question posed by Chapter 7, "Friendship at Work: Are the Rules Different?" Should friendship at work be encouraged? What are the benefits of workplace friendships? What are some of the potential drawbacks?

11. In the final chapter, Dr. Yager shares the example of Doris and her two close friends, each of whom abruptly and inexplicably cut off contact with her. What do you think of the way Doris handled this situation? Has something like that ever happened to you? How did you handle it? Have you ever cut off contact with someone you had considered a friend? Why? How do you feel about that decision now?

12. If you had to pick one concept from *When Friendship Hurts* that would be most helpful to you in the way you deal with betrayal in friendship or the way you approach friendship in your career or personal life, what would it be?

A Note to Readers:

My goal in writing *When Friendship Hurts* was to inspire dialogue about an important kind of relationship we usually take for granted. We know we are supposed to work on our relationships with our spouses and children, but we seldom think of working on relationships with our friends. Yet a true friendship can be one of life's most rewarding experiences, and I am convinced it is a relationship we should value highly.

Since, by definition, friendship requires more than one person, and since the feelings and memories that reading this book evokes may be powerful and perhaps even painful, you may want some company on your journey. Discussing these issues with a reading or support group may be an excellent way to explore the broad range of themes presented here. But please remember that this book is not intended to substitute for professional help, if that is what you need. If you are already in therapy, you might want to share this book with your therapist or group so that you can talk about your reactions to the topics, anecdotes, and examples you are reading. Most of all, I hope this book will act as a catalyst to help you find your own answers.

My web site address is: www.janyager.com. There you will find information about my research and writings, as well as information about the seminars I conduct. You can also learn about the annual National New Friends, Old Friends Week, which I founded in 1997, and which begins on the Saturday after Mother's Day, to help remind all of us that friendships, especially positive and affirming ones, are worth remembering and celebrating.

About the Author

Jan Yager, Ph.D., an internationally known relationships author and speaker, has spent the last 20 years extensively studying relationships, including friendship, which was the subject of her sociology dissertation (City University of New York, 1983). She is the author of the highly acclaimed *Friend-shifts®: The Power of Friendship and How It Shapes Our Lives,* which has been translated into five foreign editions, as well as numerous other groundbreaking books including *Single in America* and *Victims.*

Frequently interviewed by broadcast and print media, Dr. Yager conducts workshops and delivers keynote addresses in her areas of expertise, including friendship. The former J. L. (Janet) Barkas, she has taught at the University of Connecticut, Temple University, and St. John's University.

Dr. Yager, who also has a master's degree in criminal justice and did a year of graduate work in psychiatric art therapy, lives in Connecticut with her husband, Fred, and their two sons.

Visit Dr. Jan Yager's web site at www.janyager.com. Dr. Yager's mailing address is P.O. Box 8038, Stamford, CT 06905-8038; her e-mail address is jyager@aol.com.